THE HISTORY of ENGLISH

A LINGUISTIC INTRODUCTION

Scott Shay

Þe Historie of Englisch

Þæt Spell Þæt Engliscʒepeopdeʒ

ᚦᚪᛏᛦ : ᛋᛒᛁᛚᛚ ᚠ : ᚦᛗᚣᛦᛦ

ᚠᚷᛏᛁᛋ ᚲᚱᚠᛦᛗᛦ

Wardja Press

San Francisco • Washington

PUBLISHED BY WARDJA PRESS, A DIVISION OF WARDJA VENTURES, LLC
San Francisco, CA / Washington, DC

http://wardja.com

International Standard Book Number: 978-0-6151-6817-3
Library of Congress Control Number: 2007935553

Publisher's Cataloging in Publication Data
Shay, Scott.
The history of English : a linguistic introduction / Scott Shay.
    p. cm.
ISBN 978-0-6151-6817-3
1. English language—History.
PE1075.S53 2008
420'.9—dc22   2007935553

Inquiries should be addressed to: info@wardja.com

Please send error information to: errors@wardja.com

For more titles by Wardja Press, please visit us on the Web at:
http://www.wardja.com

The History of English
A Linguistic Introduction

ƿÆT ƿE ĠARDENA in geat-dagum
þeodcyninga   þrym gefrunon
hu ða æþelingas   ellen fremedon

The text above is the beginning of the epic poem, Beowulf, one of the earliest works in English literature. Yes, the words above are English, Old English, to be exact. It is English as it was spoken in the first millennium of our era. As you can see, it is quite different from the English you speak today.

In The History of English: A Linguistic Introduction, you will learn about the history of English from prehistoric times, before the advent of writing, to its Germanic ancestry, the conquest of Britain, its flowering in the Middle Ages, and its status today as an international language. While learning about its history, you will be introduced to various topics in historical and theoretical linguistics. You will learn about aspects of the grammar of the various stages of the language, and you will be introduced to authentic texts from each period.

The History of English is for everyone interested in learning more about the history of the language and for those who would like a first introduction to the study of language, linguistics.

Scott Shay is a linguist and author of books on Germanic linguistics. He received a Master of Arts degree from the University of California, Berkeley in Germanic linguistics.

In memory of my father,
Ronald Shay

ᛗᚲᚠ : ᛖᚲ ᛦᛏᛏ : ᚱᚠᚷᛁ ᛏᚹᚠᛚᛗᛗᛖ
ᛒᛦᚲᛦ : ᚹᚱᚠᛁᛏ

Contents

Preface

*T*he *History of English: A Linguistic Introduction* has literally been a lifetime in the making. My interest in the Germanic languages was sparked as a young child growing up in the Pennsylvania Dutch country of south-central Pennsylvania. I remember when I first realized that the Pennsylvania Dutch words and phrases we learned as children were an entirely separate language from English. I was immediately fascinated. I began studying German on my own in elementary school, which further sparked my interest in language and grammar. But it was only after reading Mario Pei's *The Story of Language* and *The Story of English* in junior high school that I knew I wanted to be a linguist. I had no idea up until that point that English had had such an incredible and rich history, and studying it soon became my passion.

I further honed my German and linguistic skills in Germany in high school and college, and by chance, had the opportunity to learn a modern Low German dialect (Low Rhenish) as well as some Dutch. But the highlight of my career as a linguist by far has been the opportunity to begin my doctoral studies in Germanic linguistics at the University of California, Berkeley. Studying at Berkeley was a wish come true for me, and the experience of studying with top-notch faculty and colleagues has been an incredible honor for me personally. My education in Germanic linguistics is on-going, and, hopefully, never-ending.

This is my first book that is specifically geared towards non-linguists. It is my hope that reading this book will some day spark the same passion in learning about language and linguistics that Mario Pei's books sparked in me. I hope to continue writing such books on various topics in Germanic linguistics in the future.

I'd like to take this opportunity to thank some important people in my life. First and foremost, I want to thank my mother, my family, and my friends, who have always supported me in this and many other endeavors. I'd also like to thank the German department faculty at Berkeley, and especially Dr. Rauch and Dr. Shannon, whom I am honored to have had as professors and mentors. I am eternally grateful to them for the knowledge and wisdom they have imparted to me and for giving me the chance to pursue my dream.

SCOTT SHAY
Arlington, Virginia
January 2008

Introduction

ⱧÞÆT ÞE ĠARDENA   in gear-dagum

þeodcyninga   þrym gefrunon

hu ða æþelingas   ellen fremedon

These are some of the most famous lines in English. Yes, that is right; the three lines above are the opening lines of the epic *Beowulf*, one of the greatest works in the English language. This is English as it appeared around the end of the first millennium (though the story itself is perhaps a half-millennium older than that). You may recognize a word or two in the lines above, but it is otherwise incomprehensible to a speaker of Modern English.

Most people go through school and life without ever learning about the history of our language. Many never even consider the possibility that English was ever much different from what we speak today. If you were to ask someone if she could give an example of Old English, she might, for example, name the works of Shakespeare, or the King James Bible (both Early Modern English, not all that different from our own language), or perhaps Chaucer's *Canterbury Tales* (but this work is actually written in Middle English), and there is a slight chance that she might have at least heard about *Beowulf*, an actual example of a text written in Old English, and possibly even read some of this great epic in translation. But in general, most speakers of English have no real concept of what Old English was like, much less what the stages before Old English were, or what they might have looked like. That is, most of us know very little about the history of the very language we speak every day.

The story of English is one of mystery, strife, and conquest, an epic story in its own right. From its beginnings as a language spoken by just thousands of people on an isolated island, to its mighty clashes with other neighboring languages and cultures, to its medieval and early modern flowering as a literary language, and down to its present-day status as a world language, English has reflected the culture and history of the people who have spoken it. Understanding its history is paramount to understanding who we, as speakers of the language, are today.

This book is for anyone interested in the history of our language. You will learn about the prehistory of the language thousands of years ago, about its kinship with most of the languages of Europe today, its special relationship to German, Dutch, and the Scandinavian languages, about its birth as a distinct language several hundred years into the first millennium as Germanic tribes conquered the British Isles, through continuous clashes with its Viking neighbors and its conquest at the start of the second millennium by the Norman French, and through its rebirth in the Middle Ages and flowering in the early modern era, down to its status today as the most widely spoken and understood language in the world. In addition, I will speculate about the future of the language, based on current trends. Along the way, you will learn about the culture, literature, and history of the people who spoke the language in its various stages, as well as about the structure of the language itself. All grammatical and linguistic terms will be fully explained.

This book is especially intended for those who have an interest in the history of English, but have little knowledge of linguistics, the study of language. As you learn about the various stages in the history of English, you will be introduced to linguistic terms describing the sounds and grammar of each stage, as well as other concepts in historical and theoretical linguistics.

This book is not meant to be a linguistics primer, but rather an introduction to the study of language. As such, I hope it will encourage you to learn more about the history of our language and about the study of language.

Before we move on to the first chapter about the prehistory of English, let us take another look at the opening text of this introduction from *Beowulf*. A fairly literal translation (that is, word for word) of these lines reads:

What. We of the Spear-Danes   in old days

of the people-kings,   glory heard,

how the princes   brave deeds did.

A less literal translation goes something like this:

Listen! We have heard of the glory of the Spear-Danes, of the kings of the people, and of the princes' brave deeds in days of old.

Now, let's begin the History of English!

Indo-European　　　　　　　　　　1

> Therefore is the name of it called Babel; because the Lord
> did there confound the language of all the earth: and from
> thence did the Lord scatter them abroad upon the face of
> all the earth.
>
> *–King James Bible, Genesis, Chapter 11, Verse 9*

A Riddle

I have a riddle for you. What do you use every day without thinking about using it? You use it in school or at work, and at home,
with your friends, and with your family. It can arouse feelings.
You can see it or hear it. It is something that was very easy for you to
learn as a child (you did not even have to try), but it can be quite difficult to learn as an adult. What is it? It is your language—English.

Riddles have been a part of the English language since it was first
written down over a thousand years ago. But have you ever thought
about where English, the language you use every day, comes from?
English is used by hundreds of millions of people all over the world,
but very few people know anything about its rich history. The story of
how English came to be the language we speak today is quite an interesting one—a journey with many twists and turns.

Indo-European Beginnings

All good stories start with some mystery, and the story of English is no
exception. Thousands of years ago there lived a people who spoke a
language we now call "Proto-Indo-European" (we will just call it
"Indo-European" in this book; you may also see abbreviations such as
"PIE" for the former and "IE" for the latter). No one is exactly sure
where these people who spoke Indo-European came from or when
they first appeared, but many historical linguists, people who study the
history and development of languages, trace them back to areas in eastern Europe north of the Black Sea or Asia Minor, some 1,000 to 4,000
years BCE (I will use the notation "BCE", meaning "Before (the) Common Era" to refer to what has traditionally been called "BC" and the
term "CE" or "(in the) Common Era" in place of the traditional "AD",
as these are the more common terms used today). There is no written
record of this language, but linguists have attempted to "reconstruct"

the language by working backwards from written records of its earliest descendents.

Language changes over time. Eventually, certain words, phrases, or pronunciations sound "old fashioned" to you; children and teenagers sometimes seem to have their own "language"; and new words (often related to technology or popular culture today) are created all the time (we call the creation of a new word "coining", and the new word itself is called a "neologism"). Some people you know may differentiate their use of the words "who" and "whom", while others only use the former. Accents also vary geographically—an American may have a difficult time understanding someone from northern England (and vice versa). In North America, pronunciation and words vary considerably from Canada to California, and from Texas to New England, while the same is true in the much smaller geographical space of England itself. Over hundreds and thousands of years, these small changes and differences accumulate until they are so great that we cannot easily understand our own language as it was spoken or written thousands or even hundreds of years ago.

This is what happened to Indo-European. Its speakers spread out all over Europe, the Middle East, India, and even parts of Asia, and it began to change over time. You can think of Indo-European as the "mother" of many languages you have heard of or may know today, such as Spanish, French, German, Greek, and Russian, but also Hindi, a major language spoken in India, and Farsi, the language of Iran. And, in fact, it is also the mother (or perhaps great-great-great-grandmother) of English. That's right—all of these languages were once one and the same. But they have changed so much over time that a speaker of English cannot understand a speaker of Spanish, or any of the other languages mentioned above, unless they study the language separately.

The "Discovery" of Indo-European

You may wonder how we even know about Indo-European, since it was never written down. As such, Indo-European was not actually "discovered" by someone. Its existence was first theorized by a British linguist named Sir William Jones in a lecture entitled "The Sanskrit Language" that he gave in 1786 to the Asiatic Society of Bengal in Calcutta, India. Jones lived in India at the time and had studied the ancient Indian language called "Sanskrit", which was the mother of many modern languages in India (including Hindi, Urdu, and Bengali, among many others, and is still a sacred liturgical language for Hinduism, Buddhism, and Jainism). A linguist who spoke many different languages,

Jones suggested at the time that Sanskrit, Latin, and Greek were all related, and he believed that the three might also be related to Gothic (an ancient language related to German and English which you will read about below), and Farsi (also known as "Persian"), a language spoken in the Middle East. The famous quote below is from Jones:

"The Sanskrit language, whatever be its antiquity, is of a wonderful structure; more perfect than the Greek, more copious than the Latin, and more exquisitely refined than either, yet bearing to both of them a stronger affinity, both in the roots of verbs and the forms of grammar, than could possibly have been produced by accident; so strong indeed, that no philologer could examine them all three, without believing them to have sprung from some common source, which, perhaps, no longer exists..."

Jones had studied all of these languages and had noticed many similarities in their words and grammar. In the table below, perhaps you can see some of the same similarities Jones saw over 200 years ago.

Sanskrit	Greek	Latin	Gothic	English
pita	pater	pater	fadar (fathar)	father
padam	poda	pedem	fotu	foot
bhratar	phrater	frater	brothar	brother
bharami	phero	fero	baira (bera)	bear
jivah		vivos (weewos)	qius (kweeus)	quick
sanah	henee	senex	sineigs (sineegs)	senile
virah	viro	vir (weer)	wair (wear)	were(wolf)
trí	tris	tres	thri	three
dáśa	deka	decem (dekem)	taihun (tayhun)	ten
shatá	he-katon	centum (kentoom)	hundrath	hundred

In the table above the words in parentheses in the Latin and Gothic columns spell out the actual pronunciation using Modern English spelling.

The table below shows the same table from the prior page, but with the reconstructed Indo-European words that each of the words in the columns on the right descended from. You can see the similarities in each of the daughter language columns to the original Indo-European word. The asterisk, "*", before a word means that we have no actual examples of the word written down—it was "reconstructed" by linguists, using scientific methods, much like a detective reconstructs prior events in an investigation. We will discuss how this is done below.

Indo-European	Sanskrit	Greek	Latin	Gothic	English
*pəter	pita	pater	pater	fadar (fathar)	father
*ped-	padam	poda	pedem	fotu	foot
*bʰrāter	bhratar	phrater	frater	brothar	brother
*bʰer-	bharami	phero	fero	baira (bera)	bear (to carry)
*gʷeiə-	jivah		vivos (weewos)	qius (kweeus)	quick ('the quick and the dead')
*sen-	sanah	henee	senex	sineigs (sineegs)	senile (via Latin)
*wīro	virah	viro	vir (weer)	wair (wear)	were(wolf)
*treies	trí	tris	tres	thri	three
*dekm	dáśa	deka	decem (dekem)	taihun (tayhun)	ten
*kmtom	shatá	he-katon	centum (kentoom)	hundrath	hundred

Although there are differences among the languages, you can see that there are many similarities across the languages as well. And many of the words that look different seem to show patterns in their differences. For example, if a word starts with "p-" in the first four languages, it starts with an "f-" in Gothic and English. If we looked at more words, we would see many more similar patterns. As it turns out, there are so many similarities and regular patterns that there is little chance that it could be coincidence. As Jones correctly surmised in 1786, all of the languages in the tables above must have descended from the same language. That is the language that we now call Indo-European.

Reconstructing Indo-European

You may wonder how we know what Indo-European looked like. Well, the answer is we do not know exactly what it was like, but we can make some educated guesses based on the various consonant and vowel patterns of its daughter languages that were written down, and our knowledge of common types of sound and language changes. Below you can find more detail about the relationships linguists have discovered for each word in the table above.

*pəter (Although this was the original reconstruction, linguists now believe that what has traditionally been reconstructed as the "schwa" sound, represented by an "upside-down e" and pronounced like the "a" in "sofa", was actually a sort of guttural sound, called a "laryngeal", perhaps like a very breathy "h" sound, or a more guttural sound; I will use the traditional reconstructions in this book, simply showing a later form of the word in Indo-European). As you can see, Sanskrit, Greek, and Latin all have the "p" and "t" of the reconstructed Indo-European forms, and all but Sanskrit keep the final "r". This example shows a change that happened in a branch called the "Germanic language family" (more on language families below) where "p" in Indo-European became an "f" in most cases in Germanic, which you can see in both Gothic and English, both members of the Germanic family. You can also see the change from Indo-European "t" to different sounds in Gothic (spelled "d", but pronounced like our "th" in "father"), and English. Both of these are examples of regular sound changes, according to what linguists call "Sound Laws": regular changes over time that can be predicted. This "predictable" nature of sound change is very important in historical linguistics, the study of the history of languages and language change. Because sound laws are regular, linguists can work backwards from later languages to deduce what the original may have looked like. If changes were haphazard, there would be no way to figure out what the original sounds had been.

*ped- is the stem or root for the Indo-European word for "foot". Again, you can see the regular change in the Germanic languages of Indo-European "p" to Germanic "f". Another regular change is Indo-European "d" to Germanic "t". English words such as "pedal" and "pedestrian" are also ultimately from this root, but they were borrowed into English via French and Latin (French itself is a descendent of Latin).

*bʰrāter remains very much like the original Indo-European in Sanskrit. The "bʰ" sound was probably something like a very "breathy" "b" sound. This sound became a breathy "p" sound in Greek, an "f" sound in Latin, and a non-breathy "b" in the Germanic languages. We also see the common change of Indo-European "t" to Germanic "th", as seen in Gothic and English.

*bʰer- is the root for the Indo-European word for "to carry" or "to bear" (as in "Greeks bearing gifts"). In this example you can really see the regularity of sound change. Each language exhibits the exact same consonant changes for "bʰ" as in the word for "brother" above it.

*gʷei- is the root for the word for "living". Sanskrit has a "j" in place of the "gʷ", Latin has just the "w" sound, and Germanic has a "kw" sound as in "queen" (the "q" in Gothic was pronounced as if it were "kw"). We still use this sense of "quick" in a few words, mostly antiquated now, such as the Biblical "the quick and the dead" (meaning "the living and the dead"), and in the word "quickening", which refers to the initial movement of a baby in its mother's womb before it is born, essentially the first signs of life.

*sen- refers to the concept of "old". In this example, you can see that the "s" changed to "h" in Greek, but remained the same in the other languages. The word "senile" in English was borrowed from Latin (as were related words such as "senior"). This root did not live on in English directly through its various stages.

*wiro, meaning "man", kept its initial "w" in Latin (though it is actually spelled with a "v") and Germanic, but changed to "v" in the other languages. The English word "wer" can now only be seen in the word "werewolf", meaning "man-wolf". However, there used to be many more words in English with this root, such as the antiquated "wergild", the money paid to a family to compensate for someone's murder (literally "man-money"). And even in our word "world", the "wor-" was originally from this same root; the word meant something like "life of man" or "age of man".

*treies, the word for "three", along with many of the other basic numbers, has changed very little in most daughter languages. Just like the "t" in the word for "brother", it remained the same in all of the languages but the Germanic ones, where it changed to "th".

*dekm means "ten", and once again you can see the same results for "d" in the various languages. The Latin word uses "c" in the spelling of the word, but the pronunciation is still "k". In the Germanic languages, this sound changes to a harsh guttural sound like the "ch" in Scottish "Loch Ness" or German "Bach", and eventually became an "h" sound in these languages. Note that the "m" sound in he reconstructed word is pronounced as if it had a slight schwa sound before it, somewhat like "dek-um".

*kmtom means "one hundred". The initial "k" makes the same regular changes in the other languages as in *dekm above.

These few examples give you an idea of how languages can change over thousands of years and just how difficult it can be for linguists to reconstruct an older period of a language that had not been written down. We have focused on the consonants here, but vowels also change according to sound laws, and the changes can be even more extreme than those of the consonants, as you can see in the tables above.

The Comparative Method

Linguists use what is called the "comparative method" to reconstruct dead languages based on changes in their daughter languages. Although there is no one set of steps used by historical linguists in this method, there are some basic steps that most follow. Generally, the linguist starts with examples like those in the table above with "cognate" word sets. Cognates are words in different languages that have descended from one original word. Each row in the tables in the previous section is a list of cognates, each deriving from an original Indo-European word. In general the linguist will try to use the earliest attested (that is, written) cognates in a given language—the earlier the language examples, the closer they will be to the original language, and the fewer sound changes will have crept into the language. Once the linguist has set up a list of cognates, he then tries to establish correspondence sets: which sounds are related to others in similar positions. For example, in the tables above, a "p" in Sanskrit, Greek, and Latin corresponds to an "f" in Gothic and English; a "t" in the first three languages corresponds to a "th" in the last two. The linguist will then try to establish patterns. For instance, the pattern for "p" versus "f" is easy to see: every "p" in the first three languages corresponds to an "f" in the latter two. Finally, the linguist has to decide what the most likely ancestor of these sounds in the original or "proto-" language was. This is perhaps the most difficult part of the process. It sometimes comes down to "majority rules": if most of the languages have a "p" and only a few have an "f", the most likely precursor was "p". However, many other analyses must also be made before a final decision is reached. Once the linguist has decided on a set of sounds (linguists call these "phonemes") for the proto-language, he will then also compare the system he has come up with to other known systems to see if it makes real-world sense. Obviously, this entire process is a difficult one, and there is no easy way to prove that the final results are entirely accurate, short of finding a document written in the proto-language, or the development of a time machine!

Let's take a quick look at how this might work in practice. Suppose as a linguist you are given the following data to work with, all cognates in the respective languages meaning "heart" or "middle":

Cognate List: Modern English "heart"		
Language	**Word**	**English Pronunciation**
Sanskrit	**hr̥d-**	heard-
Greek	**kard-**	card-
Latin	**cord-**	cord-
Old Church Slavonic	**sird-**	seerd-
Gothic	**hairt-**	hairt-
Old Irish	**crid-**	creed-
Hittite	**kir-**	keer-
Lithuanian	**šird-**	sheerd-

We start off by noting that these words are all cognates—they mean the same or similar things in each language, and we assume they are derived from one original Indo-European word. We are starting with the oldest attested stages for most of these languages. In one case (Lithuanian) the word is in the modern form, as Lithuanian has changed relatively little in comparison to many of the other languages. In addition, for simplicity's sake, we are only using the roots of the words above without any endings.

Next, we begin comparing the sounds in each word. We note that each word starts with a consonant sound ("h", "k", "s", or "š").

Lithuanian "š" sounds like our "sh" sound and "c" in the examples above is pronounced "k". This is followed by a vowel sound, then an "r" sound (the Sanskrit word has a "syllabic consonant", "ṛ", which simply means it sounds like an "r" with a schwa sound before it, like the "ear-" in "earth"), then a "d" or a "t" sound (with the exception of Hittite). That leaves us with a potential reconstructed form of:

$$\begin{bmatrix} h \\ k \\ s \\ \check{s} \end{bmatrix} + V + r + \begin{bmatrix} d \\ t \\ \varnothing \end{bmatrix}$$

(Brackets, [ ] enclose possible options for the beginning and ending consonants, "V" means "some vowel" and "Ø" means "nothing"). This is where the difficult part begins. Our next task is to figure out which of these sounds, if any, were the original Indo-European sounds.

Let's start with the first consonant. Again, we have the possibilities of "h", "k", "s", and "š", but how do we figure out which was the original sound? Without any other information, this would be a difficult task. However, an historical linguist familiar with various sound changes in Indo-European would recognize that these same variations are commonly seen in the daughter languages. If you look at the other tables of Indo-European daughter language examples in the previous section, we see similar variations in the words *dekm ('ten') and *kmtom ('hundred'). Indo-European linguists know that a "k" sound in Latin, Greek, Old Irish, and Hittite corresponds with an "h" in Gothic, and an "s" or "sh" sound in many other languages. In fact, this is a major subdivision in Indo-European, the "Centum vs. Satem" languages (as we saw earlier, "centum" is Latin for 'one hundred' , while "satem" means the same thing in a language called Avestan, an Iranian language). This is largely an East-West division, that is, the western Indo-European languages generally have "k" sounds in certain positions, while eastern languages have "s" or "sh". Below are some more cognates for "hundred" in various languages so that you can compare the initial sounds.

As you can see, there is a fairly regular pattern with certain languages having "k"/"h" sounds and others "s" and "sh" sounds. We already know from the prior tables that the reconstructed form for "hundred" is "*kmtom", and that a "k" has been posited as the original sound.

This original sound was likely pronounced somewhat forward in the mouth, almost like the "ky" sound in "cube", and through regular sound changes became these various sounds.

Language	Word
Tocharian	känt/kante
Old Irish	cét/céad
Old High German	hunt
Old Church Slavonic	sŭto
Sanskrit	śatam
Lithuanian	šimtas

In some Indo-European daughter languages this changed to an entirely new sound, while in others, it remained more or less a "k" sound (as we saw above, the "k" turned into a guttural sound in Germanic, like German "ch" in "Bach", and this sound eventually became "h" in the Germanic daughter language; we will discuss this in much more detail in the next chapter). This change from "k" to a new sound is not entirely unusual. In fact, in Latin itself, the original "k" sound of "centum" changed in virtually all of its daughter languages: French has "cent" (pronounced "sah" with a very nasal "ah"), Latin American Spanish has "ciento" (pronounced "see-en-to"; in Castilian Spanish it is pronounced "**thee**-en-to), and Italian has "cento" (pronounced "**chen**-to"). Based on this other comparative information and prior knowledge of a common sound change, we can assume the first consonant of the word for "heart" was "*k".

The next sound could have been either a vowel, V, or an "r" sound. In all but one example above, the vowel comes first (only Old Irish has the vowel after the "r", and this change is easily explained as a common type of sound change called "metathesis" (pronounced "muh-TATH-uh-sis"), where two sounds swap places; in fact a similar change occurred in English "bird", which was originally "brid"). In the Sanskrit example, even though no vowel is itself evident, there would have been a slight schwa sound preceding the "r", which is what the small circle under the "r" stands for. Since we assume that the majority rules here, we now posit: *kVr- (meaning "k" + some vowel + "r").

Finally we need to figure out whether the final sound in the root was a "d", "t" or nothing at all. Since it is more likely that a consonant sound disappeared from the language, as in the Hittite "kir-" rather than the opposite (that is, that a "d" or "t" came from no where in *all* of the other languages), we will assume that there was indeed a "d" or "t" in the original Indo-European word. Another well known sound change in Indo-European linguistics shows how a "d" in Indo-European becomes a "t" in Germanic (you will read more about this law, called "Grimm's Law", in the next chapter). Given this law and that fact that all of the other examples have "d" as the next sound, we can safely assume a "d" in this spot. So we now have: *kVrd-.

Figuring out the exact vowel sound for the reconstruction is a little more difficult. As you can see, the vowels in the daughter languages vary quite a bit from none at all, to "a", "e", "i", and "o". This variation is likely a result of "ablaut" which is discussed in more detail below. It basically refers to a phenomenon in which different forms of a word had a regular vowel variation, with a common one being "e/o/Ø" (with "Ø" again meaning "nothing"). Indeed, the most common reconstruction for the word heart is: *kerd-, which likely had variations of *kord- and *krd-, giving us the common "e/o/Ø" pattern. With slight changes to the vowels, it is easy to see how each of the words in our cognate list could have come from this one Indo-European word.

Though this example is somewhat simplified to show the basic comparative methodology, it should give you an idea of what historical linguists must do to reconstruct a dead proto-language such as Indo-European.

Indo-European Phonetics and Phonology

Linguists call the study of the sounds of a language "phonetics" and the study of the sound system of a language "phonology". Let's take a closer look at the sounds of Indo-European as they are most commonly reconstructed. We will concentrate on the vowels first and then the consonants.

Vowels

In the table below you can see the vowels of Indo-European as they have been reconstructed. "Short vowels" and "long vowels" are just that in Indo-European—a "short" vowel was pronounced with exactly the same *quality* as a long vowel, but its duration was simply shorter: "ah" versus "aaaah", for example, is a good idea of the difference between short and long "a". The difference here is *quantity* rather than quality. In Modern English, we do not have the same type of distinction for our long and short vowels. Our difference is actually one of quality rather than quantity. The vowel sounds in "bead" (long) and "bed" (short) are quite different, as are "time" (long) and "Tim" (short).

Indo-European Vowels	
Sound	**Pronunciation**
a ā	"a" in "father"
e ē	"a" in "day" (without the slight "y" sound at the end)
i	"ee" in "see"
o ō	"o" in "stone" (without the slight "u" sound at the end)
u	"oo" in "moon"

In the table above, a "macron", or line, over a vowel shows that it is long. In each example, the first vowel in the row is short and the second, if there is one, long. One thing you may notice here is that some of the vowels do not have long variants ("i" and "u").

Diphthongs

Next we will take a look at the diphthongs as commonly reconstructed in Indo-European. A diphthong is simply two vowel sounds spoken one right after the other, with one generally "gliding" into the other. In Indo-European, a diphthong could begin with short and long "a", "e", and "o", and end with a short "i" or "u" "glide". This gives us the following twelve combinations: "ai", "au", "āi", "āu", "ei", "eu", "ēi", "ēu", "oi", "ou", "ōi", "ōu". The "ai" diphthongs sounded something like the "i" in "five" (the the long version, "āi", simply emphasized the "ah" in "aah-ee" a little longer). The "au" diphthongs sounded a bit like our "ou" in "out": "ah-oot". The "ei" diphthongs sounded somewhat like the "ay" in "day". The "eu" diphthongs combined the "ay" sound in "day" with the "oo" in "boot": "ay-oo". The "oi" diphthongs sound like latter part of the name "Bowie", while "ou" sounds something like the "oa" in "road" (as commonly pronounced, "oh-oo"). A table of the diphthongs appears below.

Indo-European Diphthongs	
Sound	Pronunciation
ai āi	"i" in "bike"
au āu	"ou" in "out"
ei ēi	"ay" in "day"
eu ēu	"ay" in "day" + "oo" in "boot"
oi ōi	"owie" in "Bowie"
ou ōu	"oa" in "road" (with more of an "oo" sound at the end)

Consonants

The consonants of Indo-European are largely similar to consonants we have in Modern English today, with some notable differences. The following table shows you the consonants of Indo-European, grouped by phonetic category. These categories are the "voiceless stops", "voiced stops", "aspirated stops", "nasals", "fricatives", "liquids", and "glides". For the most part, these designations refer to how air is manipulated within the head and throat in the human body when these sounds are articulated.

When pronouncing a "stop" (sometimes also called a "plosive"), the air is interrupted before it can leave the oral cavity, either by the lips or tongue. A further distinction for the stops is "voicing". A "voiced" stop is one in which your vocal folds (also known as vocal cords) vibrate when you pronounce it, such as "b", "d", and "g" (try saying the words "bad", "dog", and "good", while holding your fingers on your throat—you can feel the vibration when saying the first sound). Now say the words "pin", "to", and "kin" with your fingers at your throat—there is no vibration when pronouncing the "p", "t", and "k" in these words; they are basically whispered. For this reason, we call them "voiceless" consonants.

"Aspiration" after a stop is just a slight puff of air. In Modern English, we unconsciously aspirate the voiceless stops "p", "t", and "k" when they begin a syllable. To "see" the aspiration, hold up a piece of paper just an inch from your mouth and say the word "pin".

Notice how the paper moves with the puff of air after the "p"? Now say a similar word, "bin" (it features the voiced stop "b" at the beginning, and in English we do *not* aspirate voiced stops). Now you see that the paper barely moves. In its conventional reconstruction, Indo-European had the opposite case: aspirated voiced stops but no aspirated voiceless stops. With your piece of paper in front of your mouth, try to pronounce "pin" without the puff of air (it sounds a lot like "bin"; one trick is to add an "s" before it: "spin" has an unaspirated voiceless stop, "p"); this is the Indo-European "p". Then add a puff of air after the "b" in "bin", and you will get an idea of what the Indo-European aspirated "b" may have sounded like.

As their name implies, "nasals" are sounds that utilize the nasal cavity when the sound is being articulated. Instead of just flowing through the oral cavity, air also flows through the nasal cavity with these consonants.

"Fricatives" are sounds in which the air flow through the oral cavity is only partially blocked (as opposed to the stops, where the flow is almost totally blocked). Essentially, they produce friction in the oral cavity.

"Liquids" are consonants that do not have any friction and can be prolonged like a vowel.

"Glides" (sometimes called "semivowels") are consonants that have vowel-like qualities, sometimes "acting" more like a consonant, other times more like a vowel.

The table below shows examples of the Indo-European consonants and the Modern English pronunciation for each consonant listed.

You may notice that many sounds we have in Modern English were not a part of Indo-European (for example, "z", "ch", "th", and "j"), while a few others (such as the aspirated voiced stops and the laryngeals), do not exist in Modern English, our own current incarnation of Indo-European.

The laryngeals were only proven to have existed early in the 20th century, when linguists deciphered one of the oldest Indo-European languages discovered, Hittite. Their existence had been predicted by the famous Swiss linguist Ferdinand de Saussure (1857-1913) years before Hittite was even discovered. In Hittite, the laryngeals predicted by

Saussure were represented as "h" or "hh" (as transliterated from their writing system). Their acceptance caused many "classical" reconstructions of Indo-European words to be reanalyzed.

Indo-European Consonants		
Category	**Sound**	**Modern English Pronunciation**
Voiceless Stops	p	"p" in "spin"
	t	"t" in "stop"
	k	"k" in "skin"
	k^w	"qu" in "queen"
Voiced Stops	b	"b" in "bin"
	d	"d" in "dim"
	g	"g" in "get"
	g^w	"gw" in "Gwen"
Aspirated Stops	b^h	"b" with a puff of air after it
	d^h	"d" with a puff of air after it
	g^h	"g" with a puff of air after it
	g^{wh}	"gw" with a puff of air after it
Nasals	m	"m" in "man"
	n	"n" in "noon"
Fricatives	s	"s" in "sun"
	(h_1)	(these three sounds are called "laryngeals"
	(h_2)	and their exact nature is unknown, however,
	(h_3)	they are often described as, respectively, an "h" sound, a "glottal stop" like the sound in the beginning and middle of "uh-oh", and a guttural sound, possibly like a Dutch "g" sound, a voiced version of the "ch" in German "Bach")
Liquids	l	"l" in "land"
	r	"r" in "run" though probably pronounced with a tongue trill as in Spanish or Italian
Glides	w	"w" in "win"
	y	"y" in "year"

The laryngeals influenced the vowel sounds they were near. An example of such a change can be seen in *pəter, the classical reconstruction of 'father'. The new reconstruction with the laryngeal looks like this: "ph₂ter", with the laryngeal, "h₂" eventually changing to a schwa-like sound in later Indo-European. The schwa sound accounts for the various vowel sounds that this sound eventually developed into.

Indo-European Grammar

In this section we will discuss some basics of Indo-European grammar.

Typology

The concept of "typology" in linguistics refers to the classification of languages according to their structural features. Indo-European was a highly "inflected" language, resembling Latin, Russian, or German, much more than Modern English (inflections are the grammatical endings at the end of words; in non-Indo-European languages, they can also occur in the beginning or middle of a word). Indo-European is an example of what linguists call a "fusional" language (another term for fusional is "synthetic"). Put simply, a fusional language is one that adds "affixes" (they can be "prefixes", added to the beginning of a word, "infixes" added to the middle, or "suffixes", added to the end of a word) to show grammatical relationships. A single affix can mark several grammatical categories at the same time. The other major types of languages are "isolating", and "agglutinating" languages. Modern English has become much more of an isolating language: these languages do not use affixes, but depend on word order to show relationships. The other major type, agglutinating, also makes use of affixes, but differs from fusional languages in that each affix has one and only one meaning (whereas a fusional affix can indicate more than one relationship or category at a time). Modern English is actually somewhat of a hybrid between fusional and isolating—it still makes use of affixes, such as the "-'s" of possession ("Jane's car"), and the "-ed" for the past tense of some verbs ("I walk**ed** yesterday"), but word order, rather than just word endings, also plays a large role in the grammar. For example, in Modern English, the subject of a sentence generally comes first, then the verb, then the indirect object, then the direct object. This is not the case in more fusional languages such as Russian, where word order is more flexible, and it is definitely not the case in Latin, where word order could be fairly free. Modern Chinese is a good example of a language that is even more isolating than English. This is one reason the language is well suited to written characters rather than an alphabet—it does not make use of endings added to words. Japanese, an agglutinating language with a writing system based on Chinese characters, requires special characters to represent its various suffixes. Another example of an agglutinating language is Turkish. In Turkish, the word for "house" is "ev". To make the word plural, you ad "-**ler**": "evler"('houses'). To say "**in** the house" you add "-**de**": "evde". Finally, to say "**in** the houses", it is simply the addition of the two endings "ev" + "ler" + "de": "evlerde".

Grammatical Gender, Number, and Case

Three important features of the grammar of Indo-European are the concepts of grammatical gender, number, and case. Unless you've studied other languages or linguistics, you may not be familiar with these concepts, as Modern English is totally lacking in one (grammatical gender), and makes only minimal use of another (case). The following paragraphs will help to illustrate these concepts.

The concept of "number" means just what you would expect: "singular" refers to one of something, "dual" means two of something, and "plural" means more than one.

In many languages there is more than one version of the definite article, our word "the". Spanish has "el" and "la" in the singular, and "las", and "los" in the plural. French has "le" and "la" in the singular, and "les" in the plural. German is even more complicated—there are six different words: "der", "die", "das", "des", "dem", and "den", and sixteen separate uses (some forms are used more than once). Why all of these words? These languages feature the concept of grammatical gender, in addition to number. In the more familiar use of the word "gender", it refers to whether a person or animal is male or female, that is, a type of category. In some languages, all nouns must belong to a certain category. In the case of Indo-European languages, we call this categorization "grammatical gender". In French and Spanish, the categories are called "masculine" and "feminine". However, not everything that is "masculine" gender has something to do with "maleness", nor does a word with "feminine" gender necessarily have anything to do with "femaleness". You can think of them simply as categories. For example, in French, "soleil" ('sun') is a masculine word, and "lune" ('moon') is feminine. German has *three* genders: masculine, feminine, and neuter. In contrast to French, the German word "Sonne" ('sun') is feminine, and "Mond" ('moon') is masculine. A spoon ("Löffel") is masculine, a fork ("Gabel") is feminine, and a knife ("Messer") is neuter. As it turns out, of the languages illustrated here, German is the most true to the original Indo-European, which also had the same three genders: masculine, feminine, and neuter.

In French, you use the definite article "la" before a singular feminine word: "la lune"; "le" before a singular masculine word: "le soleil"; and "les" before plurals of both: "les lunes" ('the moons'). The same is true of Spanish, except the systems is broken down even further: "el" for singular masculine, "la" for singular feminine, "los" for plural masculine, and "las" for plural feminine words.

German complicates this even further. In addition to having to know what gender and number a noun is before you can decide which version of "the" to use, you also have to know the proper "case". This word refers to the role the noun plays in a sentence. German has four different "cases", called "nominative", "genitive", "dative", and "accusative". To make what can sometimes be a complicated matter a little simpler, you can think of nominative case as being used for the subject of a sentence. In "the man sees the dog", "man" is in the nominative case because it is the subject—the thing performing the action. In this same sentence, "dog" is the thing that receives the action—it is the thing that is "seen". We say that "dog" in this sentence is in the "accusative" case (in English grammar you may have learned this as the "direct object"). You may also be familiar with the concept of "indirect objects". In the sentence "the man gave the dog a bone", "man" is the subject (nominative case), and "bone" is accusative—the direct object (that is, "bone" is what is being "given"—it receives the action). So what is the dog's role in this sentence? It is the indirect object. The bone is being given, and it is being given *to the dog*. "Dog", then, is in the dative case—dative case governs indirect objects. The final case in German is the genitive case. It is the case that governs possession or ownership. In "the man's dog is here", "dog" is the subject and "man" is in the genitive—it shows possession. In Modern English we use " 's" to show the genitive, or possessive, case.

In German, you have to know the gender (masculine, feminine, or neuter), the number (singular or plural) as well as the case (nominative, genitive, dative, accusative) of a noun before you know which version of "the" to use. Indo-European had similar requirements. Though it did not have a definite or indefinite article ("a" or "an"), each noun required a special ending, according to its gender, number, and case. You can see an example below of what this may have looked like in Indo-European when we discuss Indo-European nouns below.

Indo-European had even more cases than does Modern German, eight in all. They included the four with which you are already familiar: nominative, genitive, dative, and accusative. The other four are: "instrumental" (used with our meaning of "by means of"; for example "He killed the animal *with a knife*", in which "with a knife" would be in the instrumental case), "ablative" (this case had many uses, but the original meaning was something like "away from", so in "He sailed *from Spain* to Italy", "from Spain" would be in the ablative case), "locative" (the case for locating things: in "He lived *in Rome*", "in Rome" would be locative), and finally "vocative" (the case of address, it is used when speaking to someone directly; in the famous quote of Caesar's dying words "Et tu, **Brute**" ('And you, Brutus'), when Caesar was speaking directly to Brutus, he uses the vocative form of "Brutus", pronounced something like "broo-tay").

Ablaut

Another important feature of Indo-European is the concept of "Ablaut". This is a German word meaning something like "sound reduction" or "sound lowering", also called "apophony" or "vowel gradation". This refers to a system that was pervasive in Indo-European whereby the vowels in a given word changed in different variations of the word. An example from Greek, a descendent of Indo-European, shows these changes to the internal vowel quite clearly. The example below shows variants of the word "patēr" ('father') (as a noun and "fatherless", an adjective, in different cases). Notice the bolded vowels which show ablaut changes between the "t" and the "r" in the Greek word for "father" (notice in one case that the vowel is non-existent).

Form	Meaning
patera	father (accusative case noun)
patēr	father (nominative case noun)
patros	father's (genitive case noun)
apatora	fatherless (accusative case adjective)
apatōr	fatherless (nominative case adjective)

Although Modern English no longer exhibits ablaut in this manner, it does still exist in certain types of verbs and their corresponding noun counterparts. These verbs are called the "strong verbs" (more about these later on). One example is the verb "to sing", below.

Form	Part of Speech/Tense
sing	verb, present tense
sang	verb, past tense
sung	verb, past participle
song	noun

Note that when the word is used as a verb, the internal vowel changes as the tense changes, and it changes once again when this word is a noun. This use of ablaut is a special innovation of the Germanic branch of the Indo-European family, which we will learn more about in the next chapter.

Nouns, Pronouns, and Adjectives

As a fusional language with many types of inflectional endings, Indo-European nouns, pronouns, and adjectives were considerably more complicated than they are in Modern English. These types of words included inflectional endings for grammatical gender, case, and number. For any given noun, for example, you could generally tell by the ending what the noun's gender, case, and number were in a given sentence. We will not go into great detail here about these parts of speech, but we will go through some basic examples.

A noun describes a person, place, or thing. Examples of nouns are "Andy", "pond", and "love". Nouns can be both concrete (things you can see/feel/touch), or abstract (concepts like emotions, for example). As stated above, nouns in Indo-European were inflected (that is, they took on endings) according to their case, number, and gender. In addition to this, there were two major types of "declensions" (a "declension" is basically a grouping of words that share similar endings), and many different classes and sub-classes under these. The two declensions are called "thematic" and "athematic". In the thematic declension, a "theme" vowel was added between the root of the word and the actual inflectional ending (for example, "e" or "o"), while words in the athematic declension simply tacked on the endings directly to the root. Classes and subclasses were further groupings under the athematic and thematic declensions, often grouped based upon the root vowel or consonant endings.

Below is an example of the reconstructed forms of the word "*d^hog^{hw}-" ('day') in Indo-European, which is a thematic, masculine noun in what is called the "o-Class" (the name comes from the root vowel in the word; this just means that similary structured words with an "-o-" in the stem had similar endings). The various forms of the word are shown in the table below for number (singular and plural) and case. The isolated endings are shown as well.

If you wanted to say "(the) day is here" (Indo-European did not have a definite or indefinite article; they would just have said "day is here"), it would have looked something like:

$$\textbf{*d}^h\textbf{og}^{hw}os \text{ esti kir}$$

Indo-European Noun Declension for *d^hog^{hw}- ('day')				
Case	Singular Form	Thematic Vowel + Ending	Plural Form	Thematic Vowel + Ending
Nominative	*d^hog^{hw}os	-os	*d^hog^{hw}ōs	-ōs
Genitive	*d^hog^{hw}oso	-oso	*d^hog^{hw}ōm	-ōm
Dative	*d^hog^{hw}ōi	-ōi	*d^hog^{hw}omis	-omis
Accusative	*d^hog^{hw}om	-om	*d^hog^{hw}ons	-ons
Instrumental	*d^hog^{hw}ō	-ō	*d^hog^{hw}ois	-ois
Locative	*d^hog^{hw}oi	-oi	*d^hog^{hw}oisu	-oisu
Vocative	*d^hog^{hw}e	-e		

Since "day" is the subject, it takes the nominative case ending "-os". If you wanted to say the (somewhat nonsensical sentence) "I want (a) day", it would be

*egom wélōu $\mathbf{d^hog^{hw}}$*om*

Since "day" is now a direct object, it must take the accusative ending "-om".

Obviously, this is quite a bit more complicated than our current system of adding "-'s" for possessive and "-s" for plural. Note that there are no reconstructed forms for the ablative case for this word, nor for the vocative plural. The root for "day" is "d^hog^{hw}-", the theme vowel is "-o-" (as you can see, it comes directly after the root, in either long or short form, in almost every case), and the endings are tacked on after the thematic vowel.

Keep in mind that, although this seems quite complicated, for a child learning Indo-European, it was as easy to learn as it was for you to learn your native language. Indeed, in Modern Lithuanian, which is ultimately descended from Indo-European and has retained many grammatical features, there are two grammatical genders (masculine and feminine), five noun declensions, and seven cases (all but the ablative). The fact that four million native speakers of this "complicated" language can speak it as flawlessly as you speak English attests to the fact that languages are only "difficult to learn" if one does not learn them as a child.

Adjectives are used to modify or describe nouns. If your noun is "Andy", you can describe Andy by saying he is "tall", "funny", or "intelligent". Each of these is an adjective. In the same vein as nouns, adjectives had very similar, though not always identical endings, to the noun endings you see above.

Pronouns were also inflected in the various cases. A pronoun takes the place of a noun, and as such *refers to* a person, place, or thing. Words such as "I", "she", and "you" are pronouns. The pronouns in Modern English are the only vestige of the complicated Indo-European case system, which has been honed down from eight to three: nominative (e.g., "I" or "they"), possessive ("her", "your"), and "oblique" (direct and indirect objects; "us", "him").

Verbs

Verbs are the action words of a sentence. Some verbs describe actions that are physical, like "play", "talk", and "sing", while others involve action that is less obvious, such as "think", "lie", and "believe". Verbs were also considerably more complicated in Indo-European than in Modern English. Many of you who are familiar with Romance languages such as French, Spanish, and Portuguese are already familiar with just how complicated a verb system can be in other languages. Whereas in English verb endings are fairly uncomplicated ("-(e)s" after the verb for he/she/it, as in "I see", "she see**s**", an "-ed" to show past tense for some verbs, etc.), in Indo-European, they were as complicated as noun endings.

Before we get into some basic examples of verbs in Indo-European, let's go over some concepts related to the grammatical description of verbs. You need to know a little bit about the following concepts to understand how verbs were formed in Indo-European: "number", "person", "tense", "voice", and "mood".

"**Number**" refers to the fact that verbs can refer to the actions of one, two, or more actors. "Singular" verbs reflect action of one individual, "plural" verbs reflect the actions of more than one individual, and "dual" verbs refer to the action of two individuals. Thus, "I", "you", "he/she/it" in Modern English each refer to one individual and are considered to be singular in number. "We", "you", "they" refer to more than one individual and are considered to be plural in number. You may note that "you" in English can be either singular or plural. Modern English does not have dual forms.

"**Person**" refers to a person or thing from the speaker's perspective. Thus, "first person" includes the speaker in both singular and plural forms. Modern English "I" is a first person singular pronoun, and "we" is a first person plural pronoun. The person spoken to by the speaker is "second person". Modern English has "you" in both the singular and plural. The third person is the person or thing about whom the speaker is speaking—you can think of it as a "third party" that does not include the speaker or the person being spoken to. "He", "she", and "it" are some of the third person singular forms used in Modern English. "They" is a third person plural pronoun in Modern English.

"**Tense**" indicates *when* the action of the verb takes place, relative to the time of the utterance. Modern English has two "simple" tenses (i.e., they are not formed with any helping or auxiliary verbs): present and preterite (or "simple past"). Other tenses, such as "present perfect", "past perfect", "future", etc. require the use of auxiliary verbs—verbs that are added in addition to the main verb of the sentence, such as "have" in "I have seen that man", or "will" in "she will see him tomorrow". In both cases, the main verb of the sentence is a form of "see", while "have" and "will" are additional verbs that help to change the meaning.

"**Voice**" is a grammatical category that helps to express meaning with regards to the actors and the recipients of action in a sentence. "Active" voice is used when the actor is the subject of a sentence: "Alex baked a cake" ("Alex" is the subject, and he is the actor, while the cake is the object and receives the action.) With "passive" voice, the receiver of the action is the subject: "The cake was baked by Alex".

"**Mood**" describes the relationship of a verb with respect to reality and intent. It expresses the speaker's attitude towards what she is saying. The "indicative" mood is the usual mood you use in Modern English. Another common one is "imperative", which is used when giving commands. If you are familiar with other European languages, you may be familiar with the concept of the "subjunctive" mood, which is used for many different things, including "unreal conditions" or wishes "if I were rich…" could be said to be in the subjunctive mood (the usual form of the verb is "I was" rather than "I were"; "were" is in the subjunctive mood form here).

Indo-European verbs had three "numbers". In addition to singular and plural, it had a "dual" number, referring to two of something performing an action, something like "we two", "you two", and "those two" in Modern English. In addition, it had at least four moods (indicative, imperative, and subjunctive, as described above, plus an additional one called "optative", indicating wishes or hopes) and at least three simple tenses, generally agreed upon as present, "aorist" (from a Greek word meaning "indefinite" or "unlimited"), and "perfect". The "aorist" tense was used for completed events in the past, while the "perfect" can be thought of as showing an action that was in the past with an aspect that continues on, somewhat like our "present perfect" tense in Modern English. Just as with nouns, there are thematic and athematic classes. There are two voices, active and "medio-passive", a type of passive voice in which the verb has "stative" meaning (i.e., instead of indicating action, it indicates a state of affairs, such as "be", "have", "know", etc.) and has no expressed "actor" performing the action.

The examples below show verb "conjugations" for both a thematic and an athematic verb. A conjugation is a paradigm that simply shows all of the endings for a given verb. The thematic verb is "*bʰer-" which means 'bear' or 'carry', and the athematic verb is "dʰo-", meaning 'do'.

Indo-European Thematic Conjugation: *bʰer- ('carry')			
Number	Person	Present Indicative	Ending
Singular	1st	*bʰerō	-o
	2nd	*bʰeresi	-si
	3rd	*bʰereti	-ti
Dual	1st	*bʰerowes	-wes
	2nd	*bʰeretos	-tos
	3rd	*bʰeretes	-tes
Plural	1st	*bʰeromes	-mes
	2nd	*bʰerete	-te
	3rd	*bʰeronti	-nti

Indo-European Athematic Conjugation: *dʰō- ('do')			
Number	Person	Present Indicative	Ending
Singular	1st	dʰōmi	-mi
	2nd	dʰōsi	-si
	3rd	dʰōti	-ti
Dual	1st	dʰōwe	-we
	2nd	dʰōtes	-tes
	3rd	dʰōtes	-tes
Plural	1st	dʰōmes	-mes
	2nd	dʰōte	-te
	3rd	dʰōnti	-nti

In the tables above, the singular and third person plural endings are generally agreed upon, but the first and second person plural endings and all of the dual endings have other reconstructions as well.

You can see that the endings for the two are quite similar, with the main undisputed difference being in the first person singular. Also note in the thematic conjugation that an "e" or "o" appears between the stem and the endings in all but the first person singular—this is the "theme" vowel from which this conjugation gets its name. The lack of such a theme vowel in the second table above is characteristic of the athematic conjugation.

The paradigm for "be" is in the table below for the present indicative for all numbers and persons.

Conjugation of "be" in Indo-European				
Number	Person	Present Indicative		
Singular	1st	*bʰéumi	*ézmi	
Singular	2nd	*bʰéusi	*éssi	*órta
Singular	3rd	*bʰéuti	*ésti	
Dual	1st	*bʰeuwé	*eswé	*orwé
Dual	2nd	*bʰeutés	*estés	*ortés
Plural	1st	*bʰeumé	*ezmés	*ormé
Plural	2nd	*bʰeuté	*esté	*orté
Plural	3rd	*bʰeuṇt	*sentí	*orṇt

As you can see, the paradigm for "to be" is made up of three different roots, *bʰeu-, *es-, and *or-. With the addition of the imperative form, *wése, yet another separate form was used for this paradigm (*wes- forms were also part of the preterite paradigm). This doesn't necessarily mean that Indo-European had four different words for "be" but rather, all of these forms eventually came to have such a meaning in its daughter languages. This verb is also highly irregular in English even to this day, using all of these same roots for various forms of the verb (e.g., "be", "is", "are", "were").

Indo-European Numbers

Since the focus of this book is English, I will not go into any further detail about the structure and grammar of Indo-European (there are many good books on this subject, and the interested reader is encouraged to read further on this topic elsewhere). However, I would like to present the reconstructed numbers one through ten of Indo-European, so that you can trace the changes in subsequent chapters down to their present-day state. Each subsequent chapter will also have the numbers for the given stage of the language so you can see the exact changes over time.

	Indo-European Numbers
1	*oinos
2	*duwō
3	*treies
4	*kʷetwōr
5	*penkʷe
6	*sweks
7	*septm
8	*oktō
9	*newn
10	*dekm

The Indo-European Daughter Families

The languages that developed from the changes in Indo-European belong to ten major "language families". You can think of a language family just as your own family—a group of closely related languages that exhibit similar traits, but are still independent of each other. The ten families are:

Albanian: This is a small language family that has only one existing spoken language, Modern Albanian, spoken mainly in Albania and a few surrounding areas.

Anatolian. This family includes the Hittite language, one of the oldest Indo-European languages that was written down. It used a writing system called "cuneiform", wedge forms made mostly in clay, and was only discovered in the very beginning of the 20th century to be an Indo-European language. Its antiquity has been extremely important in reconstructing Indo-European.

Armenian: This family consists of just one living language, Modern Armenian, spoken in the country of Armenia and by many people of Armenian ancestry throughout the world.

Balto-Slavic: This family is made up of the Baltic and Slavic families. Baltic languages include Lithuanian and Latvian. Lithuanian has remained especially archaic: of all modern languages that have descended from Indo-European, it has retained perhaps the most features of the original language. The Slavic family includes such languages as

Russian, Ukrainian, Polish, Czech, Bulgarian, Bosnian, Croatian, Serbian, and many others.

Celtic. Unlike the basketball team of the same name, this is pronounced as if it started with a "k": "Keltic". At one time the Celts occupied much of Europe. Today, their languages survive largely only in Britain and Ireland: Irish and Scots Gaelic, and Welsh.

Germanic. We will talk much more about this language family in the next chapter. Germanic is the family to which English belongs, so it is very important in the history of English. Other modern-day languages that belong to this family are German, Dutch, Afrikaans, Frisian, Yiddish, Pennsylvania Dutch, and the Scandinavian languages: Swedish, Danish, Norwegian, Faroese, and Icelandic.

Greek. This family includes many ancient Greek dialects, as well as Modern Greek.

Indo-Iranian. This family consists of the Indo-Aryan languages, spoken in India today (Sanskrit and many modern Indian languages belong to this group), and the Iranian languages, including Farsi (sometimes called Persian), the language of Iran and closely related languages in many other countries in the Middle East.

Italic. Latin was perhaps the most prominent member of this language family. Latin itself is the parent language of modern Italian, Spanish, Portuguese, French, Romanian, Catalan, Romansh, and many other languages (the "Romance languages), spoken throughout Europe. Much as Indo-European broke up to become many different languages, Latin also changed as its speakers migrated out of Italy throughout Europe to become all of these modern languages.

Tocharian: This family has been extinct for a long time. It is another branch of the Indo-European tree that was not discovered until the 20th century. Its speakers lived in what is now western China, the farthest east that any Indo-European language is known to have existed.

In addition to these language families and the languages that comprise them, there are numerous other extinct languages that are Indo-European but cannot be easily classified.

As you can see, Indo-European is the mother language of most of the languages of Europe (the few that are *not* Indo-European include Basque, Finnish, Hungarian, Estonian, and Turkish), and of languages from parts of the Middle East and South Asia. Each of the languages in the language families above are "relatives" of the English you speak today.

In the next chapter, we will focus on the Indo-European daughter family to which English belongs, the Germanic family, and learn more about it and about and about English's closest linguistic relatives.

Germanic   2

ᛗ᛬ᚠᚦ᛬ᛉ᛬ᚱᛏᛏ᛬ᚱᚠᚷᛁ᛬ᛏᛂᚠᚷᛗᛗᛉ

ᛒᚱ᛬ᚱ᛬ᛂᚱᚠᛁᛏ

—ᛉᚠ᛬ᛂᚱᛁᛏᛋᚠ᛬ᚦᛗᛃᚱᛃ᛬ᛒᚱ᛬ᚱᛃ

Early Germanic

O ver time the people who spoke Indo-European spread out all over Europe, the Middle East, India, and parts of Asia. One group eventually settled in what we now call Scandinavia, most likely in the areas around modern-day southern Sweden. This was sometime around the year 1000 BCE. Today, we call these people the Germanic people, and their language "Proto-Germanic" (we will just use "Germanic" in this book). Their language was already quite different from Indo-European in many ways.

The first known written record of something distinctly "Germanic" dates to the second century, BCE in the form of a bronze helmet with an inscription in a script called Etruscan. Found in what is now the city of Zenjak in modern-day Slovenia, it is called "the Negau helmet" (Zenjak is near a city called Negova; the helmet is still referred to using the German name for the city, "Negau", as it was known at the time of its discovery). The transcribed inscription runs something like this:

harigastiteiva///ip

The first part, "harigast" is almost certainly a Germanic name; the meaning of the rest of the inscription has been debated for many years. Besides this one example, the earliest evidence is in the form of names of the various Germanic tribes in a first century CE account by the Roman historian Tacitus.

The earliest Germanic people left few written records, mostly in the form of names using their own alphabet, the runic alphabet, called the "futhark" (pronounced "FOO-thark"). It is named after the first six letters of their alphabet: f-u-th-a-r-k (there is one letter for our modern "th", called "thorn", "þ", pronounced like "th" in "thin"). Here is what those letters looked like in the alphabet itself:

ᚠ ᚢ ᚦ ᚨ ᚱ ᚲ

The letters themselves are called "runes". They were generally fairly angular letters, as they were most often carved into stone or wood. Below is an example of an early futhark, called the Elder Futhark (there were several versions over time and by different groups). In the first and fourth columns, you see the rune itself, in the second and fifth columns, the English equivalent, and in the third and sixth columns, the sound in Modern English (the bolded letters are the sound of the rune).

The Elder Futhark					
Rune	**English**	**Sound**	**Rune**	**English**	**Sound**
ᚠ	f	**f**ee	ᛁ	i	bee
ᚢ	u	**tr**ue	ᚲ	p	**p**ea
ᚦ	th	**th**in	ᛉ	z	**z**oo
ᚨ	a	**f**ather	ᛊ	s	**s**un
ᚱ	r	**r**ide	ᛏ	t	**t**in
ᚲ	k	**k**id	ᛒ	b	**b**irch
ᚷ	g	**g**ift	ᛖ	e	mak**e**
ᚹ	w	**w**in	ᛗ	m	**m**an
ᚺ	h	**h**ail	ᛚ	l	**l**ake
ᚾ	n	**n**eed	ᛜ	ng	si**ng**
ᛁ	i	thr**ee**	ᛞ	d	**d**ay
ᛃ	y	**y**ear	ᛟ	o	**o**ath

An early example of a runic inscription is from the Golden Horns of Gallehus, found in Denmark, dating to the 5th century CE:

ᛗ᛫ ᚺᛁᛗᛔᚠ᛭ᚨᛏᛁ Y ᚺᛟᛚᛏᛁ ᛟᚠ Y

ᚺᛟᚱᛏᚠ ᛏᚨᚠᛁ ᛗᛟ

A transcription in our alphabet runs as follows:

ek hlewagastiR holtijaR horna tawido

The English translation is:

I, Hlewagast (possibly "famous guest"),
(son) of Holt, made the horn.

The capital "R" seen in the transcription describes a sound that has been disputed. The original sound in Germanic was a "z" sound, which, in some of the Germanic daughter languages became an "r" sound due to a common sound change called "rhotacism" (from the Greek letter "rho", akin to our letter "r"). This phenomenon is still evident in Modern English in such contrasts as "was" versus "were" and "most" versus "more", where the first word has an "s" or "z" sound, and the latter an "r" due to rhotacism. This capital R represents a sound that was possibly something in between a "z" sound and an "r" sound, i.e., a "z" on its way to becoming an "r". Rhotacism occurred in all of the Germanic daughter languages except Gothic (more on the Germanic daughter languages below).

Examples of the changes from Indo-European to Germanic

Following are some examples of the changes from a few Indo-European words to Germanic (again, all of these forms are reconstructed; in each case, the first word is the Indo-European reconstruction and the second is the Germanic reconstruction; the arrow means "became"):

*wodr → *watr
*kwon → *χwon ("χ" is a symbol for the sound at the end of German "Bach")
*treies → *þrijiz ("þ" is pronounced like the "th" in "three", "j" like "y" in "year")
*ekwos → *eχwaz

You can already see quite a few differences. "*Watr" is of course still understandable to this day and has changed very little into Modern English 'water'. "*χwon" ('dog') is not as easily recognizable today, but it is our word "hound". A variant in IE was "*kuntos", which gave us "*χunðaz" in Germanic, and eventually "hund" in Old English, changing to "hound" by the Early Modern English period. "*Þrijiz" is possibly recognizable as our word "three", having changed little since Germanic times (it would have been pronounced something like "three-yeez). "*Eχwaz" is the only word of the four that has not survived in any form in Modern English directly from Germanic, though it did survive into Old English times as "eoh". It was eventually replaced by the word "horse". However, the word is still recognizable via the Latin borrowing "equus" in words such as "equine" in Modern English.

Characteristics of the Germanic Languages

Just as your own family might have the same eye color, hair color, the same shape of nose, etc., language families also share common traits. All of the Germanic daughter languages have certain characteristics in common. Some of these characteristics include "Grimm's Law", two simple verb tenses, a past tense with a dental suffix, and stress on the base syllable.

"Grimm's Law." You may recall the name of Jacob Grimm as the writer of fairy tales as part of the Brothers Grimm. Jacob Grimm was also a renowned Germanic linguist in the 19th century. He was the first to extensively document the regular "sound changes" we talked about in the first chapter, where an Indo-European "p" becomes "f" in the Germanic languages, and "t" becomes "th" (as in "thin", generally transcribed as "þ", the letter from the futhark). These are just a few of the changes that are a part of Grimm's Law (also called the First Germanic Sound Shift). (Though named for Grimm, the actual discoverers of the law were linguists Friedrich von Schlegel (1806) and Rasmus Christian Rask (1818), though they are rarely credited with the discovery. Grimm was the first to document the changes in detail, and as such, has become the person most widely credited with the discovery).

All of the Germanic languages exhibit this change, called a "consonant shift" (a consonant in the parent language, Indo-European, shifts, or changes to a new consonant in the daughter language, Germanic in this case). The table below shows the changes from Indo-European to Germanic according to Grimm's Law. The first word under the "Examples" heading shows a non-Germanic example (which would *not* show the shift), the second is an example of a modern Germanic language (which *does* show the shift). The following changes occurred according to Grimm's Law: the aspirated voiced stops of Indo-European became unaspirated voiced stops in Germanic, the unaspirated voiced stops of Indo-European became voiceless stops in Germanic, and the voiceless stops of Indo-European became fricatives. Note that "þ" sounds like the "th" in "thin" and "χ" sounds like "ch" in German "Bach".

Grimm's Law		
IE	**Germanic**	**Examples**
b^h	b	Sanskrit: **bh**ratar English: **br**other
d^h	d	Sanskrit: **dh**rájati English: **d**rag
g^h/g^{wh}	g/gw	Sanskrit: sti**gh**noti German: stei**g**en
b	p	Old Irish: u**b**ull Dutch: a**pp**el
d	t	Latin: **d**ecem Dutch: **t**ien
g/g^w	k/kw	Hittite: ju**g**a- English: **y**oke
p	f	Greek: **p**oda German: **F**uß
t	þ	Latin: **t**enuis English: **th**in
k/k^w	χ/χw	Latin: **c**ordis Afrikaans: **h**art

There are a few notable "exceptions" to Grimm's Law (since they are regular "laws" in themselves, they are not actually "exceptions" *per se*). You may notice the Sanskrit word "stighnoti" in the table above, which corresponds to the German word "steigen". Both come from the Indo-European root *steigh-, meaning 'to walk, to step' (both have the meaning of to walk or climb in the respective daughter languages). With Grimm's law, we would expect the "t" in *steigh- to become a "þ" in the Germanic languages, but as you can see, this is not the case. When one of the Indo-European consonants "p", "t", or "k" appears directly after "s", they do not shift in Germanic. As such, Indo-European *əster- ('star') becomes Latin, "stēlla", Greek "astēr", and Germanic "*sterzōn-", with unshifted "t". Similarly, "t" did not change to "þ" when it followed Indo-European "p" or "k" (though the "p" and "k" themselves shifted per the table above): note Greek "kleptēs" (which appears in our Modern English borrowing "kleptomaniac") and Gothic "hliftus" ('thief'); also note Latin "octō" versus Modern English "eight" where the "t" did not change in the Germanic languages as would otherwise be expected, according to Grimm's Law.

Another major "exception" is called "Verner's Law", after the noted 19th century Germanic linguist, Karl Verner, who is credited with explaining what was, at the time, considered a true exception to Grimm's Law. Linguists at the time noted that in certain instances where they expected Indo-European "p", "t", and "k" to become "f", "þ", and "χ" (this sound became "h" in all of the daughter languages), the sounds became "b", "ð" (sounds like "th" in "this"), and "g". For example, the "t" in Indo-European *pəter should have become the "th" sound in "thin" via Grimm's Law, but instead became the "ð" sound in "that" in Germanic. In the Germanic word for "to turn" (*werþ-), "þ" appears in the present tense, and in the past tense in the singular, but in the past plural, the sound becomes "ð". Verner realized that the change had to do with where the Indo-European accent fell in the word. Verner's Law went into effect if the accent fell just after the consonant in question. Thus, *pətēr, which had the accent on the second syllable was affected by this law, and instead of Germanic "*faþēr" (with the expected voiceless "þ" from Grimm's Law) we get "*faðēr", with voiced "ð". The same basic phenomenon that is responsible for Verner's Law changes can be seen in the Modern English pronunciation of "exercise" versus "exist". In "exercise", the accent falls on the first syllable: EK-ser-size and the "x" has the usual "ks" sound. However, with "exist", the accent falls in the second syllable, and the pronunciation becomes "eg-ZIST" and the "x" now has the sounds "gz". This is basically a difference in voicing: in the first example, the sounds are voiceless, in the second, they are voiced.

Two simple verb tenses. The term "simple tense" simply means that any changes to the verb are made to the word itself—no other words ("helping verbs" or "auxiliary verbs" that create a verb phrase) are needed. Indo-European had several different verb tenses that were created by changing the vowel within a verb, and/or adding something to the end of the verb.

Germanic had just two simple tenses: a present tense (for example, "I go", "she sees"), and a simple past tense ("I went", "she saw"). Most of the other Indo-European daughter languages had much more complicated verb systems. If you know Spanish or French, you know that their verb systems are complicated compared to English. The Germanic languages can still express many different tenses, but they generally use helping, or "auxiliary" verbs to do so. For example, "I **have** gone", "I **will** go", "she **will have** seen", are all examples of different tenses using auxiliary verbs ("have", "will"). It is unclear whether this characteristic is more representative of Indo-European or whether the other daughter languages with multiple simple tenses are more true to the original—both sides have been argued by linguists. However, this aspect of the Germanic verb system is a major defining characteristic of the family as a whole.

The use of a dental suffix to form the simple past tense of some verbs. A "dental suffix" simply refers to a "t" or "d" sound added to the end of a word. We call "t" and "d" "dental" because the tongue touches (or nearly touches) the teeth when these sounds are pronounced.

You know that to form the past tense of "sing" you just change the vowel, "i" to "a", and you get "sang". Likewise, to form the past tense of "run", you change "u" to "a" to get "ran". However, there are some verbs where the vowel stays the same, but you add "-ed" to form the past tense: "walk", "walked", "jump", "jumped", "bag", "bagged". Say each of these out loud and listen carefully. You should notice that for the first two words, "walk" and "jump", you actually pronounce a "t" at the end instead of a "d" (the past tenses sound like "wokt" and "jumpt"). Even though we write "-ed" on the end, the real sound is a "t". For "bag", we do add a "d" sound at the end: it sounds like "bagd". This is also a common linguistic phenomenon in which clusters of sounds tend to be entirely voiced or entirely voiceless. Since the first two words, "walk" and "jump" end in voiceless consonants, a voiceless sound is added to create the simple past; for the word "bag", which ends in a voiced consonant, another voiced consonant is appended.

This difference in types of verbs is called "strong versus weak": "strong" verbs have a vowel change in the past tense, "weak" verbs add "-d" or "-t". This change is unique to Germanic verbs: neither Indo-European, nor any other of its daughter languages exhibit this "strong" versus "weak" distinction based on the addition of a "-t" or "-d".

Stress on the base syllable. You may know that words are made up of syllables. For instance, "hi" has one syllable, while "hello" has two ("hel" + "lo"). Syllable stress simply refers to the syllable that has the most emphasis. For example, the word "emphasis", which has three syllables ("em" + "pha" + "sis"), has its stress on the first syllable. We say "EM-pha-sis". In the word "example", which also has three syllables, the stress falls on the *second* syllable: we say "ex-AM-ple", rather than "EX-am-ple" or "ex-am-PLE".

In Indo-European, the word stress could fall on any syllable, much like Modern English. However, in Germanic, stress was always on the "base" syllable, which was usually the very first syllable. The base syllable is simply the root of the word without prefixes or suffixes. This change is responsible for many other changes that occurred in the Germanic languages, most notably changes to the ending of words, which had lost any emphasis as a result of this change in stress.

There are many other changes that took place from Indo-European to Germanic that are characteristic of Germanic languages, but these will at least give you an idea of some of the major ones.

Germanic Phonetics and Phonology

Let's take a closer look at the reconstructed sounds of Germanic.

Vowels

The vowel sounds of Germanic are quite similar to those that we still have in Modern English. Take a look at the table below, where we compare the vowel sounds as they were spoken in Germanic with our Modern English vowel sounds. As in Indo-European, long vowels were simply pronounced longer than short ones. We will use a macron over a long vowel so that you will be able to distinguish long versus short vowel sounds. The long vowels with macrons look like this: ā, ī, ō, ū, ǣ. In each example below, the first vowel is short and the latter long:

Germanic Vowels		
Sound	**Example**	**Modern Pronunciation**
a ā	*swa ('as') *jā ('yes')	"a" in "father"
e	*seχs ('six')	"a" in "day" (without the "y" sound at the end)
i ī	*in ('in') *īsa ('ice)	"ee" in "see"
o ō	*oft ('often') *bōkō ('book')	"o" in "stone"
u ū	*kunnanan ('can') *χūsan ('house')	"oo" in "moon"
y	*brūnyz ('brown')	We don't have this sound in Modern English. Say "is" but pucker up your lips while saying it.
ǣ	*ǣlaz ('eel')	"a" in "ash"

Diphthongs

Next we will take a look at the diphthongs in Germanic. They are a bit more simplified than those of Indo-European.

Germanic Diphthongs		
Sound	**Example**	**Modern Pronunciation**
ai	*aikaz ('oak')	"i" in "I"
au	*baunō ('bean')	"ow" in "now"
ei	*sneikanan ('to sneak')	"ay" in "day"
eu	*keusanan ('to choose')	"ay" in "day" quickly followed by the "u" in "rune"

Consonants

The consonants of Germanic are also similar to their Modern English counterparts. For the most part, they are pronounced as they are today. The following table shows you the consonants of Germanic, along with examples and the modern pronunciation of each consonant listed.

Germanic Consonants		
Sound	**Example**	**Modern Pronunciation**
b	*bakan ('back')	"b" in "back"
d	*deupaz ('deep')	"d" in "deep"
f	*fidwōr ('four')	"f" in "four"
g	*gōðaz ('good')	"g" in "good"
γ	*daγaz ('day')	This symbol, the Greek "gamma", is the voiced counterpart to the "ch" sound in German "Bach", a guttural sound. Modern Dutch still has this sound.
γw	*sanγwaz ('song')	"γ" + "w"
χ	*χunðaz ('dog')	This symbol, the Greek "chi", is the "ch" sound in German "Bach". This sound became an "h" in late Germanic.

Germanic Consonants (continued)		
Sound	**Example**	**Modern Pronunciation**
χw	*χwō ('how')	"χ" + "w"
j	*jā ('yes')	"y" in "yes"
k	*kakōn ('cake')	"k" in "cake"
l	*līƀa ('life')	"l" in "life"
m	*matiz ('meat')	"m" in "meat"
n	*ne ('no')	"n" in "no"
ng	*kuningaz ('king')	"ng" in "finger" "ng" was pronounced as two separate sounds, even at the end of a word, as we pronounce it today in "finger".
p	*ploχaz ('plow')	"p" in "plow"
kw	*kwǣniz ('woman')	"qu" in "queen"
r	*rauðaz ('red')	This sound was probably trilled with the tongue as in modern Spanish and Italian.
s	*saiwaz ('sea')	"s" in "sea"
t	*twai ('two')	"t" in "two"
þ	*þengaz ('thing')	"th" in "thing"
ð	*unða ('and')	"th" in "the"
ƀ	*uƀan ('above')	We don't have this sound in Modern English. It is like the b/v sound in Spanish, where your lips are in position for "b" but you let air rush out like "v".
w	*wersō ('war')	"w" in "war"
z	*ainaz ('one')	"z" in "zoo"

Nouns, Pronouns, and Adjectives

Germanic was also a fusional language like its mother, Indo-European. But because of the change from a moveable accent to a fixed accent on the base syllable some time during the Germanic period, the inflectional endings of Indo-European changed considerably. In most instances, part or all of the final syllable was lost in an ending. However, nouns, pronouns, and adjectives continued to have inflectional endings for grammatical gender, case, and number. In addition, Germanic also continued the thematic vs. athematic distinction of Indo-European, with similar classes and subclasses grouped according to the root vowel or consonant ending.

Below is an example of the reconstructed forms of the word for "day" in Germanic, "*daɣaz" (just as in Indo-European, a thematic, masculine noun). It might be helpful to compare the paradigm below with that of the same paradigm in Indo-European in the prior chapter. The first table shows earlier forms, the second shows later forms.

Early Germanic Noun Declension				
Case	Singular	Ending	Plural	Ending
Nominative	*daɣaz	-az	*daɣōzez	-ōzez
Genitive	*daɣaza	-aza	*daɣōm	-ōm
Dative	*daɣai	-ai	*daɣamaz	-amaz
Accusative	*daɣan	-an	*daɣanz	-anz
Instrumental	*daɣe/u	-e/u		
Locative	*daɣi	-i		
Vocative	*daɣ	-		

Late Germanic Noun Declension				
Case	Singular	Ending	Plural	Ending
Nominative	*daɣaz	-az	*daɣōz/ōs	-ōz/ōs
Genitive	*daɣes	-es	*daɣõ †	-õ
Dative	*daɣē	-ē	*daɣamz	-amz
Accusative	*daɣa	-a	*daɣanz	-anz
Instrumental	*daɣe/u	-e/u		
Locative	*daɣi	-i		
Vocative	*daɣ	-		

† õ symbolizes a nasalized long "o" sound like French "on".

Using the late endings above, the example sentences from the first chapter, translated into Germanic, would be:

*(sa) **daɣaz** ist χer

'(the) day is here'

Since "day" is the subject, it takes the nominative case ending "-az". 'I want (a) day' would be:

*eka welō **day***a*

"Day" is now a direct object, so it must take the accusative ending "-a".

Although Germanic probably did not have a definite article in the sense that we use ours today, it did have a demonstrative pronoun, originally meaning "this" which eventually took on the meaning of "the" as well, as is evident in the Germanic daughter languages. The declension of the demonstrative is below. In the case of the plural, where there are separate forms for the different genders, they are separated as masculine/neuter/feminine.

Germanic Demonstrative			
	Masculine Singular	**Neuter Singular**	**Feminine Singular**	**Plural**
Nominative	*sa	*þatō	*sō	*þē/þō/þōz
Genitive	*þeza	*þeza	*þezōz	*þezōn
Dative	*þammē	*þammē	*þezē	*þēmiz
Accusative	*þanō	*þatō	*þiō	*þanz/þō/þōz
Instrumental	*þī			
Locative	*þiu			

As in Indo-European, adjectives had very similar endings to the noun and demonstrative endings you see above.

Pronouns were inflected in Germanic as well. The word "pronoun" literally means "for noun". In other words, it is a word that takes the place of a noun. If I say "Betty saw Tim yesterday", I could replace either name with a pronoun. For example, assuming you already know we are talking about Betty and Tim, I could then say "**She** likes **him** a lot" ("she" and "him" are personal pronouns—they take the place of a "Betty" and "Tim", respectively). Or I could even lump them both together and say "**They** are going to the party tonight". Now the word "they" takes the place of both of their names.

Pronouns were inflected for case, number, and, in the third person, gender. Below are the reconstructed personal pronouns of Germanic. Note that in the third person there were likely variants with and without an initial "h", which is reflected in the various daughter languages (North Germanic had the variants with "h", and some West Germanic dialects had them as well). Note also that in the dual, there are only reconstructed pronouns for the first and second persons.

Germanic Personal Pronouns						
Num-ber	Case	1st Person	2nd Person	3rd Person		
				masc.	neut.	fem.
Sing.	Nom.	*eka (I)	*þu (thou)	*(h)iz (he)	*(h)iu, siu (she)	*(h)itō (it)
	Gen.	*mīn	*þīn	*(h)is	*(h)izōz	*(h)is
	Dat.	*miz	*þiz	*(h)imme	*(h)izē	*(h)imme
	Acc.	*mek	*þek	*(h)inō	*(h)iō	*(h)itō
Dual	Nom.	*wit (we two)	*jit (you two)			
	Gen.	*unker	*inkwer			
	Dat.	*unkiz	*inkwiz			
	Acc.	*unkiz	*inkwiz			
Plural	Nom.	*wīz (we)	*jiz (you)	*(h)īz, siē (they)	*(h)iōz, siē (they)	*(h)iu, siu (they)
	Gen.	*unser	*izwer	*(h)izõ	*(h)izõ	*(h)izõ
	Dat.	*uns(iz)	*izwiz	*(h)imz	*(h)imz	*(h)imz
	Acc.	*uns(iz)	*izwiz	*(h)in, sian	*(h)iō	*(h)iu, siu

Verbs

The verb system of Germanic, while much more complicated than in Modern English, was considerably simpler than the system proposed for Indo-European. Some scholars view this as a simplification of a formerly more complex system. However, other scholars maintain that the Germanic system is closer to the original Indo-European system, and that the more complex systems of its other daughter languages were innovations. Under this theory, Germanic must have split apart from its sister dialects at a very early stage in the development of Indo-European. This theory is partially based on the fact that Hittite, the most ancient of the Indo-European languages found, also exhibits a similarly "simple" verbal system.

Germanic verbs continued the three number system with singular, dual, and plural. In addition, there were three moods: indicative, imperative, and subjunctive, two simple tenses: present and preterite, and two voices: active and medio-passive.

Perhaps the most prominent characteristic of the Germanic verb system was the strong versus weak distinction, an innovation peculiar to Germanic alone among the Indo-European daughter languages. This has been a much studied aspect in Germanic historical linguistics. One prominent theory as to the origin of the dental suffix in weak verbs is that it is derived from the verb "to do". As such, "walked" could essentially be analyzed as "walk-did". Still other scholars view the dental as a marker reflecting the state of the verb. The origin of the weak distinction itself (the strong being a continuation of Indo-European verb conjugation with ablaut as a major factor) seems to be a result of morphological "derivation" ("morphology" is the study of the structure of words, especially inflection and derivation of words). This simply means that a majority of weak verbs were verbs that were derived from other words, chiefly nouns or other verbs. Since they were essentially created as a new verb from some other part of speech at some point and thus did not have a "natural" preterite or past participle based on ablaut rules, a new way to show these tenses was needed. So under this theory, there was a noun "walk" (e.g., we often "take a walk", where "walk" is a noun), that eventually came to be used as a verb. Rather than create artificial ablaut patterns (walk-welk-wulken?), perhaps an ancient Germanic speaker once said "I will *do* (a) walk", and when she was done she said "I did (a) walk" (though the order must have been something more like "I (a) walk-did", and soon, this simply became "walked") (please note I am using Modern English only to illustrate the point, and not to show the actual derivation). The origin of the dental suffix is still hotly debated.

Germanic had seven classes of strong verbs (and some of these included sub-classes), most of which were based upon a specific ablaut-like pattern of vowel alternation in the different tenses and forms. There were four classes of weak verbs, distinguished by their suffixes.

The example below shows a strong verb conjugation for a thematic verb: *beranan ('to carry').

Germanic Thematic Conjugation: *beranan ('to carry')			
Number	Person	Present Indicative	Ending
Singular	1st	*beru	-u
	2nd	*biriz	-iz
	3rd	*birið	-ið
Dual	1st	*berōz	-ōz
	2nd	*beraðz	-aðz
Plural	1st	*berumz	-umz
	2nd	*bereð	-eð
	3rd	*berand	-and

The example below shows an athematic verb conjugation: *dōn ('to do'). Note that the biggest difference between the two conjugations can be seen in the first person singular: thematic "-u" versus athematic "-m", continuing from Indo-European.

Germanic Athematic Conjugation: *dōn ('to do')			
Number	Person	Present Indicative	Ending
Singular	1st	*dōm	-m
	2nd	*dōs	-s
	3rd	*dōð	-ð
Dual	1st	*dōu	-u
	2nd	*dōtz	-tz
Plural	1st	*dōmes	-mes
	2nd	*dōð	-ð
	3rd	*dōnd	-nd

In the table below you can see the conjugation for the verb "to be" in Germanic. It also utilizes four separate forms within the paradigm (with *wes as an imperative form, and *wes- forms in the preterite). It is likely that these forms were not interchangeable, and that each separate form had a certain meaning distinct from the others. Compare it with the conjugation of "to be" in Indo-European in the chapter above.

Conjugation of "to be" in Germanic				
Number	**Person**	**Present Indicative**		
Singular	1st	*beum	*im	
	2nd	*beus	*is	*art
	3rd	*beuþ	*ist	
Dual	1st	*beu	*ezu	*aru
	2nd	*beutz	*estz	*artz
Plural	1st	*beum	*ezumes	*arum
	2nd	*beuþ	*ezuþ	*aruþ
	3rd	*beun	*sind	*arun

Numbers

Here are the numbers from one to ten, as reconstructed for Germanic with the Indo-European numbers in the colum to the left of Germanic for easy comparison:

	Indo-European	Germanic
1	*oinos	*ainaz
2	*duwō	*twai
3	*treies	*þrijiz
4	*kʷetwores	*fidwōr
5	*penkʷe	*fimfi
6	*sweks	*seχs
7	*septm	*sebum
8	*oktō	*aχtō
9	*newn	*niwun
10	*dekm	*tehun

While most of these numbers follow a phonologically explicable pattern, the numbers four and five exhibit changes that are not explainable via sound changes alone. Phonologically speaking, it is very unlikely that the sound "kʷ" would become a "f" as a result of a sound law, yet this seems to have happened in the first syllable of *fidwōr and the second syllable of *fimfi. As it turns out, rather than an odd sound change, these changes were brought on by well-known types of phonological change. The "f" in *fidwōr replaced what should have been "χʷ" (via Grimm's Law) because of the influence of the beginning sound of the next number, *fimfi. The "kʷ" in *penkʷe became an "f" in *fimfi instead of the expected *finχʷi (Grimm's Law) as a result of a type of change called "assimilation". In this type of change, the "kʷ" that starts the second syllable is replaced by the sound that starts the first syllable, "f". A similar type of change happened in Latin and was passed down to its daughter languages, the Romance languages, for the number "five". Latin "quinque" (pronounced as if spelled "kween-kway") was a result of the anticipation of "kʷ" in the second syllable and substituting the original initial "p" for this sound.

The Subdivisions of Germanic

Germanic itself changed as people migrated from Scandinavia into continental Europe. It evolved into several different daughter languages, subdivided into three groups: East Germanic, North Germanic, and West Germanic. As you can guess by their names, the subdivisions are based in part on their geographical locations.

East Germanic dialects originated in the eastern part of the Germanic world, but eventually the East Germanic languages were spoken throughout much of Europe. The best known example, Gothic, which generally refers to the Gothic of Wulfila (more on him below), was spoken in Eastern Europe (in this case, in modern-day Bulgaria). No East Germanic languages survive to this day. We call the East Germanic languages "extinct" or "dead" languages.

North Germanic was spoken in the northern part of the Germanic world: Scandinavia, including modern-day Sweden, Norway, Denmark, and Iceland. The daughter language of Germanic that was the mother of modern Swedish, Norwegian, Danish, Faroese (spoken in the islands off the coast of Denmark and in Denmark itself), and Icelandic is called "Old Norse".

The third grouping of Germanic languages is called West Germanic. This is the group from which English ultimately sprang. The West Germanic daughter languages include Old High German, Old Saxon,

Old Frisian, Old Low Franconian, and Old English. Their modern-day children include High German, Low German, Yiddish, Pennsylvania Dutch, Dutch, Flemish, Frisian, and Afrikaans, in addition to English.

The Germanic Daughter Languages

Let's take a closer look at a few of the Germanic daughter languages. Figure 1. below shows approximate locations of some of the more prominent Germanic tribes during the first Millennium CE.

Figure 1: Germanic tribes, 1st Millennium CE

Gothic

The first Germanic daughter language that was written down at great length was Gothic, varieties of which were spoken throughout western, central, and eastern Europe early in the first millennium CE. Gothic is the best known member of the East Germanic languages. Other East Germanic languages include Vandalic and Burgundian.

The Goths most likely originated in southern Scandinavia (the reputed homeland of Germanic itself). Place names such as Östergötland, Västergötland, and Gotland, as well as legends and historical records all place the Goths in southern Sweden around the 1st century BCE. First and 2nd century CE accounts by the Greeks and Romans place the Goths between the Oder and Vistula rivers in modern-day Poland. They later formed settlements southwest of there to an area north and west of the Black Sea. From there, two distinct groups developed: the "Visigoths" and the "Ostrogoths". The former migrated throughout the Balkans, Italy, southern France, Spain, and Portugal. These conquerors were eventually conquered themselves by the Huns and Romans, and in other areas, they eventually assimilated into the local languages and cultures.

In the 4th century CE a Gothic bishop named Wulfila (311– 383 CE; sometimes called "Ulfilas") translated the Bible from Greek into his Gothic language. Wulfila was also a missionary. He eventually settled with his group of Christian converts in Moesia, in what is now modern-day Bulgaria.

Wulfila created his own alphabet, mostly based on the Greek alphabet and the runic alphabet (the "futhark" we saw earlier in this chapter), for his Bible translation. In Wulfila's alphabet, each letter is called a "bōka" (akin to our word "book"), and like the Greek alphabet it is partially based upon, each letter could also represent a number as well as a letter (in fact, two of the "letters" were only used as numbers).

Below you can see what the Gothic alphabet looked like with each letter's Modern English counterpart. Note that the three letters in parentheses represent the letters you will see in common transcriptions of Gothic using the Latin alphabet: "þ" for the "th" in "thorn", "j" for the "y" in "yard", and "ƕ" for "hw" of some English pronunciations of "when" ("hwen"). The numbers that each letter represented are to the right of the Latin transcription. Note that the symbols for 90 and 900 were not used as letters.

Gothic	Latin	Number	Gothic	Latin	Number
𐌰	a	1	𐌽	n	50
B	b	2	𐌲	y (j)	60
Γ	g	3	𐌿	u	70
𐌳	d	4	𐍀	p	80
Є	e	5	𐍁		90
𐌵	q	6	𐍂	r	100
Z	z	7	S	s	200
𐌷	h	8	T	t	300
𐍈	th (þ)	9	Y	w	400
I	i	10	𐍆	f	500
ï	i	10	X	x	600
K	k	20	Θ	hw (ƕ)	700
Λ	l	30	Ω	o	800
𐌼	m	40	↑		900

Besides Wulfila's Bible translation, which survives as fragmented manuscripts containing portions of both the Old and New Testaments (the most notable of which, the Codex Argenteus, is preserved in Uppsala, Sweden; a "codex" is a book made of manuscripts), there is an eight page commentary on the Gospel of John, called the "Skeireins", ('explanation', pronounced "skee-reens") miscellaneous religious texts, Latin deeds containing Gothic words and names, and Gothic names in Latin and Greek texts. In all, it is a fairly small corpus (a collection of texts). However, Gothic is extremely important in the study of Indo-European and Germanic because it is the most archaic language among the Germanic daughter languages with a corpus that goes beyond fragmented words and sentences (such as the runic inscriptions). As the oldest well-attested Germanic language, knowledge of Gothic is a must for anyone studying historical Indo-European linguistics.

Language

While Gothic does share some characteristics with both the North and West Germanic languages, it also has many features that are unique.

Rhotacism (the change from "z" to "r"), a feature of all of the other Germanic languages, was not evident in Gothic. All Germanic "z's" turned to "r" in the other languages but remained as "z" (or "s") in Gothic. Take a look at the examples below to see the correspondence between Gothic "s"/"z" and "r" in its sister Germanic languages.

Gothic	Old English	Old High German	Old Norse	Modern English
huzd	hord	hort	hodd	hoard
láisjan	lǣran	lēren		learn/teach
maiza	mā́ra	mḗro	meiri	more
razda	reord	rarta	rodd	(language)
wēsun	wǣron	wārun	váru	were

Of course, it is always possible that Gothic eventually went the way of the other Germanic languages with regards to rhotacism, but there is no textual evidence that shows this.

Another difference in Gothic is in an initial consonant cluster that is unique among the Germanic daughter languages, "þl" (you can say it by saying "Kathleen", then taking out "ka-"). Where Gothic has this cluster, the other daughter languages have "fl-": Gothic "þliuhan" ('to flee'), Old English "fleon", Old High German "fliohan", Old Norse "fljýa".

One feature that Gothic shares with Old Norse is "sharpening". Sharpening refers to a change from Germanic *jj and *ww (keep in mind that "j" is our Modern English "y" sound). In the other Germanic daughter languages, *jj and *ww became diphthongs, while in Gothic and Old Norse they changed to sounds like "d" and "g". See the examples below to compare this in several daughter languages.

Germanic	Gothic	Old English	Old High German	Old Norse	Modern English
*twajjē	twaddjē	twēgeat†	zweiio	tveggia	(of) two
*wajjuz	waddjus	wāg†		veggr	wall
*trewwjaz	triggws	trīewe	triuwi	tryggr	true
*γlawwuz	glaggws	glēaw	glau	glöggr	wise

†Note: "g" is pronounced like Modern English "y" in this context.

Lack of "umlaut" is another way in which Gothic differs from its sister languages. Most of the other languages exhibit umlaut, which simply refers to a change in the root vowel caused by a vowel in the following syllable. The most common vowels that caused umlaut were "i" (and similarly, "j" when acting as a vowel), also called "i-mutation", and "u" (or "w" when acting as a vowel). See the table below for some examples.

Germanic	Gothic	Old English	Old Norse	Modern English
*gastiz	gasts	giest	gestr	guest
*χanduz	handus	hond	hǫnd	hand
*nazjanan	nasjan	nerian		(save)

In addition to these phonological differences, there were also some other characteristics that set Gothic apart from its sister languages. These include: the retention of the masculine a-stem nominative singular marker from Germanic, the retention of a full "reduplicating" class of verbs, and a fusional passive construction, all described below.

In Germanic, as you saw in the noun declension example earlier in the chapter, the marker for the nominative singular of certain masculine nouns (Germanic "a-stem" nouns) was "-az". (These are called "a-stems" because they have an "a" in the stem; when referring to the parent Indo-European class, these are "o-stems"—this change was part of the "o → a merger" in Germanic, a change that occurred across the board, that is, all "short o" sounds in Indo-European became "short a" sounds in Germanic.) This inflection is still evident in Gothic, though with a slight change, dropping the "a" and devoicing the "z" to "s": Germanic "*daɣaz" ('day') → Gothic "dags". This sound was also changed in Old Norse, as we will see below, and dropped altogether in the West Germanic languages.

There were seven major verb classes in Germanic. Traditionally, the seventh class is the class of reduplicating verbs. "Reduplication" simply refers to the sounds in the first syllable of the word being duplicated. In this class the reduplication can be seen in the third person singular preterite indicative of "háitan" ('to call'): "haíháit" ('called'). You can see that that "hai-" is repeated (for comparison, the Modern German and Modern Dutch cognates do not show reduplication: German "heißen" and preterite "hieß" and Dutch "heten" and preterite "heette"). Another Gothic example is "slēpan" ('to sleep') with its preterite "saíslēp" ('slept'; with duplication of the initial "s") (compare with English "sleep" and "slept", Dutch "slapen", and "sliep").

The final difference we will cover here is the Gothic passive construction. As noted above in the chapter on Indo-European, the "passive" is a construction in which the subject of the sentence is not the performer of the action. For example, if I say "I hit the ball", that is an "active" sentence (we call it "active voice"). But if I say, "the ball was hit by me", "I" am still the one doing the hitting, but "the ball" is now the subject of the sentence. As you can see, in English we make this distinction by using an auxiliary verb (namely, a form of the verb "to be") plus the past participle of the verb. In Gothic (and in Germanic itself), the passive could be formed by an inflection on the end of the verb. For example, "baíran" ('to bear, to carry') becomes "baírada" ('is borne') in the third person singular present. "Nasjan" ('to save') becomes "nasjada" ('is saved'). This construction only occurred in the present tense—in other tenses the passive was created "periphrastically" (a phrase that has the same function as an inflected word), just as we do. This is perhaps a good indication that the fusionally constructed passive of Gothic was on its way out, in favor of an analytical construction, just as English has today.

Sample Texts

Following are some sample texts in Gothic to give you an idea of what the language was like in actual use. Most of these texts will be transcribed using our current alphabet. The first text will also be shown using the Gothic alphabet, to give you a flavor of what it looked like as a text.

The first text is the Lord's Prayer in Gothic (most of the ancient texts in the Germanic languages dealt with religious topics) with a transliteration in the Latin alphabet below the original text and a literal translation (that is, word for word) into Modern English. If you would like to read the text out loud, keep in mind the following pronunciation tips: the letter "þ" below has the sound of the "th" in the word "thorn", "ei" is pronounced like English "ee", "q" sounds like "qu", "h" sounds like "ch" in German "Bach", except at the beginning of a word, where it sounds like English "h", "j" sounds like "y", and "b", "d", and "g" become "ƀ", "ð", "ɣ", respectively, between vowels (see the pronunciation guide earlier in this chapter for examples of these sounds), and "gg" sounds like English "ng".

Gothic: Lord's Prayer
𐌰𐍄𐍄𐌰 𐌿𐌽𐍃𐌰𐍂 𐌸𐌿 𐌹𐌽 𐌷𐌹𐌼𐌹𐌽𐌰𐌼. 𐍅𐌴𐌹𐌷𐌽𐌰𐌹 𐌽𐌰𐌼𐍉 𐌸𐌴𐌹𐌽. 𐌵𐌹𐌼𐌰𐌹 𐌸𐌹𐌿𐌳𐌹𐌽𐌰𐍃𐍃𐌿𐍃 𐌸𐌴𐌹𐌽𐍃. 𐍅𐌰𐌹𐍂𐌸𐌰𐌹 𐍅𐌹𐌻𐌾𐌰 𐌸𐌴𐌹𐌽𐍃 𐍃𐍅𐌴 𐌹𐌽 𐌷𐌹𐌼𐌹𐌽𐌰 𐌾𐌰𐌷 𐌰𐌽𐌰 𐌰𐌹𐍂𐌸𐌰𐌹. 𐌷𐌻𐌰𐌹𐍆 𐌿𐌽𐍃𐌰𐍂𐌰𐌽𐌰 𐌸𐌰𐌽𐌰 𐍃𐌹𐌽𐍄𐌴𐌹𐌽𐌰𐌽 𐌲𐌹𐍆 𐌿𐌽𐍃 𐌷𐌹𐌼𐌼𐌰 𐌳𐌰𐌲𐌰. 𐌾𐌰𐌷 𐌰𐍆𐌻𐌴𐍄 𐌿𐌽𐍃 𐌸𐌰𐍄𐌴𐌹 𐍃𐌺𐌿𐌻𐌰𐌽𐍃 𐍃𐌹𐌾𐌰𐌹𐌼𐌰. 𐍃𐍅𐌰𐍃𐍅𐌴 𐌾𐌰𐌷 𐍅𐌴𐌹𐍃 𐌰𐍆𐌻𐌴𐍄𐌰𐌼 𐌸𐌰𐌹𐌼 𐍃𐌺𐌿𐌻𐌰𐌼 𐌿𐌽𐍃𐌰𐍂𐌰𐌹𐌼. 𐌾𐌰𐌷 𐌽𐌹 𐌱𐍂𐌹𐌲𐌲𐌰𐌹𐍃 𐌿𐌽𐍃 𐌹𐌽 𐍆𐍂𐌰𐌹𐍃𐍄𐌿𐌱𐌽𐌾𐌰𐌹 𐌰𐌺 𐌻𐌰𐌿𐍃𐌴𐌹 𐌿𐌽𐍃 𐌰𐍆 𐌸𐌰𐌼𐌼𐌰 𐌿𐌱𐌹𐌻𐌹𐌽.

Gothic	English Translation
Atta unsar þu in himinam,	Father ours thou in heaven
weihnai namo þein.	be hallowed name thine
qimai þiudinassus þeins.	come kingdom thine
wairþai wilja þeins,	become will thine
swe in himina jah ana airþai.	as in heaven also on earth.
hlaif unsarana þana sinteinan	bread ours the daily
gif uns himma daga.	give us this day.
jah aflet uns þatei skulans sijaima,	and forgive us that sinners we are
swaswe jah weis afletam	as also we forgive
þaim skulam unsaraim.	the sinners ours.
jah ni briggais uns	and not bring us
in fraistubnjai,	in tempting
ak lausei uns af þamma ubilin.	but deliver us from the evil one.

Although this may look very strange at first glance, you will notice certain similarities to English. For example, the word "þein", pronounced "theen", sounds a lot like the word "thine", which you may have encountered in certain editions of the Bible, or in a Shakespeare play (and, in fact, until just before Shakespeare's time, they were pronounced similarly). "Namo" (pronounced "NAH-mo") is easily identified as "name", "wilja" (WEEL-ya) as "will", and even "airþai", which was pronounced something like "AIR-thigh" sounds quite a bit like "earth", even if it does not look like our word at first glance. "Weis" (pronounced "wees") sounds an awful lot like English "we", "þatei" (THAHT-ee) is similar to "that", "uns" is a lot like "us", and even "briggais", which is pronounced "BRING-ice", is obviously "bring". With all of these similarities, it is easy to see that Modern English and Gothic are related.

Below are a few verses from the Wulfila Bible translation, Matthew, chapter 5, verses 16-18, from the *Codex Argenteus*, the "silver codex", so named because of its silver binding. Created in the 6th century from Wulfila's 4th century translation, parts of it were rediscovered at the abbey of Werden in the German Rhineland in the 16th century CE and other parts came to rest in the library of Emperor Rudolph II in Prague. It ended up in Uppsala, Sweden, in the 17th century, where it remains today. My translation here is a less literal one, but take a look to see where you can find matches between the Gothic and English texts.

Gothic	English Translation
swa liuhtjai liuhaþ izwar in and-wairþja manne, ei gasaihvaina izwara goda waurstwa jah hauh-jaina attan izwarana þana in himi-nam.	So let your light shine before men, that they may see your good works and praise your Father in heaven.
ni hugjaiþ ei qemjau gatairan wi-toþ aiþþau praufetuns; ni qam gatairan, ak usfulljan.	Do not think that I have come to destroy the law or the prophets; I have not come to destroy them but to fulfill them.
amen auk qiþa izwis: und þatei usleiþiþ himins jah airþa, jota ains aiþþau ains striks ni usleiþiþ af witoda, unte allata wairþiþ.	For I tell you truthfully, until heaven and earth disappear, not the smallest letter ('iota'), not the least stroke, will in no way disappear from the law until everything is fulfilled.

The Goths and their dialects spread all over the European continent. However, by the end of the first millennium, they had largely died out, having been overtaken by the descendents of Latin. However, Gothic dialects may have survived all the way into the 18th century in an area of modern-day Russia known as the Crimea. In the 16th century CE, a Flemish ambassador wrote down a list of approximately 80 words he had heard spoken in the Crimea, along with a few details about the grammar. Today, this language is generally acknowledged to have been a surviving vestige of the East Germanic languages.

Below are the numbers in Gothic, along with the Germanic and Indo-European counterparts for comparison.

	IE	Germanic	Gothic
1	*oinos	*ainaz	ains
2	*duwō	*twai	twai
3	*treies	*þrijiz	þreis
4	*kʷetwores	*fidwōr	fidwor
5	*penkʷe	*fimfi	fimf
6	*sweks	*seχs	saihst[†]
7	*septm	*sebum	sibun
8	*oktō	*aχtō	ahtau[†]
9	*newn	*niwun	niun
10	*dekm	*tehun	taihun[†]

[†]Note that in Gothic, the spelling "ai" sometimes represents an "ay" sound in "day" (without the "y" sound), and "au" a sound like the "a" in "awe".

Old Norse

Next, let's take a look at Old Norse. There is an extensive amount of literature written in Old Norse dialects. It was the language of the Vikings, who wrote many stories, called *sagas* and *eddas* about Viking heroes. The eddas, written in Iceland as both prose and poetry, were written down in the 13th century CE. They are an important source of our knowledge of Old Norse mythology. The sagas were epic tales written in prose, detailing early Germanic and Scandinavian history, Viking voyages, the migrations to Iceland, and feuds among the various clans in Iceland. The sagas were written down from the 10th to the 14th centuries.

Over time, various tribes were differentiated within Scandinavia, and eventually they migrated to various parts of their homeland and beyond. The Danes moved south out of the presumed Germanic homeland in southern Sweden, to present-day Zealand and the Jutland peninsula, once it was vacated by the Angles and other peoples who moved to England. The Swedes spread throughout the southern and central territory we now call Sweden, conquering other groups such as the Geats (a well-known people in Germanic literature—Beowulf, whom we will hear more about later was a "prince of the Geats"). The Norwegians moved to the North and West settling in modern-day Norway (from the words "North" and "way").

In the middle of the 8th century CE the Vikings began their excursions, with Norwegian Vikings striking Ireland and England. The Danish Vikings began their attacks early in the 9th century, attacking northern Germany, the Netherlands, Belgium, and northern France. The Danes eventually conquered most of England, and for a time, a Danish king ruled the country. The Duchy of Normandy in the north of France was also ruled by the descendents of the Vikings (the name itself comes from "north men") who eventually assimilated into French culture. The Vikings also founded settlements in Iceland and Greenland, and it is evident that they were the first Europeans to land in North America with settlements discovered in Newfoundland.

Once Christianity made its way to Scandinavia beginning late in the 10th century with the Danes and ending with the conversion of the Swedes by the mid 12th century, the Viking threat diminished.

Language

As a North Germanic language, Old Norse was defined by characteristics not found in the East or West Germanic languages, though it also shared characteristics with both groups as well.

One of the characteristics it shared with West Germanic was umlaut, as discussed in the last section. Old Norse had three types of umlaut: a-umlaut, which changed the quality of certain vowels when these vowels preceded a syllable with an "a" (and some other vowel sounds), i-umlaut, which changed the quality of some vowels when the following syllable contained "i" or "j", and finally u-umlaut, which transformed vowels that were *not* pronounced with rounded lips, into vowels that were pronounced with rounded lips. These fairly drastic changes resulted in vowels that differ greatly from their East and West Germanic counterparts.

Like Gothic, Old Norse was also subject to sharpening, though Germanic *jj and *ww both became "gg" in Old Norse. Unlike Gothic, Old Norse *was* subject to rhotacism of Germanic *z. An intermediate stage in Old Norse between *z and "r" is often represented as "R" as seen earlier in the chapter in the runic transcriptions.

Old Norse also kept the masculine a-stem singular nominative ending from Germanic, but it changed due to rhotacism. Germanic "*daɣaz" ('day') → Runic "dagaR" → Old Norse "dagr" (compare Gothic "dags", Old English "dæg", Old High German "tac").

One of the characteristics that sets apart Old Norse (and its modern descendents) from the other Germanic languages is a "post-posed" definite article. In English (and, indeed, in all of the other Germanic languages), the definite article always precedes the noun it modifies: "*the* gift", "*the* tree". But in Old Norse the definite article often *followed* the noun it modified—we call this a "post-posed" article, for example, "gjǫf" ('gift') and "gjǫfin" ('the gift'), "tré" ('tree') and "tréit" ('the tree'). The article was often attached to the noun itself.

Sample Texts

Below are some sample texts from Old Norse. The first is an example of the Lord's Prayer in Old Norse, for comparison with the other Germanic daughter languages. The translation is a literal one.

The first thing you may notice is Old Norse made use of some letters that were not in the Latin alphabet: "ð", called "eth" is pronounced like the "th" in "the", "þ" is "th" in "thorn", and "æ", called "ash", is pronounced like the "a" in "ash". These symbols were also used above in describing the sounds of Germanic. The "accents" over the vowels (such as "í", "ó", "á") simply mean that the vowel is a long vowel.

Take a look at the Old Norse words, and you may notice some familiar ones: "Faþer" is nearly identical to English "father"; "til" was actually borrowed into English from Scandinavian, and has given us "until and '"till"; "kome" is again, nearly identical to our word; "þin", like its Gothic counterpart looks very much like English "thine", and even words such as "iarðu", pronounced "yarthu" and "fyr gefom", pronounced something like "feergayfoam" can easily be seen as related to our language, especially once you say them out loud. So, what at first glance looks quite foreign, still has many words that are recognizable in English today. Just as with Gothic, you can see that this language is indeed related to English.

Old Norse	English Translation
Faþer vár es ert í himenríki,	Father our who is in heavenly kingdom,
verði nafn þitt hæilagt	become name yours holy
Til kome ríke þitt,	To come kingdom yours,
værði vili þin	become will yours
sva a iarðu sem í himnum.	so on earth same in heaven
Gef oss í dag brauð vort dagligt	Give us today bread ours daily
Ok fyr gefþu oss synþer órar,	And forgive us sins ours
sem vér fyr gefom þeim er viþ oss hafa misgert	Same we forgive them who against us have committed wrong
Leiðd oss eigi í freistni, heldr leys þv oss frá öllu illu.	Lead us not in temptation, rather free thou us from all evil

The text below is the prologue to *Snorri's Edda*, also known as the *Prose Edda*, written by Snorri Sturluson around 1220 CE.

Old Icelandic	English Translation
Óðinn hafði spádóm ok svá kona hans, ok af þeim vísendum fann hann þat, at nafn hans myndi uppi vera haft í norðrhálfu heims ok tignat um fram alla konunga. Fyrir þá sök fýstist hann at byrja ferð sína af Tyrklandi ok hafði með sér mikinn fjölda liðs, unga menn ok gamla, karla ok konur, ok höfðu með sér marga gersamliga hluti. En hvar sem þeir fóru yfir lönd, þá var ágæti mikit frá þeim sagt, svá at þeir þóttu líkari goðum en mönnum. Ok þeir gefa eigi stað ferðinni, fyrr en þeir koma norðr í þat land, er nú er kallat Saxland. Þar dvaldist Óðinn langar hríðir ok eignaðist víða þat land.	Odin had the power of divination, and so did his wife, and from their foreknowledge he found that his name would be exalted in the northern part of the world and honored above all other kings. Therefore he was eager to begin his journey out of Turkland and had many people, young and old, men and women, with him and they had many expensive things. And wherever they went over the lands, great things were said of them, so that they were said to be more like gods than men. And they did not stop on their journey before they came north into that land which is now called Saxland. There Odin remained a while and subjugated the land.

The language of the text is most properly called "Old Icelandic". The English translation is a non-literal translation of the text. It is a snippet of the story of how the god Odin, the chief god in the Germanic pantheon, came from the land of the Turks to the northern Germanic territory and conquered it. Known in English as "Woden", his name is the source of one of the days of the week in English: "Woden's day" has become "Wednesday".

As we will see below, Old Norse had some influence on its contemporary sister language, Old English, resulting from continual incursions by the Vikings onto English soil.

The Old Norse period lasted until approximately 1300 CE. Various dialects eventually become Modern Danish, Norwegian, Swedish, Faroese, and Icelandic (the most conservative of all existing Germanic languages; modern Icelanders can read the language above about as easily as we can read more antiquated versions of Early Modern English, that is, it has changed comparatively little in a millennium).

Below are the numbers in Old Norse, with the Indo-European and Germanic counterparts for comparison. The two forms for "one" are a result of inflection for gender.

	IE	Germanic	Old Norse
1	*oinos	*ainaz	einn, eitt
2	*duwō	*twai	tveir
3	*treies	*þrijiz	þrír
4	*kʷetwores	*fidwōr	fjórir
5	*penkʷe	*fimfi	fimm
6	*sweks	*seχs	sex
7	*septm	*seƀum	siau
8	*oktō	*aχtō	átta
9	*newn	*niwun	nío
10	*dekm	*tehun	tío

West Germanic

The largest group of languages comes from the West Germanic family. From Old High German (OHG) we have today's Modern German (also called "New High German"), its various dialects, Pennsylvania Dutch (a mixture of High German dialects spoken in the US and Canada), and Yiddish (actually derived from Middle High German, the German language of the Middle Ages, though it is written in Hebrew script); from Old Saxon (OS), we have various "Low German" dialects spoken in Northern Germany; from Old Low Franconian (OLF), we have modern Dutch, Flemish, and Afrikaans (spoken in South Africa); from Old Frisian (OF), we have modern Frisian, spoken in the northern parts of the Netherlands and Germany; and from Old English (OE), we have Modern English and Scots English (considered a separate language by some, it is best known among speakers of English in the song "Auld Lang Syne", literally "old long since", meaning "long ago").

Old High German

Old High German is the language that would eventually become Modern German. Although it is more closely related to English than Gothic or Old Norse, you may find it most difficult to pick out familiar words from an Old High German text than any other Germanic texts. This is because Old High German underwent further sound changes that no other Germanic languages did: the "High German Consonant Shift" (more on this below). "High" in the term "High German" simply refers to the geography of the land the various tribes occupied—it was in the southern part of modern Germany, Switzerland and Austria, among others; in general, hilly or mountainous areas (i.e., "high" ground), as opposed to the Low Germans who occupied low-lying land in the North.

The speakers of Old High German dialects originated in the middle and lower regions surrounding the Elbe river. These speakers included Franconian, Thuringian, Bavarian, Suebi/Suevi, and Alemannic tribes. They came in constant contact and conflict with the Romans and other Germanic tribes for several centuries in the same general area of modern Germany today. Many of the dialects of Old High German bear the names of the tribes who spoke them. These dialects include Ripuarian (around modern-day Cologne), Moselle Franconian (around Trier), Rhenish Franconian to its southeast, and East Franconian to the east of this area, all Franconian (also called "Frankish") tribes (related to the ancestors of the speakers of Old Low Franconian). Northeast of the East Franconian area was East Middle German. To its south was Bavarian, and west of Bavarian were Swabian and Alemannic.

Language

The High German Consonant Shift, often called the "Second Germanic Sound Shift", is in many ways parallel to the First Germanic Sound Shift (Grimm's Law). With this second shift, the voiceless stops "p", "t", and "k", as well as their voiced counterparts, "b", "d", and "g" were affected. In the table below, you can see these changes.

High German Consonant Shift		
Germanic	Old High German	Examples
p	1: pf/ph* 2: ff	Old English: helpan OHG: helphan Old Saxon: slāpan OHG: slaffan
t	1: z 2: ʒ/ʒʒ†	Old English: tīen OHG: zehan OLF: etan OHG: eʒʒan
k	1: ch 2: ch/hh‡	Old English: corn OHG: chorn Old Frisian: makia OHG: mahhōn
b	(p)	Old English: beran OHG: peran
d	t	Old Saxon: dag OHG: tac
g	(k)	Old Saxon: gast OHG: kast

*This sound, spelled these two ways, sounds like the "p-f" in "up for".
†The sound represented by "z" is pronounced like the "ts" in "hats"; "ʒ" is pronounced somewhat like "s" in "so".
‡The first "ch" is pronounced "kχ" (the "k" + "ch" in German "Bach"), the second "hh/ch" is pronounced like "χχ".

In the Old High German column in the table above, the first instance occurs when the corresponding Germanic sound appeared word-initially, medially after certain consonants (l, r, m, n), and when doubled (referred to as "1." above). The second instance of each sound is the change that occurred when the corresponding Germanic sound appeared "medially", that is, between vowels, or word final after a vowel (referred to as "2." above). The Examples column shows examples of Old High German words with cognates in its sister West Germanic languages, including Old English, Old Saxon, Old Low Franconian (OLF), and Old Frisian. In the Old High German examples you can see the consonant shift, while in the other languages, you can see that the original consonants from Germanic remain.

Germanic "p" became "pf", often written "ph" in 1. This sound, still heard in Modern German, can be heard in English if you say "up for" very quickly. In 2., "p" became a geminated "ff". Germanic "t" became "z" (pronounced like the "ts" in "hits") in 1., and became a special "s" sound, written with a special letter, "ʒ", in 2. This would eventually become a regular "s" sound in Modern German, sometimes written "ss", and under certain circumstances, with "ß". Germanic "k" only became "ch" (pronounced "kχ" ; recall that "χ" is the sound of "ch" in German "Bach") in 1. in the southernmost dialects (Upper Germanic); it is still often heard in many modern dialects of Swiss German. In 2. it became "ch" (often spelled "hh", pronounced "χ") in all but the northernmost dialects, such as some Franconian dialects. Germanic "b" became "p" and "g" became "k" only in the southernmost dialects. The change of "d" to "t" however, was widespread.

The High German Consonant Shift seemed to begin in the mountainous regions in the southern and southwestern parts of this area and spread northward. This is why only certain "Upper German" dialects, like Alemannic, embraced the entire sound shift, including the full shift of Germanic "k". As the changes drifted northward, they had a lesser and lesser effect.

Old High German also shared some characteristics with its other sister languages. Like Old Norse, it exhibited i-umlaut of "a", "o", "u", and their diphthongs, such as "ou" and "uo". Old High German was subject to rhotacism, but not the sharpening of Germanic *jj and *ww we saw in Gothic and Old Norse.

In addition to the High German Consonant Shift, another major difference between these dialects and their West Germanic siblings is in the personal pronouns of the third person singular. Most of its siblings have forms beginning with "h", but these are completely absent in Old High German

Another characteristic of Old High German (and several other of its sister languages) is called "final devoicing". This affected the voiced stops "b", "d", and "g". When one of these sounds came at the end of a word, it was "devoiced" (i.e., pronounced as if it were its voiceless counterpart, "p", "t", "k", respectively). In Old High German, this was generally also seen in the orthography (its writing system; "k" was usually written "c"). Therefore, you will see "ge**b**an" ('to give') with "b", but "gi**p**" (the imperative, 'give!') with "p" since the sound now appears at the end of the word in this form. Likewise you will see "ta**g**es" ('day' in the genitive case,) but "ta**c**" in the nominative. Note that the change in spelling does not always occur, but these sounds are nonetheless devoiced finally regardless. In Modern German, the spelling does not change, but these consonants are still devoiced in final position. The common "Guten Tag!" ('good day', 'hello') is actually pronounced "gooten tah**k**".

The Old High German period lasted from the 9th to 11th centuries CE. To this day, however, the division of dialects within Germany, Austria, and Switzerland still reflects the various groups and their associated dialects from late in this period.

Sample Texts

The dialects we collectively call Old High German varied widely. Below are four sample texts of the Lord's Prayer in some of the most prominent dialects of the period. These will show you the degree of variation among the various dialects. Note that in my transcriptions in this book, I use a macron for long vowels for consistency throughout. However, if you go on to read more about Old High German, Old Saxon, and Old Low Franconian elsewhere, many texts use a circumflex accent, such as "â, ê, î, ô, û" to show long vowels.

Alemannic	English Translation
Fater unseer, thu pist in himile,	father ours thou art in heaven
uuihi namun dinan,	hallowed be name thy
qhueme rihhi diin,	may come kingdom thy
uuerde uuillo diin,	become thy will
so in himile sosa in erdu.	so in heaven as in earth
prooth unseer emezzihic kip uns hiutu,	bread ours continual give us today
oblaz uns sculdi unsero,	forgive us our debts
so uuir oblazem uns skuldikem,	as we forgive our debts
enti ni unsih firleiti in khorunka,	and not lead us in temptation
uzzer losi unsih fona ubile.	but deliver us from evil.

Bavarian	English Translation
Fater unsēr dū pist in himilum	father ours thou art in heaven
kauuīhit sī namo dīn	hallowed be name thy
piqhueme rīhhi dīn	may come kingdom thy
uuesa dīn uuillo	be thy will
sama sō in himile est sama in erdu.	same as in heaven is same in earth
pilipi unsraȥ emizzīgaȥ	food ours continual
kip uns eogauuanna	give us always
enti flāȥ uns unsro sculdi	and forgive us our debts
sama sō uuir flāȥȥamēs unsrēm scolōm	same as we forgive our debts
enti ni princ unsih in chorunka	and not bring us in temptation
uȥȥan kaneri unsih fona allēm suntōn	but deliver us from all sins

The two texts above are from Upper German dialects from what is today modern-day Switzerland and Bavaria. For the most part, they show the full implementation of the High German Consonant Shift. The texts below, both from Middle and Central German dialects, show evidence that the consonant shift was not complete in these more northern areas.

Rhenish Franconian	English Translation
Fater unsēr, thu in himilom bist,	father ours thou in heaven art
giuuīhit sī namo thīn.	hallowed be name thy
quaeme rīchi thīn.	may come kingdom thy.
uuerdhe uuilleo thīn,	become thy will,
sama sō in himile endi in erthu.	same as in heaven and in earth
Brooth unseraz emezzīgaȥ gib uns hiutu.	bread ours continual give us today
endi farlāȥ uns sculdhi unsero,	and forgive us our debts,
sama sō uuir farlāȥȥēm scolōm unserēm.	same as we forgive our debts.
endi ni gileidi unsih in costunga.	and not lead us in temptation
auh arlōsi unsih fona ubile.	also deliver us from evil.

East Franconian	English Translation
Fater unser, thū thār bist in himile,	father ours thou who art in heaven
sī geheilagōt thīn namo,	be hallowed thy name
queme thīn rīhhi,	may come kingdom thy
sī thīn uuillo,	be thy will
sō her in himile ist, sō sī her in erdu,	as here in heaven is so be here in earth
unsar brōt tagalīhhaz gib uns hiutu,	our bread daily give us today
inti furlāz uns unsara sculdi	and forgive us our debts
sō uuir furlāzemēs unsarēn sculdīgōn,	as we forgive our debts
inti ni gileitēst unsih in costunga,	and not lead us in temptation
ūzouh arlōsi unsih fon ubile.	but deliver us from evil.

You may be able to see some similarities to English in the Lord's Prayer examples ("fater" is "father", "namo" is "name", "uuillo" is "will", "sama" is "same") but many of the words are hard to decipher because of the High German Consonant Shift. Also notice the differences among each of the examples. For instance, the Alemannic and Bavarian texts often use "p" where the others use "b" ("pist" versus "bist" ('(thou) art'), "prooth" versus "brōt" ('bread')), and "k" where others use "g" ("kauuīhit" versus "giuuīhit" ('hallowed'), "kip" versus "gip" ('give')).

The example below is one of the earliest known poetic works of Old High German, the *Wessobrunner Gebet* ('Wessobrunn Prayer'), written ca. 790 CE, author unknown. It is named after the monastery at Wessobrunn in modern-day Bavaria. The poem consists of two parts: the first is nine lines of alliterative verse, and the second is the actual prayer (for the wisdom and strength to avoid sin) in free prose. The title, in bold italics below, is in Latin.

Old High German	English Translation
De Poeta	*Of the Creator*
Dat gafregin ih mit firahim firiuuizzo meista	That I discovered among men (as the) greatest wonder
Dat ero ni uuas noh ufhimil	That (there) was (once) neither earth nor heaven above
noh paum [nohheinig]* noh pereg ni uuas	nor was (there)[any] tree [at all] nor mountain
ni [sterro] nohheinig noh sunna ni scein	neither any [star] at all nor (did the) sun shine
noh mano ni liuhta noh der mareo seo	nor (the) moon glow nor (was there) the great sea.
Do dar niuuiht ni uuas enteo ni uuenteo	But when (there) was nothing there, no ending nor turns'
enti do uuas der eino almahtico cot	ends there was the one almighty God
manno miltisto enti dar uuarun auh manake mit inan	of all beings (the) greatest (in) grace and there were many with him
cootlihhe geista enti cot heilac [ist]	glorious spirits and God [is] holy
Cot almahtico, du himil enti erda gauuorahtos enti du mannun so manac coot forgapi forgip mir in dina ganada rehta galaupa enti cotan uuilleon uuistom enti spahida enti craft tiuflun za uuidarstantanne enti arc za piuuisanne enti dinan uuilleon za gauurchanne.	God Almighty, who wrought heaven and earth and who gave so much good to men in your grace give me right belief and good will, wisdom, and knowledge and power to withstand devils and turn from evil and to work your will.

*Brackets, [...], show places where words are missing; presumed original words are inserted in these instances.

Below are the numbers in Old High German, along with the Indo-European and Germanic counterparts for comparison with the other Germanic daughter languages.

	IE	Germanic	Old High German
1	*oinos	*ainaz	ein
2	*duwō	*twai	zwēne
3	*treies	*þrijiz	drī
4	*kʷetwores	*fidwōr	fior
5	*penkʷe	*fimfi	fimf
6	*sweks	*seχs	sehs
7	*septm	*sebum	sibun
8	*oktō	*aχtō	ahto
9	*newn	*niwun	niun
10	*dekm	*tehun	zehan

Old Saxon

Next we will take a look at Old Saxon. This language, sometimes known as "Old Low German", is perhaps best known for a work called *"Heliand"*, ('savior'). It is a retelling of the Biblical gospels from a distinctly Germanic perspective, with Jesus as a Germanic hero, written in alliterative verse (we will talk more about this specific type of poetry in the chapter on Old English). It was written in the early to mid 9th CE.

The Saxons were first written about in the middle of the 2nd century CE, at the time occupying modern-day Holstein in Germany and the northeastern part of the Netherlands, from the North Sea coast to the lower Elbe. They were bordered by Slavs to the east, Danes to the North, Frisians to the northwest, and Franks to the south and west. The Saxons got their names from the *sahs*, a short sword or dagger that was essentially their trademark weapon. The Saxons of the North Sea area were the very same people who eventually helped to settle England. Towards the end of the 3rd century CE the Saxons began invasions of Roman occupied northern Gaul (modern-day France) and southeastern England. While the former were eventually integrated with the Franks (with whom they had a sometimes amicable, but mostly adversarial relationship), the latter, along with other North Sea Germanic tribes (the Angles and Jutes) continued to settle modern-day England.

Beginning in 772 CE, Charlemagne, king of the Franks, began a series of invasions into Saxon territory to conquer it and convert the Saxons to Christianity. However, it was not until 804 CE that the last of the Saxon nobles finally surrendered and the Saxons were integrated into Charlemagne's Holy Roman Empire.

Language

Old Saxon spelling uses "th" for the "þ" sound (in "thin") as well as for the "ð" sound (in Modern English "the"); in some documents, though, "ð" is also sometimes used. When "th" appears word-initial, word-final, or before a voiceless consonant, it is pronounced "þ", otherwise it is pronounced "ð". Old Saxon also has a new letter, "ƀ", which stood for the same "v"-like sound we saw for this character in Germanic. It alternated with "f" in a regular fashion: "ƀ" appeared medially between vowels, and "f" elsewhere (word-initial, word-final, medially before a voiceless consonant). The letter "g" represents several different sounds: "g" in "go" when word-initial, "γ" when medial after a "back" vowel ("a", "o", "u"), a "y" sound similar to that in "yes" when medial after a "front" vowel "i" or "e", and "χ" word-finally, except after "n", when it was pronounced as "k". Old Saxon uses "uu" for the "w" sound.

As a West Germanic language, Old Saxon shares many features with its West Germanic sister languages. The absence of the High German Consonant Shift distinguishes it from Old High German: Old Saxon has "bōk", "opan", "tunga" versus Old High German "buoch", "offan", "zunga", and "bist", "dag", "geƀa" versus (Upper German) "pist", "tac", "keba". Like its sister North Sea dialects Old English and Old Frisian, Old Saxon drops nasal consonants that come before the fricatives, "s", "þ", and "f": "ōthar" ('other'), "fîf" ('five') versus Old High German "andar", "fimf" (compare the Old Saxon words with Old English "ōþer", "fîf" and Old Frisian "ōther", "fîf"). Old Saxon, along with Old English and Old Frisian, did not distinguish person in the verb plural endings: first, second, and third person plural verbs shared a common ending for all tenses and moods.

Sample Texts

The *Heliand* is the only literary text available in Old Saxon. Although the original manuscript no longer survives, it is estimated that it would have been about 6000 lines of verse. Surviving are three larger manuscript copies (one, perhaps the oldest, was relatively recently discovered in a library in Leipzig, Germany in April, 2006), and three fragments.

The text of the *Heliand* is somewhat problematic in linguistic terms. There are obvious influences from Old English, Old Frisian, and Old High German. Some have argued that the text is written in a sort of pidgin to appeal to a wide majority of people. However, a simpler answer would be that the text was influenced by a possible original in another language (such as Old English) and by scribes of other languages copying the text imperfectly, allowing their own dialects to influence their writing.

Old Saxon	English Translation
Fadar ūsa firiho barno,	Father ours of mens' sons,
thu bist an them hōhon himila rīkea	thou art in the high heavenly kingdom
geuuīhid sī thīn namo uuordo gehuuilico.	hallowed be thy name (with) every word.
Cuma thīn craftag rīki.	May come thy mighty kingdom.
Uuerða thīn uuilleo oƀar thesa uuerold alla,	Become thy will all over this world,
sō sama an erðo, sō thar uppa ist	as same on earth, as (it) is there up
an them hōhon himilo rīkea.	in the high heavenly kingdom.
Gef ūs dago gehuuilikes rīd, drohtin the gōdo,	Give us of days every support, Lord the good,
thīna hēlaga helpa, endi alīt ūs, hebenes uuard,	thy holy help, and absolve us, heaven's guard,
managoro mēnsculdio, al sō uue ōðrum mannum dōan.	of many offenses, as we to other men do.
Ne līt ūs farlēdean lēða uuihti	Do not let us lead astray evil little creatures
sō forð an iro uuilleon, sō uui uuirðige sind,	so forth in their will, if we worthy are,
ac help ūs uuiðar allun uƀilon dādiun.	but help us against all evil deeds.

The *Heliand* text is a good example of how epic poetry was written at the time. The first text, above, an example of the Lord's Prayer, is relatively straightforward. The next example, the Biblical story of the Annunciation of the angel Gabriel to Mary that she would bear a child, is a bit more difficult to understand. In this poetic language, whole phrases and clauses that would always be close to the nouns or phrases they modify in Modern English, often appear separated. As such, I have created a near word-for-word translation first to help you read through the text, and then a less literal one below so that you can more clearly see how each piece fits together.

Old Saxon

Thō ni uuas lang aftar thiu, ne it al sō gilēstid uuarð,

sō he mancunnea managa huīla,

god alomahtig forgeƀen habda,

that he is himilisc barn herod te uueroldi,

is selƀes sunu sendean uueldi,

te thiu that he hēr alōsdi al liudstamna,

uuerod fon uuītea. Thō uuarð is uuisbodo

an Galilealand, Gabriel cuman,

engil thes alouualdon, thar he ēne idis uuisse,

munilīca magað: Maria uuas siu hēten,

uuas iru thiorna githigan. Sea ēn thegan habda,

Ioseph gimahlit, gōdes cunnies man,

thea Dauides dohter: that uuas sō diurlīc uuīf,

idis anthēti. Thar sie the engil godes

an Nazarethburg bi namon selƀo

grōtte geginuuarde endi sie fon gode quedda:

"Hēl uuis thu, Maria," quað he, "thu bist thīnun hērron liof,

uualdande uuirðig, huuand thu giuuit haƀes,

idis enstio fol. Thu scalt for allun uuesan

uuībun giuuīhit…"

English Literal Translation

Then it was not long after that, no it all so done was

so he to mankind for a long time,

God almighty to give had

that he is heavenly child hither to the world,

is the same son to want to send,

to those that he here redeemed all people

people from punishment. Then became trusted messenger

to Galilee, Gabriel came,

angel of the Creator, who he one woman knew,

lovely maiden: Mary was she called,

was a well-grown maiden. She had a thane,

spoken for by Joseph, man of good kin,

the daughter of David: that was such a praiseworthy woman,

woman pledged. There her the angel of God

at the city of Nazareth by name

greeted face to face and to her spoke of God:

"Hale be thou, Mary," said he, "thou art dear to your Lord,

worthy to the Ruler, for thou hast understanding,

woman full of grace. Thou shalt be before all

women blessed…"

English Translation

It was not long after that that God wanted to send his heavenly child to the world to redeem mankind from punishment.

Then he sent his trusted messenger Gabriel, angel of the Creator, to Galilee, to the lovely maiden: Mary she was called, a well-grown woman. She was spoken for by Joseph, a man of good kin. This daughter of David was such a praiseworthy woman, pledged to her husband.

There at the city of Nazareth the angel of God greeted her face to face by name and spoke to her from God: "Hale be thou, Mary, woman full of grace" said he, "thou art dear to your Lord, worthy to the Ruler, for thou hast understanding. Thou shalt be blessed above all women…"

Below are the numbers in Old Saxon, along with the Germanic and Indo-European counterparts for comparison.

	IE	Germanic	Old Saxon
1	*oinos	*ainaz	ēn
2	*duwō	*twai	tuuē
3	*treies	*þrijiz	thria
4	*kʷetwores	*fidwōr	fiuuuar
5	*penkʷe	*fimfi	fīf
6	*sweks	*seχs	sehs
7	*septm	*sebum	sibun
8	*oktō	*aχtō	ahto
9	*newn	*niwun	nigun
10	*dekm	*tehun	tehan

Old Low Franconian

Old Low Franconian is the oldest form of the modern Dutch dialects in the eastern part of the Dutch language area (it is not a direct predecessor to Modern Dutch, which is one of the reasons it is usually not referred to as "Old Dutch"). The name "Franconian" refers to the Franks—the same ancient Germanic tribe discussed in the section on Old High German. The Franks, though a Germanic tribe, eventually gave their name to the people we now call "French" (from Old English "frencisc", pronounced "frenchish"), though the French language is an Italic language, coming to us via Latin. The term "Old Low Franconian" is the most common one used to denote this language but another term is also gaining acceptance: "Old Low Frankish". You may also come across the term "Old Netherlandic". The Old Low Franconian era lasted from approximately the 9th to the 12th centuries CE.

As the Roman empire was dying in the 3rd and 4th centuries CE, a new federation of Frankish tribes, including the Salians, Ripuarians, and Hessians began to systematically invade Roman territory in the areas of the present-day Netherlands, the German Rhineland, and the Moselle river valley, conquering these areas by the mid 5th century. It was the Merovingian king Clovis (also known as "Chlodwig") who eventually became the king of all the Franks by late in the 5th century. Clovis conquered a considerable amount of land in central Europe, conquering a large portion of modern France in addition to increasing the size of his territory in Germany. By the mid 6th century, the Franks had conquered the Bavarians, Burgundians, and Thuringians, pushing far to the south of modern-day Germany. Perhaps the height of Frankish power was reached on Christmas Day, 800 CE, when the Carolingian king Charlemagne was crowned emperor of the Holy Roman Empire. Charlemagne was not only a great king, but also a patron of the arts, and was ultimately responsible for the creation of many of the texts of his day.

It is important to keep in mind that the Franks in the former Roman Gaul (modern-day France) also spoke an Old French dialect, which had evolved from vulgar Latin (that is, Latin as spoken by the people, or the "colloquial" language) and was influenced by the Germanic dialects surrounding it. In addition, it is important to understand that, although certain Frankish dialects are considered to be Old Low Franconian and others Old High German, the key difference among these was simply the High Germanic Consonant Shift, which affected the latter to certain degrees, but not the former. That their current incarnation is as dialects of separate languages (Dutch in the one case and German in another) shows that the boundaries of what is a dialect versus what is a language can be somewhat arbitrary and fluid.

Old Low Franconian is thus a dialect that was spoken in the eastern territory of the modern-day Netherlands and the areas of modern-day Germany bordering this area along the Rhine, just north of Cologne. Modern Dutch is related to these dialects, but it was the dialects of the western part of the modern-day Netherlands that have evolved into the standard language. The eastern dialect discussed here, however, is nonetheless quite similar and has the most extensive written records for the earliest period (though even these are quite sparse). As such, it has become the standard dialect studied by historical linguists.

Perhaps the most common words associated with Old Low Franconian are the following:

> **Hebban olla vogala nestas hagunnan hinase hic
> enda thu uuat unbidan uue nu.**

The English translation is:

> **All birds have started making nests, except me
> and thee, what are we waiting for now.**

Written in the 12th century CE, by a Flemish monk in the margin of a Latin manuscript in the abbey of Rochester, Kent, England, there is some question as to whether this is indeed an Old Low Franconian dialect or an Old English dialect (the two were quite similar). It is often cited as the oldest text in Dutch, however, fragments from the Salic Law (6th century) and the Wachtendonk Psalms (10th century) are considerably older.

Language

Old Low Franconian exhibits some features that are unique among the West Germanic daughter languages. The consonant cluster "-ft-" sometimes became "-(c)ht-" (with a "χ" sound): Old High German "stiften" ('to found') versus Old Low Franconian "stihtan". The cluster "-chs-" became "-(s)s-": Old High German "fuhs" ('fox') and Old Saxon "fohs" (on both cases, "h" sounded like "χ") versus Old Low Franconian "fus". Another unique feature of Old Low Franconian is the first person singular ending for the verb, "-on", in the present indicative: Old Low Franconian "ic macon" ('I make') versus Old English "ic macie", Old Frisian "ic makie" (but note Old High German "ih mahhōn", the normal ending for a certain class of weak verbs—the common ending in Old Low Franconian was possibly changed to this for all verbs by analogy based on these fairly high frequency verbs) .

One feature that Old Low Franconian shares with Old High German, setting them both apart from the other Germanic languages, is the lack of a masculine a-stem plural ending in "-s" (which became the basis for the Modern English plural: Gothic "dagōs" ('days'), Old Norse "dagar" (with rhotacism of the Germanic "z"), Old English "dagas", Old Saxon "dagos", versus Old High German "taga", Old Low Franconian "daga". Old Low Franconian also exhibits final devoicing, generally shown in the orthography, just like Old High German (though, like Modern German, it is not shown as such in Modern Dutch): Old Low Franconian nominative "wort" ('word') versus genitive "wordes", imperative "gif!" ('give') versus infinitive "gevon". However, unlike Old High German, Old Low Franconian does exhibit a personal pronoun beginning with "h-": "he"/"hie" ('he'), versus Old High German "er". Unlike its neighboring North Sea Germanic languages, Old Low Franconian had three distinct endings for each person in the plural forms of the verb, as did Old High German.

Sample Texts

The vast majority of texts from Old Low Franconian come from the Wachtendonk Codex, which is now lost. It was discovered late in the 16th century, and five fragmentary copies survive (one of which is actually an Old High German translation). The original work was a Latin psalter (that is, a book containing the Biblical Psalms) that included hymns and creeds in addition to the Book of Psalms, with a word for word translation into Old Low Franconian written between the lines.

Below is a sample of an Old Low Franconian text, from the Wachtendonk text, Psalm 60. My translation here is a fairly literal one (though not word-for-word), to show you just how close the language is to English, with some modern cognates in parentheses.

Old Low Franconian	English Translation
Gehōri, got, gebet mīn, thenke te gebede mīnin.	Hear, God, my prayer: think on my prayer,
Fan einde erthen te thi riep, so sorgoda herte mīn. An stēine irhōdus-tu mi;	From the ends of the earth to thee cried my heart so sorrow-fully. On a stone thou hast ex-alted me;
Thū lēidos mi, uuanda gedān bist tohopa mīn, turn sterke fan antscēine fiundis.	Thou hast led me, for thou art my hope, a tower of strength against the face of the enemy (fiend).
Uuonon sal ic an selethon thīnro an uueroldi, bescirmot an getheke fetharaco thīnro.	I will live forever in thy taberna-cle, protected by the cover of thy wings (feathers).
Uuanda thu, got mīn, gehōrdos gebet mīn, gāui thu erui forhtin-don namo thīnin.	For thou, my God, hast heard my prayer, thou hast given an inheri-tance to those who fear thy name.
Dag ouir dag cuningis saltu ge-fuogan, jār sīna untes an dag cun-nis in cunnis.	Day over day shall you give to the king, his years even to generation in generation.
Foluuonot an ēuuon an gegi-nuuirdi godis; gināthi in uuār-hēide sīna uua sal thia suocan?	(He) abides forever in the pres-ence of God; who will seek his mercy and truth?
Sō sal ic lof quethan namin thīnin an uuerolt uueroldis, that ik geue gehēita mīna fan dage an dag.	So shall I sing praise to thy name forever and ever (world of worlds), that I may give my vows from day to day.

The second text is from the *Leiden Willeram*, a copy in Old Low Franconian of an Old High German commentary on the Biblical "Song of Songs" (also known as the "Song of Solomon"). The original was by

Williram von Ebersberg in an East Franconian dialect of Old High German. The original was written in the mid 11th century; the Leiden copy was likely written towards the end of the same century. The text in italics below is Latin.

Old Low Franconian	English Translation
Vox Christi ad ecclesiam	*The voice of Christ to the church*
Sino, scona bistu, friundina min sino, scona bistu; thin ougan sint duvan ougan.	Beautiful art thou, my friend; beautiful art thou; thine eyes are dove's eyes.
Scona bistu an guoden werkan, scona bistu an reynan gethankon. Thin eynualdigheyd skinet an allan thinan werkon, wanda thu ueychenes ande gelichnisses niet neruochest.	Beautiful art thou in (thy) good works, beautiful art thou in pure thoughts. Thy sincerity shines on all of thy works, for thou pursuest not deception or hypocrisy.
Vox ecclesiae	*The voice of the church*
Sino, scone bistu, wine min, ande eerlich.	Beautiful art thou, my beloved, and honest.
Thu quithes, thaz ich scona si, auor al mina sconheyd thiu is mer uan thich cuman. Thu bist sunderlicho scone *pre filiis hominum,* beythe *et per diuinitatem et per uirgineam natiuitatem.*	Thou sayest, that I be beautiful, but all my beauty is come from thee. Thou art especially beautiful *above the children of man,* also *by your Godly nature and your virgin birth.*

Below are the numbers in Old Low Franconian, along with the Germanic and Indo-European counterparts for comparison. You may notice that several of these are reconstructed forms since Old Low Franconian studies suffer from a lack of source materials.

	IE	Germanic	Old Low Franconian
1	*oinos	*ainaz	ein
2	*duwō	*twai	twē
3	*treies	*þrijiz	thrī
4	*kʷetwores	*fidwōr	*fēr
5	*penkʷe	*fimfi	*fīf
6	*sweks	*seχs	*sehs
7	*septm	*seƀum	sivon
8	*oktō	*aχtō	*ahto
9	*newn	*niwun	*nigun
10	*dekm	*tehun	tēn

Old Frisian

Frisian (pronounced "FREE-zhun"), a language spoken along the coasts and on the islands off the coasts of the Netherlands, Germany, and Denmark is English's closest living relative. The Frisian people were the closest kin to the Anglo-Saxons who left the area around the North Sea for England in the 5th century, CE. A common poem shows you how close these languages are even today:

> **Modern Frisian:** Brea, bûter, en griene tsiis is goed Ingelsk en goed Frysk.

> **Modern English:** Bread, butter, and green cheese is good English and good Frisian.

The Old Frisian period lasted from approximately the 11th to the 16th centuries CE, putting it alongside the "middle" versions of most of the other Germanic languages. Keep in mind that this does not mean that Old Frisian was not spoken until the 11th century, but rather that the first attestations of the language did not occur until then.

The Frisians initially occupied the coastal areas of Friesland and Groningen in the modern-day Netherlands. They were subjugated by the Romans late in the 1st century BCE according to the Roman historian Tacitus (whose writing is responsible for quite a bit of our initial knowledge of the early Germanic tribes). This subjugation lasted several centuries. They likely mixed at this time with the Angles and Saxons who would eventually leave the continent for Britain. The Frisian territories were eventually annexed by the Franks, after which the Frisians converted to Christianity. For a period in the late 9th century, the area was ceded to Viking conquerors. Eventually the Frisians spread out further, eventually occupying the coastal areas of northern Germany and up the Jutland peninsula in modern-day Denmark. Although there are still small populations of Frisian speakers in these areas today, for the most part the Frisians have been absorbed into the local cultures and languages. However, Frisian is currently making a small comeback in the Netherlands, partially due to the emphasis the European Union has placed on preserving minority languages and cultures. Frisian is also a co-official language of the Netherlands in the province of Fryslân.

Language

Old Frisian, as expected, shares many similarities with Old English. One of the similarities is the "palatalization" of "k" and "g" (this simply means changing a sound by bringing your tongue closer to the hard palate in your mouth, that is, up front). Whereas Germanic had "eka" ('I') and Old English originally had "ic" (pronounced "eek"), this sound was eventually palatalized to sound like "each". Similarly, Old Frisian palatalized this sound to something like "ts" in "hats" or "ch" in "cheese". Compare Old English "cīese", (with "c" pronounced "ch"; 'cheese') and Old Frisian "tsyse"; Old English "drencean" (again with "ch"; 'to water'; note Modern English "drench") and Old Frisian "drentza". Also similar to Old English, a "g" appearing before an "i" or "e" becomes "y" as in "yell" (spelled "g", or sometimes "j"). The descendant of the Germanic *gj (seen largely in weak verbs) also become an affricate, "dz" (like the "ds" in "lids"), or "dʒ" like the "g" in "gym". Note Old Frisian "ledza" ('to lie') versus Old Saxon "liggian", Old Frisian "sedza" ('to say') versus Old Norse "segja" (and compare Old English "secgan", prounced, "sedge-ahn").

Vowel and consonant changes in general from Germanic to Old Frisian are often quite similar to the changes that occurred in Old English. One difference which it coincidentally shares with Old Norse is the deletion of the final "n": Old Frisian "bidda" ('to ask'), Old Norse "biþia" versus Gothic "bidjan", Old English "biddan", Old Saxon "biddian", Old High German "bitten". Such coincidences must be carefully considered when analyzing linguistic data before jumping to conclusions. Rather than a sign of Norse influence, this change most likely happened independently, as this is a fairly common occurrence in the Germanic languages. Indeed, Modern Dutch is generally spoken without final "n" after a schwa (though it is still written), and many dialects of Low and High German today feature infinitives with just a schwa ending resulting from a dropped "-n".

Sample Texts

Below is a sample of an Old Frisian text, the Ten Commandments:

Old Frisian	English Translation
Thet erste bod: minna thinne god fore feder ende moder mith inlekere herta.	The first commandment: love thy god before father and mother with (thy) whole heart.
Thet other bod: minna thinne euncristena like thi selwm.	The second commandment: love thy fellow Christian as thyself.
Thet thredde bod: fira thene sunnandei and there helche degan.	The third commandment: celebrate Sunday and the holy days.
Thet fiarde bod: minna thine feder end thine moder, hu thu longe libbe.	The fourth commandment: love thy father and mother as long as thou livest.
Thet fifte: thet thu thi nowet ne ower hore.	The fifth: thou shalt not commit adultery.
Thet sexte: thet thu nenne mon ne sle.	The sixth: thou shalt not slay a man.
Thet sogende: thet thu nowet ne stele.	The seventh: thou shalt not steal.
Thet achtende: thet thu thi nowet ne vrsuere, ne nen falesk withscip ne driue.	The eighth: that thou shalt not swear nor bear false witness.
Thet niugende: thet thu nenes thines euncristena wiues ne gereie.	The ninth: that thou shalt not covet your fellow Chrisian's wife.
Thet tiande: thet thu nenes thines euncristena godes ne ierie.	The tenth: that thou shalt not covet your fellow Christian's goods.

The text below is from a legal document by Charlemagne to the Frisian people, admonishing them to obey his law and Biblical law. It was likely written in the early 9th century. Latin text is in italics; text in brackets is assumed.

Old Frisian	English Translation
Hec est instructio Fresonum.	*These are instructions to the Frisians*
[1] *Hic est scriptum.* Hir is escriwen, thet wi alsadene landriucht halde, sa God selua erest [sette and] bad, thet wi alle afte and alle riuchte thing helde.	[1] *Here it is written.* Here it is written, that we hold the law of the land such as God himself first (set and commanded), that we (should) hold all legal and all lawful things.
[2] Efter tham beden hit and bonden alle ertkeningan. Julius [and] Octauianus, [sa heten] tha furma, ther [to] Rome [keningan] weren.	[2] Afterwards it was commanded by all kings of earth. Julius [and] Octavianus, [so were called] the first [ones], who were kings in Rome.
[3] God ief Moysi twa stenena tewla; ther weren on escriwen tha tyan bode and alle tha riucht, ther tha israheliske lude heden, tha se in ther westenia weren. And alsa God sine liude latte fon Egyptra londe, alsa lat hi alle thene to tha himele, ther tha riuchte fulgiat. And hwasa thet riucht brecht, sa bislute hine God in there helle, alsa hi bislat tha Egypteran in tha Rada Se, tha se sina liude vrdera wolden. Bi thio bislut thene God in there helle, ther tha riuchte brekat. Want hit selua scref mith sine h ondum and bad alle sine liudum to haldan.	[3] God gave Moses two stone tablets; there were ten commandments written on them and all the laws, that the Israeli people had when they were in the desert. And as God led his people from the land of Egypt, so he leads them all to heaven, who follow the law. And whoever breaks the law, God will seal him in hell, as he sealed the Egyptians in the Red Sea, because they wanted to harm his people. Therefore God shuts them in hell, those who break the law. For he wrote it with his own hands and commanded all his people to keep it.
[4] Alsa helden hit Aaron ende Samuel anta keningan Dauid and Salomon, ther er Christus berde weren.	[4] Likewise Aaron and Samuel kept it, and kings David and Solomon, before Christ was born.

Below are the numbers in Old Frisian, along with the Germanic and Indo-European counterparts for comparison.

	IE	Germanic	Old Frisian
1	*oinos	*ainaz	ēn, ān
2	*duwō	*twai	twā, twēne
3	*treies	*þrijiz	thrē
4	*kʷetwores	*fidwōr	fiūwer
5	*penkʷe	*fimfi	fīf
6	*sweks	*seχs	sex
7	*septm	*sebum	sigun
8	*oktō	*aχtō	achte
9	*newn	*niwun	nigun
10	*dekm	*tehun	tiān

In the next chapter, we will take a look at one more Germanic daughter language, Old English, in much more detail. This is the language that would eventually become the English you and I speak today.

Old English   3

ƿæꞇ Ic ᵹꞃefna cẏꞅꞇ   ꞅecᵹan ƿẏlle
ƿæꞇ me ᵹemæꞇꞇe   ꞇo miꝺꞃe nihꞇe
ꞅẏꝺþan ꞃeoꝛꝺbeꞃenꝺ   ꞃeꞅꞇe ƿuneꝺon

—*The Dream of the Rood (author unknown)*

History

When you hear the phrase "Old English", what do you think of? Many people are familiar with phrases such as "Ye Olde Book Shoppe" and believe that this is "Old English". But it is not. To be sure, it is an *older* form of English than what we speak today, but it is actually just a slightly earlier form of our Modern English with slight spelling variations. (The "y" in "ye" is, in fact, a misspelling of "þ" (the letter "thorn"), which we already know was pronounced like "th", so "ye" is actually "the").

Other people think of the great English playwright William Shakespeare, but his language was also just an earlier version of what we speak, called Early Modern English. We will talk more about Shakespeare and his language in a later chapter. Still others think of a man named Geoffrey Chaucer when they hear "Old English". Chaucer was a poet and author in England in the 14th century CE. Though that was quite a long time ago, even Chaucer's language was not Old English—we call it "Middle English", and it is the subject of the next chapter.

Old English, also called "Anglo-Saxon", was spoken from approximately the 5th century to the 11th century, CE. If you recall from chapters one and two, there were constant migrations of peoples in Europe for thousands of years. The people who spoke Old English came from continental Europe, along the coasts of what are now the Netherlands, Germany, and Denmark. There were likely three different Germanic tribes that made the trek across the sea to Great Britain: the Angles, Saxons, and Jutes. These tribes of Germanic peoples began populating the British Isles in the late 4th century CE, coming in many waves of settlers. They settled into a number of different kingdoms, which comprised four different dialect areas: Mercian in central England and the East, Northumbrian to the North of Mercian (both of these areas made up the Anglian dialect area), Kentish in the Southeast (generally assumed to be where the Jutes settled), and West Saxon in the South and Southwest. Though there were distinct differences among these dialects, a speaker of one dialect could easily understand speakers of another (thus, we say they were "mutually intelligible"). West Saxon became the dialect in which most texts were written (due to political reasons, not the least of which was that it was the dialect of King Alfred the Great, about whom you will read below).

Figure 2: Dialects of Old English

In the map above, you can see the general outlines of the dialect areas of Old English in Great Britain.

Britain had been conquered many times in the past. People who spoke Celtic dialects had settled the area long before the Angles and Saxons arrived. Their descendents survive to this day—the modern-day Irish, Scots, and Welsh. The land was populated even before the Celts, though little is known about these people or their language. After the Celts came the Romans, when Julius Caesar invaded in 55 BCE. After the Romans came the Angles, Saxons, and Jutes in the middle of the 5th century CE.

One of the earliest historians to write about the history of the Anglo-Saxons was Bede (ca. 672– 735 CE; also known as the Venerable Bede). Bede was a Benedictine monk from Northumbria. His most famous work was written in Latin (the ecclesiastical and scholarly language of the day): *Historia ecclesiastica gentis Anglorum* ('The Ecclesiastical History of the English People'), completed in 731. In it, Bede tells the history of England, beginning with Roman times. It was Bede who first mentions the three groups of peoples who settled Britain.

Here is an example of Old English, specifically the West Saxon dialect: the familiar Lord's Prayer:

Old English (West Saxon)	English Translation
Fæder ure þu þe eart on heofonum	Father ours thou who art in heaven
si þin nama gehalgod	be thy name hallowed
to becume þin rice	come thy kingdom
gewurþe ðin willa	become thy will
on eorðan swa swa on heofonum.	on earth as as in heaven.
urne gedæghwamlican hlaf syle us todæg	our daily loaf give us today
and forgyf us ure gyltas	and forgive us our offenses
swa swa we forgyfað urum gyltendum	so as we forgive our offenders
and ne gelæd þu us on costnunge	and not lead us in temptation
ac alys us of yfele soþlice.	but release us from evil truly.

English has obviously changed greatly over the past 1,000 years. Nonetheless, when you compare the above on a word-for-word basis, you can easily see that they are similar.

In some cases, the spelling might cause the familiar to seem unfamiliar: a "d" in "father", though still pronounced much as we pronounce it today with the "th" sound, "heofonum" ('heaven') with an "f", though this was pronounced as a "v" in this position, and many cases in which vowels have changed in our present language ("þu" vs. "thou", "swa" vs. "so", "hlaf" vs. "loaf", and "yfele" vs. "evil"). In many cases, words have disappeared or their meaning has changed ("rice", pronounced "**reach**-a", might be familiar to those who know the German word "Reich", meaning 'kingdom' or 'empire'), "gyltas", our modern word "guilt", meaning "offenses", "syle" became "sell" and its meaning has since changed, and even the word "soþlice" (pronounced "**soath**-leach-a", literally "sooth-like" ("soothly" is an archaic word now in Modern English, but means something like "true") meaning "amen".

Norse Influence

In the 9th and 10th centuries CE, other Germanic tribes from Scandinavia waged countless raids against the Anglo-Saxons. We know them today as the Vikings—the Anglo-Saxons called them "Danes". The Vikings pillaged and plundered the east coast of England for two centuries. For a time, a part of the country was established under Viking rule, and was known as the "Danelaw". It was through this contact with the Vikings that Old English itself was influenced by the language of these invaders. The Vikings spoke Old Norse dialects, which you know are sister languages to Old English. The Anglo-Saxons and Vikings could probably understand each other, and they also borrowed words from each other. Viking influence can be seen in the names of towns ending in "-by" and "-thorp", both Norse words for "town" (in fact, the term "by-laws" originally meant "town laws"). Many Old Norse words entered the Old English vocabulary at this time, including such basic words as "sky", "skirt", "egg", and even the pronouns "they", "their", and "them". The mixing of these two languages gave English some interesting word pairs which survive to this day: in the following examples, the first term is from Old Norse, the second from Old English: "nay" vs. "no", "fro" ("to and fro") vs. "from", "skirt" vs. "shirt", and "raise" vs. "rear". The Old Norse word "egg" competed with the Old English "ey" (rhymes with "hay") until the Early Modern English period, when the Old Norse word won out—it is the word we use today. One theory also states that the mixing of Old Norse and Old English may have helped to change the very grammar of the language itself while it was on its way to becoming "Middle English" (discussed in the next chapter).

The Influence of Latin

Another great influence on Old English was that of Latin. While there was some Latin influence on the language even since the time of Germanic itself, its greatest influence came after the Christianization of England.

Latin was the language of the church and of scholarly pursuits. It was the language of instruction (although at that time, only the most privileged children went to school), and it was the language of legal documents. The Anglo-Saxons were originally a pagan people who worshipped the Teutonic (another name for the common Germanic) gods. This pagan influence is still evident in our language today in our names for the days of the week: Sunday is the day of the Sun, Monday of the moon, Tuesday honors the god Tiu (or Twia), god of war and the sky, Wednesday honors the god Woden, the leader of the gods, Thursday honors the god Thor, god of thunder, and Friday honors the goddess Freya (or Fria), goddess of love, beauty, and fertility. Only Saturday, honoring the Roman god Saturn, the god of agriculture, does not refer to Teutonic paganism.

Once the conversion to Christianity of the pagan Anglo-Saxons began late in the 6th century and into the 7th century CE, Latin gained more and more of an influence over Old English. Since Latin was the language of the church, many of the words borrowed at this time dealt with ecclesiastical and religious topics: abbot, altar, angel, ark, candle, chalice, cleric, deacon, disciple, hymn, martyr, mass, noon, nun, offer, organ, palm, pope, priest, psalm, rule, shrift, shrine, temple, and tunic. However, since the church at that time greatly influenced the daily lives of even the common people, many every-day words were also added, such as: items of clothing and similar materials (cap, mat, silk, sock, purple, sack), food (beet, to cook, lobster, mussel, oyster, pear, radish), plants (aloe, balsam, lily, pine, plant), education (grammar, master, school, verse), and various other words, such as anchor, circle, elephant, fever, giant, place, and sponge.

Latin also influenced the writing system, which had been rune-based. The Latin alphabet we use to this day was eventually adopted to replace runes, though a few runic letters persisted through much of the Old English period, including thorn (þ), eth (ð), and wynn (ƿ) (more on these letters below).

Latin had one more indirect influence on Old English, in the form of an event called the Norman Conquest. As you may recall from the first chapter, Latin is part of the Italic branch of Indo-European, and French is one of its many daughter languages (along with Spanish, Portuguese, Italian, Romanian, and many other languages and dialects). In the 11th century CE, French speaking Normans conquered England. As a result of this conquest, grammatical changes which had already begun prior to this event seemed to speed up, and a large number of French words were added to the vocabulary. Take a closer look at that last sentence. Most of the "big" words, such as "result", "grammatical", "changes", "conquest", "large", "number", and "vocabulary" were borrowed into English from Latin and French, while the "small" words you use every day, such as "as", "a", "which", "had", "the", "and", and "up" come to us directly from Old English.

We will discuss the Norman Conquest and its implications for the language in much more detail in the next chapter, as it marks the transition period from Old English to Middle English.

Literature

During the Old English period, many different types of literary works blossomed, including religious texts, chronicles of events, epics, legal works, and poetry. In all there are some 400 manuscripts written in the language which survive to this day.

Cædmon's Hymn, a poem about the Biblical creation story, is considered to be the oldest surviving text in Old English. It dates from the 7th century CE.

The Anglo-Saxon Chronicle is a collection of chronicles that report on the history of the Anglo-Saxons. For each year there is a brief description of the significant events that occurred. Originally commissioned by King Alfred the Great in the late 9th century CE, the Chronicles were kept until the latter part of the 12th century. Alfred (849 - 899) was a very learned man and was also responsible for a translation of parts of the Bible into Old English. He was a great champion of the English language, and its use in literary works thrived during his reign. Alfred was the king of Wessex from 871 until his death in 899 and is the only English king to be called "the Great". He is best known for his defense of his kingdom against the Vikings

Because of his patronage of culture and the arts, and a similar sounding name, Alfred is sometimes confused with Ælfric of Eynsham (ca 955 – ca 1010; often referred to simply as "Ælfric", pronounced "AL-freech"). Ælfric was the abbot of Cerne in moder-day Dorset in the southwest of England. He was one of the most prolific writers in Old English, having authored many homilies, biblical commentaries, hagiographies (stories about the lives of the saints), grammars, and many other types of literature.

The most widely known work from this period is the epic poem, *Beowulf*, the story of a young hero from a Germanic tribe in southern Sweden called the Geats. It describes the hero's travels to Denmark to help defeat a terrible monster called Grendel. In essence, *Beowulf* is a story about the history of the Germanic people who were the ancestors of the Anglo-Saxons. While the story itself is believed to have been composed in the 8th century CE, the oldest *Beowulf* manuscript dates to around 1000 CE. As with most epic poetry of the time, *Beowulf* was meant to be heard, rather than read. For centuries, poets, or *scops* (pronounced "shopes") as they were called, recited the story from memory, often adding to it as they went along. This in itself was quite a feat, as the poem as originally written down consists of almost 3200 lines.

Much of the poetry written in Old English times, including *Beowulf*, has a very specific format that is quite unlike most poetry you think of today. The Anglo-Saxons did not use end rhymes in poems. Instead, they often used "alliteration", which means that the beginning sounds of certain words in a line are the same.

An example of alliterative verse can be seen in this popular translation of an Old English poem, *The Seafarer*. The translation is from the early 20th century by J. Duncan Spaeth. The first two lines are as follows (the letters in bold simply show which syllables are emphasized when spoken aloud):

> **True** is the **tale** that I **tell** of my **trav**els,
>
> **Sing** of my **sea**faring **sor**rows and **woes**;

You will notice that many of the words in the first line begin with a "t" sound, and several in the second line start with "s". This gives you an idea of what an alliterative poem must have sounded like to the Anglo-Saxons.

Since much of the literature of that time was meant to be heard rather than read (most of the population was illiterate), the use of alliteration may have helped those telling the stories to more easily remember them in the days before they were written down.

Perhaps one of the most interesting forms of literature from this period is the Old English riddle—over 90 have survived. These poems come in various lengths, from just a few lines to over a hundred. The word itself comes from Old English "rædels", ('opinion, riddle, counsel, conjecture') and is related to our word "read". The riddles were very much like riddles we have today—the reader tries to identify an object, animal, natural phenomenon, or process from the often playful description in the riddle. The riddles that survive are part of the *Exeter Book*, one of four poetic codices (the plural of "codex") written between 975 and 1025 CE. Below is an example, Riddle 47 (the riddles are generally identified by number; the "/", called a "virgule", is akin to our modern comma).

Old English	Modern English
Moððe word fræt / me þæt þuhte	A moth ate words / that seemed to me
wrætlicu wyrd / þa ic þæt wundor gefrægn,	strangely weird / when I heard this wonder
þæt se wyrm forswealg / wera gied sumes,	that the worm swallowed / some man's speech
þeof in þystro, / þrymfæstne cwide	thief in the dark / glorious speech
ond þæs strangan staþol. / Stælgiest ne wæs	and its strong foundation. / the thief was
wihte þy gleawra, / þe he þam wordum swealg.	not at all wiser / that he swallowed the words.

A less literal translation would be something like this:

A moth ate some words. That seemed very strange to me when I heard about this, that some worm, a thief in the dark, swallowed a man's speech, so glorious and with a strong foundation. The thief was none the wiser that he had swallowed the words.

Perhaps you can you guess what the answer to this riddle is? What kind of moth or worm can eat words? The answer is...a bookworm. The bookworm is a "moth" or "worm" that eats words—the pages of a book.

Language

In this section, we will learn a little bit more about the Old English language itself, including its sounds, sound system, and grammar.

Old English Phonetics and Phonology

First, let's take a closer look at the sounds of Old English.

Vowels

The vowels of Old English were pronounced quite differently from their modern-day counterparts. In the table below you can compare the letters and their sounds as they were spoken in Old English with their modern pronunciations. The Anglo-Saxons did not generally use any distinguishing marks to show whether a vowel was long or short, but many transcriptions of Old English texts today use a macron over a long vowel so that modern readers will know how to pronounce it correctly. In each example below, the first vowel is short and the latter long:

Old English Vowels		
Letter	**Example**	**Modern Pronunciation**
a ā	ac ('and') bān ('bone')	"a" in "father"
e ē	bedd ('bed') wēn ('belief', 'hope')	"a" in "day"
i/y ī/ȳ	binn ('bin') bītan ('to bite')	"ee" in "see"
o ō	on ('on') bōc ('book')	"o" in "stone"
u ū	cunnan ('can') hūs ('house')	"oo" in "moon"
y ȳ	lyft ('air') hȳd ('hide', 'skin')	We don't have this sound in Modern English. Say "lift" but pucker up your lips while saying it.
æ ǣ	æsc ('ash') ǣfre ('ever')	"a" in "ash"

Note that the "y" is sometimes used for the "i" sound, and other times stands for a sound that has since been lost in our language. You may note that the short vowels still have the same quality of the long vowels—they sound the same but are just shorter in length. It is possible that at some point in the Old English period the short vowels started to change in quality to be closer to our current short vowel sounds. This is historically especially evident for "e" and "o", where their sounds may have been more like Modern English "e" in "bed" and "o" in British English "pot".

Diphthongs

Next we will take a look at the diphthongs in Old English

Old English Diphthongs		
Letters	**Example**	**Modern Pronunciation**
ea ēa	eald ('old') eac ('also')	"a" in "sat" followed quickly by the "a" sound in "sofa"
eo ēo	eorðe ('earth') beo ('bee')	"a" in "say" quickly followed by either the "o" in "bone" or "u" in "rune"
ie	ierfa ('heir')	This sound probably started as a diphthong, something like the "ia" in the name "Mia". Eventually it shifted to a sound similar to the "i" in "sit".
io īo	fioh ('money') bīoþ ('are')	"ee" in "beet" quickly followed by either the "o" in "bone" or "u" in "rune"; this is usually just a variant of "eo"/"ēo".

Consonants

The consonants of Old English are very much like their modern-day counterparts: for the most part, they are pronounced as they are today. The following table shows you the consonants sounds of Old English that are either non-existent in our alphabet, or that have a different pronunciation from ours today. The table also shows examples and the modern pronunciation of each consonant listed.

The "c" can represent two different sounds: a "k" sound and a "ch" sound. The "s" sound we often have in Modern English for "c" (for example, "cent") does *not* occur in Old English. The "ch" variant is often written as a "c" with a single dot above it in modern transcriptions to help with the distinction: "ċ". "C" is usually pronounced "ch" when it comes before or after an "i" or "e" and like a "k" elsewhere: "ic" ('I') is pronounced "each", "eac" is "æ-uk" (the "æ" is like "a" in "cat"); "cēap" ('price') is pronounced "chææ-up", while "cald" ('cold') is "kahld". There are many exceptions to this rule, but you can often use the word's modern counterpart as a guide if there is a modern descendent.

"F" is used for both the "f" and "v" sound; Old English did not have the letter "v". The "v" sound occurs when "f" comes between vowels or before voiced consonants.

Old English Consonants		
Letters	**Example**	**Modern Pronunciation**
c	cald ('cold')	"c" in "cold"
	cild ('child')	"ch" in "child"
cg	ecg ('edge')	"g" in "age"
f	for ('for')	"f" in "for"
	ofer ('over')	"v" in "over"
g/3	gear ('year')	"y" in "year"
	frogga ('frog')	"g" in "good"
	agan ('to own')	This is the "γ" sound we saw in Germanic.
h	helpan ('to help')	"h" in "help"
	niht ('night')	Say "hue" and over-emphasize the "h"; German "ch" in "nicht".
	naht ('nought')	This is the "χ" sound we saw in Germanic.
ng	cyning ('king')	"ng" in "finger"
		"ng" was always pronounced as two separate sounds, even at the end of a word, as we pronounce it today in "finger".
r	read ('red')	This sound was probably trilled with the tongue as in modern Spanish and Italian.
s	sæ ('sea')	"s" in "sea"
	wesan ('to be')	"z" in "zoo"
sc	scip ('ship')	"sh" in "ship
	ascian ('to ask')	"sk" in "ask"
þ	þing ('thing')	"th" in "thing"
	þa ('the')	"th" in "the"
Ð/ð	æðele ('nobleman')	"th" in "this"
	bæð ('bath')	"th" in "bath"
x	seax ('knife')	This was pronounced like the "h" in "naht" above + "s" (rather than the "ks" of today).
w/ƿ	wynn ('joy')	"w" in "win" (the use of "w" instead of "ƿ" is a later development)

The letter "g" can stand for a whole range of sounds, from the familiar "g" sound of "go" to a "y" sound, and even a sound we no longer have: the sound in the word "agan" changed to a "w" sound in Middle English—the current spelling for this word is "own". There is some question as to the exact nature of the sound in certain environments. The "g" in "go" was most likely the pronunciation when it came before or after a consonant ("gnorn" ('sad'), "sang" ('sang')), or was doubled as in "frogga" below. The sound becomes a "y" sound in most cases before or after an "e" or "i". When "g" comes between vowels, especially "a", "o", and "u", it is pronounced as a "γ" (a voiced "ch" of German "Bach"). At the beginning of a word before "a", "o", and "u", it was pronounced as "γ" during the early Old English period, but this changed to the "hard g" of "go" later on. The "y" variant, like "c" above, often has a dot above the "g" in some modern transcriptions: "ġ".

"H" can have the usual sound we hear today in "have", but syllable-final (including before consonants) it had the same variants as Modern German "ch": the "h" sound in "hue", exaggerated a bit (usually after "i" or "e"), and the "χ" sound (after "a", "o", and "u"; just like the sounds and variation in German "ich" versus German "Bach"). Neither sound exists in our language today.

Old English also lacked the letter "z". The letter "s" was used in its place and could have both the usual "s" sound in "so", or the "z" sound in "zoo". The "z" sound usually occurred when "s" was between vowels or when it was around voiced consonants.

The combination "sc" usually represents the "sh" sound "ship", but in certain circumstances, it retained its two individual sounds, such as in "ascian" which survives today as "ask" (there was also a variant, "acsian", akin to the modern dialect pronunciation "aks").

We have seen some of the four archaic letters before. The letter "þ", called "thorn" could represent both "th" sounds in English, the "th" of both "thin" and "this". Another letter, "Ð" (the capital version) or "ð" (the lowercase version), usually called "eth" but possibly called "ðæt" by the Anglo-Saxons, could also have both pronunciations. For the most part, these letters were used interchangeably by the Anglo-Saxons. The "th" sound in "that" usually occurred between vowels but was also possible at the beginning of a word (as was the "thin" sound: use Modern English as your guide).

Another new letter is "ȝ", called "yogh" (its name has various pronunciations, but you can call it "yogue"). An adoption from the Irish alphabet, this letter often appeared in the place of "g" and had its various pronunciations as seen above.

The final archaic letter, "ᵽ", called "wynn" ('joy'), survived from the runic alphabet and retained its "w" sound. This letter was mainly used in earlier texts; the use of "w" occurs in later ones.

Old English Grammar

The grammar of Old English, like Indo-European and Germanic may seem more "complicated" in many ways than is Modern English. If you have ever tried to learn another language, you have probably encountered many things that seemed to make the language more "difficult" than English. Although all languages are complex in a certain respect, there are certainly languages that can be harder *to learn* for speakers of certain languages than others. Learning Old English is probably about as difficult to learn as is learning Latin for a native speaker of Modern English.

Old English was largely a fusional language—as you will see, just as with Indo-European and Germanic, word endings played a key role in the grammar.

The Definite Article

One example of this complexity in Old English can be seen in its definite article. In Modern English, using "the" is quite simple—it never changes, no matter what. (At least that is true for the written word—if you listen to yourself and others carefully when you speak, you may notice that we often *pronounce* two distinctly different versions of the definite article; in my dialect of American English, I usually pronounce "the" as if it were pronounced something like "thuh", with the "-a" sound in "sofa" at the end. But, if the word that comes after it starts with a vowel sound, like "a", "e", "i", "o", or "u", the sound changes to "thee". I say "thuh man", but "thee apple". Next time you have a conversation with someone, listen carefully to see if their pronunciation changes as well, or try it yourself).

As explained in prior chapters, during older periods of our language speakers had to take into account concepts such as number, gender, and case when dealing with nouns and adjectives. Old English was much more like Modern German with regards to grammar—it also had the same three genders and the same four cases, and in some instances, a fifth case, the "instrumental" case. This case was only used very early in the period and died out during the Old English period, replaced by periphrastic constructions such as "with" + a noun phrase.

Below are the forms of the definite article in Old English:

Old English Definite Article				
	Masculine Singular	Neuter Singular	Feminine Singular	Plural
Nominative	se	þæt	sēo	þā
Genitive	þæs	þæs	þære	þāra
Dative	þæm	þæm	þære	þæm
Accusative	þone	þæt	þā	þā
Instrumental	þy	þy		

Below is an example of how to use the definite article in Old English, with the definite articles bolded:

Se cyning seah **þone** hund.

In Modern English, this would be "the king saw the dog". Since "cyning" is a masculine noun and it is the subject, it is in the nominative case. There is just one of them, so it falls in the very first column at the upper left of the table above: singular, masculine, nominative: so the proper article to use is "se". "Hund" is also masculine and singular (there is just one in this sentence), but it is the thing receiving the action in the sentence above, so it is in the accusative case. Therefore, the correct article is "þone". Now, let's try changing things around.

If I write:

Þone hund seah **se** cyning.

what do you think this sentence means? If you said "the dog sees the king", you are *wrong*. The beauty of having case system inflections is that you can "mark" words with their proper function (subject, object, indirect object), regardless of where they occur in a sentence. The sentence above actually *still* reads "the king sees the dog." How can this be? Well, you may have noticed that the articles before "hund" and "cyning" did not change in either version—"se" *always* marks the subject and "þone" *always* marks the object. So no matter what order these words occur in, it is still the king performing the action and the dog receiving it. Modern German works much the same way, as do many other languages.

As you know, things have changed greatly in this respect in Modern English. Since we no longer "mark" the noun's role in the sentence with inflections, speakers of English had to come up with another way to tell what the subject is and what the direct object is. In Modern English, we simply use word order for that purpose: the subject comes before the verb and the direct object comes after it in most instances.

Note that the definite article in Old English was actually more versatile than it is in Modern English, and is more properly referred to as a "demonstrative pronoun", in that it could be used as both a definite article as well as a pronoun similar to "that" and "this".

It is also important to note that Old English did not have an indefinite article (Modern English "a"/"an"). Our modern indefinite article is derived from the word "one". In Old English, using the adjective "ān" ('one') specifically meant that you were talking about one and only one of whatever it was modifying. To say "he saw a boy" the Anglo-Saxons would have just said something like "he saw boy"; the "indefiniteness" was implied.

Nouns and Adjectives

The definite article was not the only place where case and gender markings came into play. Nouns and adjectives also had gender and case markers in Old English. Here is an example of all of the different endings a single noun could have. We will look at the word "stān", a masculine noun meaning "stone", "scip", a neuter noun meaning "ship", and "sorg", a feminine noun meaning "sorrow".

These are just a few of the examples of different "declensions" of nouns in Old English (a "declension" simply shows all of the possible endings a word can have). Again, it may look like Old English was a pretty "difficult" language, but keep in mind, little children who lived during that time period learned it as easily as you learned Modern English; it might be difficult for a modern speaker of English to learn Old English, but that is not a reflection on the language itself.

Old English Noun Declension		Masculine	Neuter	Feminine
Singular	**Nom.**	stān	scip	sorg
	Gen.	stānes	scipes	sorge
	Dat.	stāne	scipe	sorge
	Acc.	stān	scip	sorge
Plural	**Nom.**	stānas	scipu	sorga/sorge
	Gen.	stāna	scipa	sorga
	Dat.	stānum	scipum	sorgu
	Acc.	stānas	scipu	sorga/sorge

Adjectives followed fairly similar declensions to the nouns. In addition, there was a distinction of "weak" versus "strong" use of adjectives. An adjective uses the weak declension if it follows a demonstrative pronoun, possessive adjective, genitive noun, or noun phrase, otherwise it uses the "strong" declension (e.g., if there is no other word before the adjective). Following are examples of both the strong and weak declensions of adjectives, using the word "gōd" ('good'). The first table below shows the strong declension.

Old English Strong Adjective Declension		Masculine	Neuter	Feminine
Singular	**Nom.**	gōd	gōd	gōd
	Gen.	gōdes	gōdes	gōdre
	Dat.	gōdum	gōdum	gōdre
	Acc.	gōdne	gōd	gōde
Plural	**Nom.**	gōde	gōde, gōd	gōde, gōda
	Gen.	gōdra	gōdra	gōdra
	Dat.	gōdum	gōdum	gōdum
	Acc.	gōde	gōde, gōd	gōde, gōda

The table below shows the weak declension for adjectives.

Old English Weak Adjective Declension		Masculine	Neuter	Feminine
Singular	**Nom.**	gōda	gōde	gōde
	Gen.	gōdan	gōdan	gōdan
	Dat.	gōdan	gōdan	gōdan
	Acc.	gōdan	gōde	gōdan
Plural	**Nom.**	gōdan	gōdan	gōdan
	Gen.	gōdra, -ena	gōdra, -ena	gōdra, -ena
	Dat.	gōdum	gōdum	gōdum
	Acc.	gōdan	gōdan	gōdan

As an example, if you wanted to say "I see (a) good dog", it would be:

Ic sēo gōd**ne** hund.

In the example above "good dog" is masculine, singular, accusative. It uses the strong declension because there is no other determiner before the noun phrase "good dog".

"They see long ships" would be:

Hīe sēoþ lang**e** scipu.

In this case, "long ships" is neuter, plural, accusative.

To see the difference from the strong declension examples above, we will change the example sentences slightly by adding determiners before the adjectives, necessitating the use of the weak adjective forms. "I see **the** good dog", would be:

Ic sēo þone gōd**an** hund.

"They see **those** long ships" would be:

Hīe sēoþ þā lang**an** scipu.

In addition, endings also varied somewhat based on the length of the stem vowel of the adjective (the above examples are "long stems").

Adjectives also had "comparative" and "superlative" forms, as they do today. The comparative is used to compare two things: "the girl is tall**er** than the boy". The "-er" on "tall" shows that you are using the adjective to compare two things. In a similar manner, more than two things can be compared in the superlative: "Terry is the tall**est** boy". The "-est" ending shows the superlative comparison. The comparative and superlative in Old English are similar to those used today, with one major exception. The comparative was formed with "-ra" (or just "-r-", with the proper ending if the adjective directly modified a noun), while the superlative was formed with "-ost" or "-est", depending on the vowel sound in the adjective. So for example, the word "hālig" ('holy') has a comparative "hāligra" ('holier'), and superlative "hāligost" ('holiest'); "eald" ('old') had "ieldra" ('older'; note the now somewhat archaic 'elder') and "ieldest" ('oldest' or 'eldest'). Old English did *not* make use of our common "more" and "most"; this change did not occur until the Middle English period.

Pronouns

Below is a table showing the Old English pronouns. You may not be surprised to learn that case plays a role in the pronouns and their forms as well.

There are several things to note in this table. In the first person, we see that most of the words are still recognizable in Modern English. The word for "I", "ic" (pronounced "each", later "itch") was not capitalized as it is today. "I", "mine", "me", "we", "our", and "us" have clearly descended from the pronouns you see in the table. The second person pronouns are not quite as straightforward.

You might have noticed that there are two separate words for "you", one for the singular (based on "þū"), and one for the plural (based on "gē"). "Þū", pronounced "thoo", is the word "thou", which you may be familiar with from the Bible or other religious texts, as well as from Shakespeare. It was used until the 18th century but has all but died out. You might know "gē", pronounced "yay", from the texts just mentioned as well: it is the word "ye", but also a form of our current word "you"—if you look at the dative and accusative forms, "ēow", pronounced "ay-oh", you might notice a resemblance to our word today: it is a sort of mixture of the nominative, dative, and accusative forms: "yay" + "ay-oh".

Old English Personal Pronouns						
Number	Case	1st Person	2nd Person	3rd Person		
				masc.	neut.	fem.
Singular	Nom.	ic	þū	hē	hit	hēo
	Gen.	mīn	þīn	his	his	hire
	Dat.	mē	þē	him	him	hire
	Acc.	mē, mec	þē, þec	hine	hit	hīe
Plural	Nom.	wē	gē	hīe		
	Gen.	ūre	ēower	hira		
	Dat.	ūs	ēow	him		
	Acc.	ūs	ēow	hīe		

But perhaps the greatest differences from Modern English can be seen in the third person pronouns. In the singular, the masculine pronouns have changed very little, while the neuter and feminine forms are quite a bit different. The feminine pronouns "hēo" ("hay-oh") and "hīe" ("hee-a") are now "she" and "her", respectively. Perhaps the most baffling change was from "hēo" to today's "she": an "h" doesn't usually change into a "sh" sound, even over hundreds of years. As you saw in the chapters on Indo-European and Germanic, there are indeed sound "laws" that explain changes from one sound to another, but from a linguist's point of view, this change is unexpected. The answer may be, however, that the "sh" may not have actually come from a sound change at all. Instead, a new word may have taken the place of "hēo" (just as the dative form "hire" came to be used for the accusative today).

As you can see, the words for "he" and "she" in Old English were not terribly different: the only difference is a single "o" on the end of the word for "she". A common change in English that is happening even today is that sounds at the end of a word often change and are eventually dropped (this explains why we no longer have all of the endings you saw in the noun examples). Eventually, it was probably difficult for people speaking Old English to know whether a person was saying "he" or "she". The answer was to "adopt" another word to take the place of one of them. Many languages often use the definite article in place of personal pronouns, and that was likely the case in Old English. Since "sēo" was more easily distinguished from "hē", it may have won out over "hēo". The "s" in "sēo" would have had to have changed to "sh" (though "s" *can* become "sh" before "e", this is the most debated step in this explanation) and it would eventually come to be pronounced "shay-uh" then "shay". It changed to the present "she" just before Shakespeare's time. Some linguists dispute this account of how we got the pronoun "she", but it seems to be the most likely explanation.

Quite a few changes also took place in the third person plural. The words "hīe", "hira", and "him" all sounded somewhat similar (or even identical in the case of "him") to third person *singular* pronouns. Again, this could have eventually caused confusion. Words were borrowed from another language, in this case, from the Viking conqueror's language, Old Norse. These two languages were still close enough that a speaker of either language could likely make himself understood to a speaker of the other language. The Old Norse third person plural pronouns began with a "th" sound that made them sound much different from the Old English pronouns starting with "h". In addition, Old English already had this sound in other common words, such as the definite article and the demonstratives. For a while, both forms existed together, with the "th" forms more common in the north of England, and the others, elsewhere. However, by the late Middle English period, the "th" versions had won out, and those are the ones we use today. (As a side note, many speakers of English still may be using a version of the former third person plural pronouns when they shorten "them" to "em", as in, "Go get 'em!").

Old English also had dual forms for the pronoun in the first and second person, but these died out during the Old English period.

Verbs

Like most of other parts of speech, verbs in Old English were a bit more complicated than in Modern English. Before we get into specific examples of verbs in Old English, let's go over some further concepts related to the grammatical description of verbs. These concepts are: "infinitive", "present participle", and "past participle".

The most basic form of a verb is called the "**infinitive**". The infinitive is the form used when naming the verb (this is the form of the verb you will look up in a dictionary of Old English). In Modern English, the infinitive has "to" in front of the verb: "to help", "to think", "to do". In Old English, the infinitive is a single word, and usually ends in "-an" (but some common verbs simply end in "-n"). The Old English counterparts to the Modern English infinitives above are: "helpan", "þencan", and "tuon". The stem of the infinitive is the basic form from which all other verb forms are derived. The stem can be derived by simply taking the "-(a)n" ending off of the infinitive.

The "**present participle**" form of a verb in Modern English is the verb form ending in "-ing": "helping", "thinking", "doing". It can be used as a verb in our "progressive tense" ("I am walk**ing**") or as a verbal adjective ("a bounc**ing** ball"). The present participle of the verb in Old English is formed by adding "-ende" to the verb stem. Thus, the present participle of "helpan" is "helpende". The present participle was used in Old English only as a verbal adjective, not as an auxiliary to form progressive tenses as we do in Modern English today. For example, you could say "a helping hand": "helpende hand", but not "I am helping her"; in Old English you simply said "I help her". Modern English also uses the present participle form as a verbal noun (called a "gerund"): "seeing is believing". Old English used the infinitive for this purpose.

The "**past participle**" form of the verb in Modern English ends in either "-d" or "-t" (for weak verbs) or has an internal vowel change plus either "-(e)n" or no suffix (for strong verbs). Like the present participle, it can be used as part of a verb phrase in Modern English: "I have **seen** him", "She has **given** it to him", "They have **helped** me", or as a verbal adjective "a **painted** wall", "a **sewn** handbag". The past participle in Old English is formed by optionally prefixing "ge-" to the verb stem, in addition to a dental suffix ("-(e)d/-od" or "-(e)t") for weak verbs, or by optionally prefixing "ge-" to the stem of a strong verb, with a possible vowel change in the stem, and a suffix of "-en". The past participle of "hælen" ('to heal', a weak verb) is "(ge)hæled"; the past participle of "wrītan" (strong) is "(ge)writen". It was used in much the same manner as Modern English.

Now let's take a look at the two most basic paradigms for Old English verbs: the strong and weak conjugations:

Old English Strong Verb Conjugation: singan ('to sing')			
Infinitive:	singan ('to sing')	**Past Participle:**	(ge)sungen
Present Participle:	singende	**Imperative:**	sing singaþ
Indicative		Subjunctive	
Present	Preterite	Present	Preterite
ic singe þū singest hē singeþ	ic sang þū sunge hē sang	ic singe þū singe hē singe	ic sunge þū sunge hē sunge
wē singaþ gē singaþ hīe singaþ	wē sungon gē sungon hīe sungon	wē singen gē singen hīe singen	wē sungen gē sungen hīe sungen

One thing to note in the table above is the different vowels of the preterite singular and plural, and that the second person singular preterite has the vowel of the plural.

An example of a weak conjugation is in the table below:

Old English Weak Verb Conjugation: lufian ('to love')			
Infinitive:	lufian ('to love')	**Past Participle:**	(ge)lufod
Present Participle:	lufiende	**Imperative:**	lufa lufiaþ
Indicative		Subjunctive	
Present	Preterite	Present	Preterite
ic lufie þū lufast hē lufaþ	ic lufode þū lufodest hē lufode	ic lufie þū lufie hē lufie	ic lufode þū lufode hē lufode
wē lufiaþ gē lufiaþ hīe lufiaþ	wē lufodon gē lufodon hīe lufodon	wē lufien gē lufien hīe lufien	wē lufoden gē lufoden hīe lufoden

There are also separate classes within both the strong and weak paradigms, each with slight variations. However, the examples above give you an idea of what each conjugation looks like. A few things to note are: 1. the plural forms are always the same for all three numbers, and 2. the plural endings are the same in both weak and strong conjugations.

Following is the paradigm for the common word "habban" ('to have'):

Old English Conjugation of "habban" ('to have')			
Infinitive:	habban	**Past Participle:**	gehæfd
Present Participle:	hæbbende	**Imperative:**	hafa habbaþ
Indicative		**Subjunctive**	
Present	**Preterite**	**Present**	**Preterite**
ic hæbbe	ic hæfde	ic	ic
þū hæfst/hafast	þū hæfdest	þū hæbbe	þū hæfde
hē hæfþ/hafaþ	hē hæfde	hē	hē
wē habbaþ	wē	wē	wē
gē habbaþ	gē hæfdon	gē hæbben	gē hæfden
hīe habbaþ	hīe	hīe	hīe

Below is the paradigm for the word "bēon" ('to be'). Note that "bēon" is highly irregular. Although there are different forms for "to be", they were not all used interchangeably. The use of separate forms that are not genetically related (i.e., they do not ultimately come from the same word) in a paradigm is called "suppletion" (or "suppletive forms"; another example of suppletion in English is the verb "to go" in which we have "go" in the present but "went" in past tense forms; both of these forms originated from entirely separate words with similar meanings). The most common forms used in the present tense indicative are those on the left under "Present" tense in the table below. The "wesan" forms are rarely used in the present indicative, while the "be-" forms generally refer to future action (though conjugated in the present tense). The preterite indicative and subjunctive use only the "wes-" forms. If you recall, each of these forms has its roots in the various forms that have come down from Germanic via Indo-European.

Old English Conjugation of "bēon/sindon/wesan" ('to be')	
Infinitive:	bēon/sindon/wesan
Present Participle:	bēonde, wesende
Past Participle:	gebēon
Imperative:	bēo/wes bēoþ/wesaþ

Indicative			
Present		**Preterite**	
ic	eom/bēo/wese	ic	wæs
þū	eart/bist/wesst	þū	wære
hē	is/bið/wes(t)	hē	wæs
wē	sindon/bēoþ/wesaþ	wē	wæron
gē	sindon/bēoþ/wesaþ	gē	wæron
hīe	sindon/bēoþ/wesaþ	hīe	wæron

Subjunctive			
Present		**Preterite**	
ic	sie/beo/wese	ic	wære
þū	sie/beo/wese	þū	wære
hē	sie/beo/wese	hē	wære
wē	sien/beon/wesen	wē	wæren
gē	sien/beon/wesen	gē	wæren
hīe	sien/beon/wesen	hīe	wæren

Numbers

Following is a table of the number system in Old English. Keep in mind that various spelling variations for the numbers were possible.

The numbers "ān", "twēgen", and "þrīe" were declined like adjectives (i.e., they took on gender, case, and number endings when they came before a noun), as were the ordinal numbers (these are the numbers of order: first, second, third, etc.). The various forms of two and three are a used for the different adjective declensions.

Old English Numbers			
1	ān	20	twentig
2	twēgen/ twā/tū	21	ān and twentig
3	þrīe/ þrēo	30	þrēotig/ þrītig
4	fēower	40	fēowertig
5	fīf	50	fīftig
6	siex	60	siextig
7	seofon	70	hundseofontig
8	eahta	80	hundeahtatig
9	nigon	90	hundnigontig
10	tīen	100	hundtēontig/ hund/ hundred
11	endleofan	200	tū hund
12	twelf	1000	þūsend
13	þrēotīene	2000	tū þūsendu

You may have noticed that the numbers are fairly similar to Modern English up to the number 70. At this point, Old English adds the prefix "hund-" (obviously related to our current word "hundred", and itself meaning 'hundred' in Old English). This, along with the differences in the numbers eleven and twelve (versus the "teen" numbers) shows that the original number system may have had a basis of twelve, rather than our current ten. After 60 (five times twelve), the expected forms have a prefix of "hund-". This basis of twelve is also evident in our modern world where certain items still come in dozens (twelve) and grosses (twelve times twelve), though it should be noted that this so-called "duodecimal" (from Latin "two" and "ten") theory has been disputed.

Another stark difference was the way that numbers such as 21, 33, or 67 were created. You may recall the old children's nursery rhyme "Sing a Song of Sixpence", which starts out:

> Sing a song of sixpence a pocket full of rye,
>
> **Four and twenty** blackbirds baked in a pie.

Although this particular version comes to us from Early Modern English, the convention of building numbers beyond twenty was the same in Old English: the smaller number comes before the larger number, with an "and" linking them. This originated in Germanic (and, indeed, most of the Germanic languages today still use this formula, with the other main exceptions being Swedish and Norwegian), and continued to be used until the Modern English period. Thus, Old English has "ān and twentig" (literally "one and twenty") for 'twenty-one', "fēower and fēowertig" for 'forty-four', etc.

Sample Texts

Following are some sample texts in Old English from various times within the period, showing poetry as well as prose.

The first text sample is from *Cædmon's Hymn*, written in the 7th century CE. As the story goes, Cædmon was a herdsman attached to an abbey who was ashamed that he could not sing vernacular songs of his time. One night, he dreamt that he was ordered to create a song about the biblical creation story. The next day, still remembering the dream song, he wrote it down and added to it. He later became a devout monk and poet of religious works. Cædmon's Hymn, as the poem came to be called, is one of the earliest attestations of Old English. His story was related in Bede's *Ecclesiastical History of the English People*. The poem is one of the earliest recorded examples of poetry in a Germanic language.

The poem follows below with underlined words that have survived in Modern English glossed at the end of the text ("glossing" simply means explaining or translating the words).

| Cædmon's Hymn (Lines 1– 9) ||
Old English	Modern English Translation
Nu sculon herigean heofonrices weard,	Now (we) should praise the heavenly kingdom's guardian,
meotodes meahte and his modgeþanc,	the creator's might and his mind's thought,
weorc wuldorfæder, swa he wundra gehwæs,	the work of the father of glory, how he each of the wonders,
ece drihten, or onstealde.	the eternal Lord, established in the beginning.
He ærest sceop eorðan bearnum	He first created for the children of men
heofon to hrofe, halig scyppend;	heaven as a roof, the holy Creator;
þa middangeard moncynnes weard,	then middle-earth mankind's guardian,
ece drihten, æfter teode	the eternal Lord, afterwards made,
firum foldan, frea ælmihtig!	the earth for men, the Lord almighty!
shall, heaven-Reich (German), ward, might, mood-thought, work, (glory-) father, wonders, shape, earth, bairn (Scots English), heaven, roof, holy, middle-yard, man-kin, almighty	

The next text sample is from *Beowulf*, the greatest epic poem in English, which we discussed earlier. This translation, from a 1910 translation by Francis Gummere (a typical Victorian-era translation) is fairly non-literal (as such, I have not tried to line it up with the original). The underlined words focus on those words that have survived in the modern language (though their forms and meanings today may differ from the original). Their modern-day counterparts are at the bottom of the text.

Besides the use of alliteration, this poem makes use of "kennings". A kenning, also common in Old Norse literature, is a compound word that creatively describes an every-day concept. For example, in the text below, "hron-rāde" (literally 'whale-road') is used instead of the word for "sea" (you can imagine how the sea could be metaphorically referred to as a "road of whales").

Beowulf, Author Unknown (Lines 1–11)	
Old English	**Modern English Translation**
Hwæt! wē Gār-<u>Dena</u> in <u>gēar</u>-<u>dagum</u> þēod-<u>cyninga</u> þrym gefrūnon, hū þā <u>æðelingas</u> ellen fremedon. <u>Oft</u> Scyld Scēfing sceaðena <u>þrēatum</u>, <u>monegum</u> mægðum <u>meodo</u>-setla oftēah. Egsode <u>eorl</u>, syððan ǣrest wearð fēa-sceaft <u>funden</u>: hē þæs frōfre <u>gebād</u>, <u>wēox</u> under wolcnum, weorð- myndum ðāh, oð þæt him ǣghwylc þāra ymb- sittendra <u>ofer</u> hron-<u>rāde</u> <u>hȳran</u> <u>scolde</u>, gomban gyldan: þæt wæs <u>gōd</u> <u>cyning</u>!	Lo, praise of the prowess of people-kings of spear-armed Danes, in days long sped, we have heard, and what honor the athelings won! Often Scyld the Scefing from squadroned foes, from many a tribe, the mead-bench tore, awing the earls. Since erst he lay friendless, a foundling, fate repaid him: for he waxed under welkin, in wealth he throve, till before him the folk, both far and near, who house by the whale-path, heard his mandate, gave him gifts: a good king he!
what, Danes, year, days, kings, athelings, often, threat, many, mead, earl, found, bad (verb), wax, over, road, hear, should, good, king	

The final text sample is an example of Old English prose. The Anglo-Saxon Chronicles recounted the history of the Anglo-Saxons in Britain with annual recordings of significant events in the Anglo-Saxon world. The chronicles also record history prior to the Anglo-Saxon conquest of Britain, including the Roman conquest of Britain and the life of Christ (obviously recorded well after these events occurred). The chronicles were actually started in 890 CE at the request of King Alfred the Great (mentioned earlier in the chapter). The chronicles continued to be written for over 300 years from their inception. The lines below are from the years 455 and 457 CE, chronicling part of the Anglo-Saxon conquest of Britain, and the (perhaps mythical) undertakings of twins Hengest and Horsa (note that these names are the words for 'stallion' and 'horse'). Underlined words are glossed at the end of the text.

Anglo-Saxon Chronicles	
Old English	**Modern English Translation**
455 Her Hengest Horsa fuhton wiþ Wyrtgeorne þam cyninge, in þære stowe þe is gecueden Agælesþrep, his broþur Horsan man ofslog; æfter þam Hengest feng to rice Æsc his sunu.	455 CE. Here Hengest and Horsa fought against Vortigern the king on the spot that is called Aylesford. His brother Horsa was slain; Hengest and his son Ash afterwards took hold of the kingdom.
457 Her Hengest Æsc fuhton wiþ Brettas in þære stowe þe is gecueden Crecganford þær ofslogon .iiiim. wera, þa Brettas þa forleton Centlond mid micle ege flugon to Lundenbyrg.	457 CE. Here Hengest and Ash fought against the Britons on the spot that is called Crayford, and there slew four thousand men. The Britons then left the land of Kent, and in great consternation fled to London.
here, fought, with, king, brother, slaughtered, Reich (German), son (four thousand), men (were- from "werewolf"), with, flew	

In the next chapter, we will take a look at the next stage of the language, Middle English.

Middle English   4

And for ther is so gret diversite
In Englissh and in writyng of oure tonge,
So preye I God that non mywrite the,
Ne mysmetre for defaut of tonge.

—*Geoffrey Chaucer, Troilus and Criseyde*

History

The year 1066 is one of the most important in the history of England, and for the history of the English language. That year marked the Norman Conquest, in which William, the Duke of Normandy, defeated the Anglo-Saxon king Harold at the Battle of Hastings.

King Harold had only recently defeated an invasion by King Harald of Norway in late September of that year, when England was invaded by Normans from the north of France. Harold's troops had been worn down by their recent battles, but put up a strong fight against the Normans. On October 14th, 1066, Harold was killed and his army fled. Harold had no living heir. William gained control of the country by the end of October and was crowned King of England on December 25th, 1066 at Westminster Abbey.

The Normans themselves were actually distant kinfolk of the Anglo-Saxons. Their moniker comes literally from the words "north men", the descendents of Vikings who had been invited to settle northern France in 911 CE, in the hopes of staving off future Viking attacks. Within a century, they had adopted the language and culture of the region, including the northern variant of Old French, called "langue d'oïl", adding their own Norse influence.

Normans quickly became the feudal rulers of England, and they instituted their language as the language in which official business was done. The Anglo-Saxon aristocracy was quickly replaced by Normans, as were those in the hierarchy of the Church. But by the time of the Black Death in the mid-14th century CE, the Normans had been almost completely integrated into English society.

The effect of the Norman Conquest on the English language has been much debated. There is no denying that in the period starting at the end of the 11th century, a vast number of French (and Latin) words became a part of the vocabulary. This was especially the case for terms dealing with government and law, but it was even more pervasive than that; eventually the vocabulary became a mixture of its base of Anglo-Saxon with the French language of the conquerors.

Some scholars in the past have argued that the Norman Conquest was the reason for the vast changes which would soon occur in the language, including simplification of the case system and the elimination of the grammatical gender system almost entirely. However, there is linguistic evidence that such changes were already well underway by the time of the Norman Conquest, and it is likely that this event and the following influx of French simply hastened a process that was already inevitable.

The Middle English period is generally considered to be from about 1100 CE to the latter part of the 15th century CE. During this time, French was the language of the ruling class, as well as the language of law, government, and literature. However, the common people still spoke English. Over time, as the Norman conquerors intermarried and mixed with the common classes, French gave way to English, though the latter would be much changed by this point.

Literature

Whereas in the Old English period, the West Saxon dialects of Wessex dominated the literary and scribal traditions, the Middle English period is characterized by more diversity in the literary dialects and scribal styles. Despite the dominance of Anglo-Norman French, English was still a vibrant literary language during this period. Over time, Northumbria, East Anglia, and London each had their turn as major sources of Middle English literature.

One of the first great works of this period is the Piers Plowman dream-vision, written in the mid-14th century CE. Attributed to William Langland, this allegorical narrative uses alliteration, much like the works of the Old English period. Also reminiscent of the Old English period is the religious theme of the poem. In it, the narrator has a series of dream-visions, where he meets allegorical characters such as Truth (God), Wrong (the Devil), Conscience, Liar, and Reason. In the end, he embarks on a search for Dowel ("do well"), Dobet ("do better"), and Dobest ("do best"), in a quest for the meaning of "true" Christianity.

Another great writer of the period was the author of several important works, including *Sir Gawain and the Green Knight, Patience, Cleanness,* and *Pearl*. As such, he is known as the "Gawain Poet" or the "Pearl Poet". Little is known about the poet himself. He wrote in the Cheshire dialect of north-west England. His poetry also followed the alliterative religious and mythological traditions of the prior era.

Sir Thomas Malory was best known for his works regarding the Arthurian legend. He was the author and compiler of *Le Morte d'Arthur* (Middle French for "the death of Arthur"), a retelling of prior stories including his own original stories about Arthur. Malory was an interesting character in his own right, having served in Parliament, but also in prison for various crimes, including burglary, rape, and theft. His stories of the Arthurian legend are perhaps the best known in the English language, and the basis for many of the modern retellings of these tales.

No description of Middle English would be complete without mention of William Caxton, the first Englishman to work as a printer. Caxton was born in Kent, worked in London, and worked and traveled extensively as a businessman in continental Europe. His travels took him to Belgium and Germany, where he learned about the newly created printing industry. He set up his own printing press in Bruges, in the Dutch-speaking part of Belgium (called Flanders), where he collaborated to create the first book to be printed in English in 1475 CE: *Recuyell of the Historyes of Troye*, which Caxton himself translated. In 1476 he set up his own printing press at Westminster. The first book known to have been printed there was *Dictes or Sayengis of the Philosophres* ("Sayings of the Philosophers"), printed November 18, 1477 CE. Perhaps the most important works printed by Caxton were *Le Morte d'Arthur*, by Malory (see above), and Geoffrey Chaucer's *Canterbury Tales*.

Caxton is an important figure in the history of English in much the same way Johannes Gutenberg was for German—as the initial printer of widely read works, he was able to set certain standards for the written language. The spoken language of the time was one in flux, and the works he printed consisted of a variety of dialects and styles. The task of standardizing the printed language was largely up to Caxton himself, and he is credited today with a great amount of influence in shaping the standardized language.

Finally, the man whose literary works are practically synonymous with the term "Middle English" is Geoffrey Chaucer. The author of *The Canterbury Tales*, Chaucer was most likely born in London around 1343 CE. He lived there and in Kent, the county in which Canterbury is situated. A contemporary of William Langland and the Pearl Poet, Chaucer's earliest careers included courtier, diplomat, and civil servant. He traveled extensively throughout continental Europe, visiting such places as France, Flanders, Spain, and Italy. It was during these travels that he came upon the literary traditions that would later influence his own writings—those of France and Italy. His own work is often divided into three periods: French, Italian, and English. He was originally known for his translations of both French and Italian works. But he is best known world-wide for his work in English, the most prominent being the *Tales*, his unfinished frame narrative. Those works were heavily influenced by the French and Italian traditions with which Chaucer was most familiar.

Begun in the late 1380's CE and not completed until a decade later, Chaucer's *The Canterbury Tales* is perhaps the best known work of Middle English literature. It is a collection of tales, two in prose, the rest in verse, told by 31 men and women (including Chaucer himself) on a pilgrimage from the Tabard Inn in Southwark (a borough of London) to St. Thomas à Becket's shrine at the cathedral in Canterbury. In order to make their journey go more quickly, the inn's host suggests that each pilgrim tell two tales during the journey to the cathedral, and two each on the return trip, with the best storyteller earning a free supper upon their return. With twenty-four actual tales, the work was never fully completed as planned.

This literary device, based on contemporary devices used in continental European literature (most notably Boccaccio's *Decameron*, from which Chaucer borrows liberally for several tales), allows Chaucer to illustrate the lives of the common people from various perspectives, some comical, others serious, using the common language of the people (many times using the "bawdy" language of the day). It is an intriguing snapshot of life in 14th century England.

A big difference between Chaucer's works and those of his contemporaries is the style in which he wrote, called "accentual-syllabic meter", an alternative to the alliterative style of Old English and many of his contemporaries. He was also one of the first to use the "iambic pentameter" (in which a line contains five stressed syllables) in English, which eventually became quite common.

Chaucer is often credited as one of the most important influences in helping to appoint the dialect of London, a combination of Kentish and Midlands dialect, as the standard for English.

Language

Middle English is the first stage of the language that is somewhat accessible to speakers of Modern English without the need for extra training in grammar or vocabulary. If you try to read a Middle English text, you will be able to get at least the gist of its meaning—something you cannot do with Old English without further training.

The language of Middle English is still very much grounded in Germanic with a noticeable influx of French vocabulary. The grammar itself is quite a bit different from that of Old English. It has often been characterized as having become more "simplified". The richness of the inflectional system did indeed become much simpler. But, with a decrease in inflections came an increase in the importance of "syntax" (the structure of a sentence) and an increase in the use of prepositional phrases which took up the former work of the inflections.

Two simple examples of this change from inflections to periphrastic constructions (which to this very day have not been fully implemented) are in the use of the genitive and dative cases. In Old English, possession was shown by the use of genitive case endings. In the Middle English period, the vast array of genitive endings leveled out to essentially just one: "-(e)s" (the "e" was most commonly used earlier in the period, less commonly later on) added to the end of a noun. In addition, a periphrastic construction came into much greater usage, involving the preposition "of". For example, today we can say "the girl's book" (using inflection), or "the book **of** the girl" (periphrastic). Many languages make use of just one or the other, whereas Modern English allows more flexibility (although there are often stylistic issues to take into consideration when employing one or the other).

The indirect object, governed by the dative case in Old English, along with its various inflectional endings, also changed during this period. During the earlier part of the period, the inflectional endings merged into a final "-e", which was lost entirely by the latter part of the period. By the end of the period, inflection no longer distinguished a noun acting as an indirect object—it had to be shown by other means, namely via syntax or a phrase. In Modern English, we can now say "the woman gave the boy some candy", and we know that "the boy" is the indirect object because of its place in the sentence (if we said "the woman gave some candy the boy" this would not make sense and would in fact be grammatically incorrect; if we changed it further and said "the boy gave the woman some candy" the entire meaning is changed, whereas in languages with riche inflectional endings than Modern English, such as German or Russian, you could use this approximate word order and the sentence would still have the meaning of the woman giving candy to the boy). Periphrastically, you can say "the woman gave some candy *to the boy*" in which case a prepositional phrase is used to indicate the indirect object. Again, Modern English allows for more options than many other languages in this respect.

Many other aspects of the complicated inflectional grammar of Old English also became more simplified in Middle English. Grammatical gender disappeared almost entirely, the case system became much more simplified (nouns had just two cases, possessive and non-possessive, while some pronouns also retained "oblique" forms used for direct and indirect objects), and verb conjugations simplified (though the verb itself, in some respects became more complicated with the increased use of auxiliary verbs and an increase in the number of verb tenses). It was in this period that the language began to change from a mostly fusional language like Latin to a more isolating one.

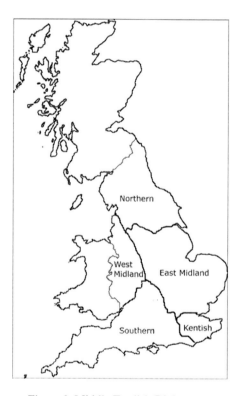

Figure 3: Middle English Dialects

A common question is "why did these changes happen"? Linguists do not have a definite answer. Language is, of course, constantly changing, but the sweeping changes that occurred during this period of the language have caused many to search for a source. The Norman conquest and introduction of French into England is often cited as a prime reason for these changes. However, linguists have shown that many of the changes that took place in this period began well before the 11th century CE. Surely, the changes brought about by the new Norman influence may have helped to speed up the pace of change. The exact answer to why the changes occurred will probably never be precisely known.

The dialect areas of England changed as well, but five main areas are generally cited: Northern, East Midlands, West Midlands, (some scholars group the two together as simply "Midlands"), Southern, and Kentish. The London dialect, an East Midland dialect, grew dominant by the latter part of the period (due to the rise of London, and acclaimed authors such as Chaucer who spoke this dialect). It is from this dialect that standard Modern English is directly descended, rather than the dominant West Saxon of the Old English era. A map of the Middle English dialect areas is above.

To see a clearer picture of the changes in the language, here is the Lord's Prayer, which we saw in Old English in the last chapter, in Middle English. This version is from the Wycliffe Bible, circa 1390. Modern English glosses appear for underlined words.

Middle English	Glosses
Oure fadir that art in heuenes	
halewid be thi name	
thi kyngdoom come to	
be thi wille don	
in erthe as in heuene;	heaven
ȝyue to vs this dai oure breed ouer othir substaunce,	give, us, over
and forȝyue to vs oure dettis, as we forȝyuen to oure dettouris;	forgive, debts
and lede vs not in to temptacioun, but delyuere vs fro yuel.	deliver evil
Amen.	

Note that you can already read this text without any help. Although the orthography and syntax may be a little different from that of Modern English, you can see that this language is not so different from your own.

Middle English Orthography

During the Middle English period, French scribes began to influence the orthography and spelling of English. The letters "ash" and "eth" were dropped but "thorn" and "yogh", the other "non-Latin" letters from Old English, remained for some time. However, the French scribes' aversion to non-Latin letters soon won out completely, as "thorn" and "yogh" eventually became digraphs (two letters that stand for a single sound), "th" and "gh" respectively. In addition, new letters were added to the alphabet from French: "j" (varied with "i"), "v" (at first used for "u" in initial position, "q" (in combination with "u" to represent the former Old English "cw"), and "z", which varied with "s".

Middle English Phonetics and Phonology

Vowels

In general, the vowels of Middle English did not change considerably from the Old English period. One of the most important changes was the growing dominance of the schwa sound (the "a" in "sofa"), replacing other vowel sounds in unaccented syllables (as it does to this day). With the accent generally on the initial syllable (a trait carried down from Germanic), vowels in final syllables, especially, turned to a schwa sound, and then eventually were dropped altogether (the "silent "-e" on the end of so many words in Modern English is a testament to this change). By the latter part of the Middle English period, most final "-e's" were likely silent. In Chaucer's own works, one can usually ascertain from the meter whether a given final "-e" was pronounced or not, but it is debatable whether those examples where final "-e" is pronounced in his works were pronounced simply to make the meter "work" or whether some words at the time still kept this pronunciation.

Although the change had most likely begun in the Old English period, a change in the concepts of "long" and "short" vowels was solidified in the Middle English period to something approximating what we have today—a change in quality rather than quantity. If you recall, in Old English long vowels were simply pronounced somewhat longer than short vowels, but they otherwise sounded the same. In Middle English, long and short are distinguished by a different quality of sound altogether, although the quantity distinction was not lost altogether during this period for some vowels. An example of the quality difference was the long "i" sound "shire" (pronounced "sheer") and the short "i" in "this" (pronounced as it is today).

Following is a more detailed look at the individual vowel sounds of Middle English. In each example, the first letter is the short vowel, and those following are long vowels.

Middle English Vowels		
Spelling	**Example**	**Modern Pronunciation**
a a	that name	short "a" in "father", like American English "o" in "hot" "a" in "father"
e ee (closed) ee (open)	bed sweete ('sweet') heeth ('heath')	"e" in bed "ay" in "sway" (without the "y" sound at the end) "e" in "bed" drawn out: "hehhhth"
i i	this shire	"i" in this "ee" in "sheer"
o oo (closed) oo (open)	oft good boot ('boat')	"o" in British English "hot" "oa" in "road" "ou" in British English "bought"
u u (rounded) ou	but nature flour ('flower')	"u" in "put" "u" in French "tu", "ü" in German "für" (only in French loanwords) "oo" in "floor"

You may have noticed that both the "e" and the "o" have "closed" and "open" pronunciations that were different (though the spelling was usually the same). The closed "e" usually came to be spelled "ea" in Modern English while the closed "o" is usually spelled "oa" in Modern English words that originally had these sounds. The "ou" spelling for the long "u" sound was a convention from Norman French.

Diphthongs

The diphthongs are fairly different from the Old English diphthongs. However, only one was entirely new, the "oi" diphthong in the table above. It came into the language via Norman French, and was evident only in loanwords. Note the two slightly different pronunciations for the oi/oy/oj spelling. Also note that, although many of the Middle English examples below look like (and in many cases are identical to) their modern-day counterparts, the pronunciation was quite different. Remember when trying to pronounce the diphthongs that the sounds are not pronounced separately, but rather the first sound "glides" into the second sound in a smooth transition.

Below are the diphthongs of Middle English.

Middle English Diphthongs		
Spelling	**Example**	**Modern Pronunciation**
ai/ay/ei/ey	day	"a" in "dad" + "ee" in "deed"
au/av/aw	cause	"ou" in house
eu/ev/ew	newe ('new')	"e" in "bed" + "oo" on "boot"
iw/eu/ev/ew	tiwesday ('Tuesday')	"ee" in "deed" + "oo" in "boot"
o/ou/ov/ow	ought	"ou" in British English "bought" + "oo" in "boot"
oi/oy/oj	joy point	"oy" in "joy" "u" in "put" + "ee" in "deed"

Consonants

The consonants of Middle English were even closer to their modern day counterparts than those of Old English. The inventory of consonant sounds was almost identical with that of our language today.

One change, likely the result of the influx of Norman French words, was that the f/v and s/z sounds became "phonemic". You may recall that in Old English, "f" represented both "f" (unvoiced) and "v" (voiced) sounds, while "s" represented both "s" (unvoiced) and "z" (voiced) sounds. You could tell which sound, voiced or unvoiced, was appropriate according to its place in the word. For instance, if an "f" occurred between vowels or with a voiced consonant, it had the "v" sound, but in all other instances (e.g., word initial, word final, among voiceless consonants), it had the "f" sound. The same was true for "s"—"s" sound "initially", "finally" and with voiceless consonants, and "z" between vowels ("medially") or among voiced consonants. With the introduction of words from Norman French, these rules were no longer valid—a "v" sound could start a word, as could a "z", for example. When separate sounds that were once considered "the same sound" (i.e., they varied in complementary positions, such as Old English "s" versus "z" or "f" versus "v") are no longer considered one sound, we say that they have now become separate phonemes. In Middle English, since an "f" vs. a "v" and an "s" vs. a "z" could occur in environments that were no longer predictable, we say they became phonemic.

An example from Modern English where we have two separate sounds, but do not *consider* them to be separate, is in the "p", "t", and "k" sounds. You may recall from the first chapter that we noted the difference between the "p" in "pin" versus the "p" in "spin" (i.e., the first is pronounced with a puff of air, the second is not, and sounds more like "b"). We call this difference one of aspiration—the first example uses an aspirated "p", the second does not. The same is true of "k" and "t" (say "kin" versus "skin" and "tone" versus "stone"). To speakers of English, the "p" in "pin" is regarded as the same sound as the "p" in "spin". In fact, you probably never noticed a difference before until you tried the "paper test" from the earlier chapter, or listened carefully to your own pronunciation just now. We call these different "p" sounds "allophones" of the phoneme "p". The aspirated allophone occurs when it is word- (and often syllable-) initial, the unaspirated allophone occurs after "s". So it is entirely predictable when you pronounce it one way versus the other. If you *did* pronoun "pin" *without* aspiration, or "spin" *with* aspiration, it would sound a little funny to most people, but no one would be confused—as native speakers of English, we still consider all allophones of a phoneme (just think of this as "regular variations of a phoneme") to be "the same sound", i.e., they never change the meaning of the word. This is not the case for these sounds in other languages. For instance, in Thai, the word "phaa" (*with* aspirated "p") means "forest", whereas "paa" (without aspiration) means "split". Thus, in Thai, these two sounds are *not* allophones of the same phoneme—they are considered separate phonemes entirely. With the influx of words from Norman French into Middle English that violated the former "f/v" and "s/z" variations, these four sounds also became separate phonemes in the language.

Middle English Grammar

As mentioned above, the Middle English period marked the beginning of the transition of English from a mostly fusional language to a more isolating language. This was a result of the massive loss of inflectional endings for every part of speech that had them, including nouns, adjectives, and verbs. The following pages document Middle English grammar in more detail, showing the changes from the Old English period.

Articles

You may recall that in Old English, the definite article was quite complicated, with many different possibilities, depending on number, case, and gender. In Middle English, all of these possibilities coalesced into a single definite article: "þe", later spelled as it is today, "the". Middle English also saw the introduction of "an" as an indefinite article, derived from the Old English word for "one". Because of its very nature as an unstressed word in a sentence, the "n" was eventually dropped except when it appeared before a word beginning with a vowel sound, just as it is today.

These are some very significant changes that occurred over the space of a few centuries at most. The loss of endings in the articles shows how the emphasis on the initial syllable of a word in English, as well as the frequency of a word that generally had little to no stress *within a sentence*, helped to whittle away the sounds at the end of the word (i.e., the inflectional endings), until they were gone completely. There were likely other factors involved in this leveling from many options to one, in the case of the definite article, such as the contact with both Scandinavian and French languages later in the Old English period, though these effects were probably more limited than is sometimes assumed.

Nouns and Adjectives

Nouns also underwent drastic changes similar to the definite article: only two basic inflections survived, the plural marker and the possession marker. The plural marker became "-(e)s" for most words, though in some dialects, the "-(e)n" plural was more commonly used. However, in dialects where "-(e)s" was the usual plural, the "-(e)n" plural was still used, more commonly used than it is today (there are only a handful in use in Modern English: "children", "oxen", and "brethren" among them). In Middle English, such common words as "eye", "too" ('toe'), "ear", "shoe", and "hand" had these plurals: "eyen", "toon" (though "toos" was also possible), "earen", "shoen", and "handen".

The genitive case gave way to what is now commonly called the possessive case. All nouns added "-(e)s" to show possession (if the noun ended in a vowel, the "e" was not added—our Modern English " 's " comes from this Middle English convention; the apostrophe is simply a place holder for the former "e") and for noun plurals.

In the table below, you can see how noun declensions changed from the Old to Middle English periods. The table uses the Old English and Early and Late Middle English words for Modern English 'stone'.

Noun Declension: Old, Early Middle, and Late Middle English				
Number	Case	Old English	Early Middle English	Late Middle English
Singular	Nom./Acc.	stān	ston	stoon
	Dat.	stāne	stone	
	Gen.	stānes	stones	stoon(e)s
Plural	Nom./Acc.	stānas		
	Dat.	stānum	stonen, -es	
	Gen.	stāna	stone, -es	

Among adjectives, there were also great inflectional losses that were even more extensive than among nouns: no adjective inflections survived the Middle English period, save a vestigial "-e" on the end of monosyllabic adjectives. Whereas the adjective could move a bit more freely in Old English (before or after the noun it modified), the adjective in Middle English became firmly planted before the adjective, with a few exceptions of usage from Norman French, which generally had the adjective *after* the noun it modified (many have survived to this day; e.g., "surgeon general", "court martial", etc.). The following table shows the leveling of adjectives in Middle English.

Middle English Adjective Declension		
	Strong Declension	Weak Declension
Singular	good	goode
Plural	goode	goode

The Old English comparative "-ra" became "-re", then "-er". Old English "-ost"/"-est" for the superlative became "-est". In addition to these minor changes, a new periphrastic comparative and superlative came into being from the influence of Norman French: the use of "more" + adjective for the comparative and "most" + adjective for the superlative. The general rule was that adjectives of two syllables or less used the endings to form the comparative and superlative, while adjectives with more than two syllables used "more" and "most". In the

Middle English period (and through the Early Modern Period, as evidenced in Shakespeare's writings), "double comparatives" and "double superlatives" were in common use. One could find: "sweeter", "more sweete", and even "more sweeter". Likewise, the superlative could be "sweetest", "moste sweete", or even "moste sweetest".

Pronouns

The personal pronouns also changed from the Old English to Middle English periods. However, these were probably the least drastic changes of all. In fact, it is the personal pronouns alone that to this day mark the former object cases in English. Middle English personal pronouns preserved the three gender categories (although they changed from "grammatical" gender, which was largely arbitrary, to "natural" gender, whereby male people and animals are "masculine", female people and animals are "feminine", and inanimate things, or animals of indeterminate gender are "neuter"). It preserved two of the three numbers (singular and plural; the dual number denoting two of something was already gone late in the Old English period), and person distinctions (first, second, and third persons). The major change was in the case system. Whereas with nouns, adjectives, and determiners (articles and demonstratives) all case distinctions were lost, save a "possessive" case for nouns, the personal pronouns kept a possessive as well as an *oblique*, or object case, wherein the dative and accusative cases coalesced to form a single case. The linguistic term for this coalescence in the case system is called case "syncretism".

Middle Englsh Personal Pronouns						
Number	**Case**	**1st Person**	**2nd Person**	**3rd Person**		
				masc.	neut.	fem.
Singular	**Nom.**	i, ich	þou	he	it, hit	sche
	Pos.	my, myn	þy, þyn	his	his	her
	Obl.	me	þee	him	it, hit	hir(e)
Plural	**Nom.**	we	ye	þei		
	Pos.	oure	youre	þeir, hire		
	Obl.	us	you	þem, hem		

The personal pronouns of Middle English appear in the table above. The first person singular nominative pronoun was initially "ich", (pronounced much like our word "itch"). Its unstressed form, "i" (not always capitalized at this point) was pronounced like the "i" in "bit", and its stressed for was pronounced like "e" in Modern English "he". In the possessive case, "my" (pronounced like Modern English "me", and still pronounced as such in some dialects in the UK) was the usual form, but "myn" occurred before nouns that began with a vowel sound, just like the "a" vs. "an" distinction at the time. For example, "my eyes" would have been "myn eyen". In the first person plural, "we" was pronounced close to modern "way", "oure" rhymes with "poor", and "us" rhymed with "puss".

In the second person pronouns, there was still a distinction of singular versus plural, however, the singular forms were only used with close acquaintances, family members, and subordinates. The plural form began to be used even when addressing a single person to show deference or respect. The was likely a result of Norman French influence, which also developed the distinction (French has the distinction to this day in it is singular familiar "tu" versus plural and formal "vous"). "Þou" was pronounced "thoo", "þy" and "þyn" were pronounced as "thee" and "theen" (with the same distinctions as "my/myn"), and "þee" sounded like our modern "they". In the plural, "ye" rhymed with modern "yay", and "youre" and "you" already had their modern pronunciations.

In the third person pronouns, the masculine possessive and oblique pronouns were pronounced as they are today, while the nominative rhymed with modern "hey". The neuter pronouns began to lose their initial "h-" in the nominative and oblique, and retained the use of "his" for the possessive. An early feminine form of "heo", gave way to "sche", as explained in the last chapter. "Sche" would have rhymed with "Shay", the possessive would have sounded somewhat like modern "hair" (though with a vowel sound closer to the "e" in "get"), and the oblique case would have sounded much like our word "here".

The third person plural pronouns exhibit some of the most drastic changes. The introduction of pronouns borrowed from Old Norse became solidified in the Middle English period. While languages often borrow liberally from each other, it is fairly rare for a language to borrow an entire set of pronouns, as happened in late Old and early Middle English. The nominative "þei" was pronounced something like our modern pronunciation (although the vowel sound would have been slightly more like the "a" in "mat" + "e" in "me"), the possessive had two forms, "þeir" and "hire", with the former eventually winning out, and "þem" and "hem" in the oblique case, again with the latter eventually disappearing. The loss of the pronouns with initial "h", as explained in the last chapter, was likely due to the fact that these pronouns eventually became identical in sound to some of those in the masculine and feminine singular. Borrowing the "þ-" pronouns from Old Norse, a language which was still quite close to Old English, helped to differentiate the plural versions from those of the singular.

Verbs

The verbs in Middle English changed quite a bit from the Old English period as well. In some senses, the verb was simplified, while in others it became more complex. Following are examples of the strong and weak conjugations in Middle English, using the same example verbs as in the last chapter for easier comparison.

Below is the conjugation for strong verbs in Middle English.

Middle English Strong Verb Conjugation: singen ('to sing')			
Infinitive:	singen ('to sing')	**Past Participle:**	(y)sung(e)(n)
Present Participle:	singende, singing	**Imperative:**	sing singeþ, singes
Indicative		**Subjunctive**	
Present	**Preterite**	**Present**	**Preterite**
i singe	i sang		
þou sing(e)st/ singes	þou sung(e)	*sg.* sing(e)	*sg.* sunge
he singes/ singeþ	he sang		
pl. singes/ singe(n)/ singeþ	*pl.* sunge(n)	*pl.* singe(n)	*pl.* sunge(n)

Note that the plural forms in the indicative present above are *not* variations for person, but rather dialectical variations: in each individual dialect, the plural was the same for all three persons in the plural. Next, take look at the conjugation for weak verbs in Middle English below.

Middle English Weak Verb Conjugation: luvien ('to love')			
Infinitive:	luvien ('to love')	**Past Participle:**	(y)luvet
Present Participle:	luvende, luving	**Imperative:**	luv luveþ, luves
Indicative		Subjunctive	
Present	Preterite	Present	Preterite
i luve þou luv(e)st/ luves he luves/ luveþ *pl.* luves/ luve(n)/ luveþ	i luved(e) þou luvedest he luved(e) *pl.* luved(e)(n)	*sg.* luve *pl.* luve(n)	*sg.* luved(e) *pl.* luved(e)(n)

The paradigms above show the various dialectical differences in Middle English. In the infinitive ending (originally "-an" in Old English), the vowel sound weakened to a schwa sound, represented by "e"; the final "-n" was eventually dropped as well late in the period (as it had been in other parts of speech), until the bare infinitive eventually came to be what it remains to this day: essentially the verb stem. The strong past particle likewise lost its final "-en" in some instances, but kept it in others. The "ge-" prefix, which had already declined in Old English, became a simple "y" or "i", and was also commonly dropped altogether. The present participle remained the same as it had been in Old English in some dialects, but gradually evolved into the "-ing" form we have today during this period. In the present tense, there was competition between "-est" and "-es" in the 2nd person singular, and "-es" and "-eþ" in the 3rd person singular, the former being favored in the North of England, and the latter in the South. The plural forms also had several different dialectical possibilities (although the same form was used for all three persons, as it had been in Old English).

A major change from the Old English period was the introduction of more complexity to the verb tense system. You may recall that Old English had only two simple tenses, present and preterite. Through the addition of periphrastic constructions, Middle English added more tenses, including the present perfect (sometimes called simply "perfect"), past perfect (sometimes called "pluperfect"), future, and progressive tenses. These new tense constructions make use of an auxiliary verb, such as "habben"/"haven" ('to have'), "be(n)" ('to be'), "shullen" ('shall'), and "willen" ('will') plus a an infinitive or participle.

The present perfect tense used a present tense form of "habben"/ "haven" or "be(n)" plus the past participle. It was used to denote action that began in the past that is not yet completed (the following are all examples from Chaucer's *Canterbury Tales*):

The droghte of March **hath perced** to the roote.
The drought of March **has pierced** to the root.

But finally **yecomen is** the day...
But finally the day **has come**... (literally 'is come')

"Habben"/ "haven" was used with transitive verbs (in general, verbs that can take a direct object), while "be(n)" was used with intransitive verbs (verbs which are more abstract, generally do not have objects, and often refer to motion, such as "go", "come", etc.).

Similarly, the past perfect tense described action that began in the past and was completed in the past. It made use of the same "habben"/ "haven" versus "be(n)" distinction, but this construction used a preterite form of these verbs, plus the past participle.

At nyght **were come** into that hostelrye...
At night **had come** into that hostelry...

So **hadde I spoken** with hem everychon...
So I **had spoken** with them, everyone...

You may recall that Old English had no future tense in its verb system—an adverb of time was simply used with a present tense verb. Speakers of Modern German often do the same thing where an English speaker would use the future tense. Even in Modern English itself, we often do this: "I **am going** to school tomorrow" (rather than "I **will go**..."). Middle English acquired a new periphrastic future tense via the use of the auxiliary verbs "shullen/shal" and "willen/wil" plus the main verb's infinitive form. The confusion over the "proper" verb to use for different persons and circumstances ("shall" vs. "will") arose in the Middle English period. In the 14th century, students in English schools used "willen" to translate the Latin "velle" ('wish'), and "shullen" where

Latin used its inflected future tense. Even at this time, there was a greater propensity to use "willen" over "shullen" for simple future meaning. A distinction eventually arose in which "shall" was to be used for the first person, and "will" for second and third person for simple future tense: "I shall go" vs. "they will go"), while the reverse was the case for instances of "willfulness" or "insistence" ("we *will* return" vs. "he *shall* return"). This distinction, an artificial, "prescriptive" rule, has been lost in North American English, and has been greatly eroded in most other English dialects as well.

Following are examples of future tense usage in Middle English:

> For by my trouthe, if that I **shal** nat **lye**...
> For by my truth, I shall not lie...

> Thanne **wil** I **be** bynethe, by my croun...
> Then I **will be** beneath it, by my crown...

At this time a new "progressive" aspect also arose, with the use of a form of "be(n)" ('to be') plus the present participle. How this construction came into being is fairly easy to surmise. Initially the present participle in "I am going" would have been seen as simply an adjective, describing "I". Eventually, it was "reanalyzed" as being part of the verb and extended to be used with most verbs.

Below is the conjugation for "habben"/"haven" ('to have') in Middle English.

Middle English Conjugation of "habben/haven" ('to have')			
Infinitive:	habben/haven	**Past Participle:**	yhaved/yhadde/(y)had
Present Participle:	habbende/ habbing/ havende/having	**Imperative:**	habbe/have habbeþ/haveþ
Indicative			
Present		**Preterite**	
i þou he pl.	habbe/have/ha havest/hast haveþ/haþ habbeþ/habben/ habbes/haveþ/ have(n)/han	i þou he pl.	hafde/havede/hadde had(d)est/had(e)st hafde/havede/hadde had(d)e(n)

Middle English still had several forms for the verb "be(n)". The "bēon" verbs of Old English made up the infinitive, participles, and imperative forms, and were used to a lesser extent in the present indicative (though more commonly in the present subjunctive). The "wesan" forms are used throughout the preterite in both indicative and subjunctive. The "sindon" forms survive in the present indicative singular and the present subjunctive singular. In addition, a new plural form arose in the present indicative, giving us forms that start with "ar-". These forms arose from the "earon"/"aron" forms of the Old English dialects of Northumbria and Mercia (possibly influenced by Old Norse forms, though these forms were also part of Germanic and may have simply arisen directly without outside influence). You can see the conjugation for "to be" in Middle English below.

Middle English Conjugation of "be(n)" ('to be')			
Infinitive:	be(n)	**Past Participle:**	ben/(y)be(n)
Present Participle:	beand(e)/being	**Imperative:**	be bes/beþ
Indicative			
Present		**Preterite**	
i þou he *pl.*	am/em/be art/ert/es/bes(t) es/is/be(o)þ ar(e)/arn/es/be(o)þ	i þou he *pl.*	was/wes was/wore/were/ wast/weore was/wes wer/war(e)/were(n)
Subjunctive			
Present		**Preterite**	
sg. *pl.*	be/si(e) be/ben	*sg.* *pl.*	war(e)/were war(e)/were(n)

Numbers

Following is a table of the number system in Middle English. As you can see, the numbers in Middle English are strikingly similar to those of today—the spelling has changed very little, though the pronunciation was quite different. Many of the numbers had two forms, with an "-e" inflection added to numbers that stood after a noun or alone. Note that the Germanic construction for numbers greater than twenty was still used in Middle English.

Middle English Numbers			
1	on/an/o/a	20	twenti
2	two/to/tweine	21	on and twenti
3	þre	30	þretti/ þritti
4	four(e)	40	fourti
5	fif/five	50	fifti
6	six(e)/sex(e)	60	sixti
7	seven(e)	70	seventi
8	ei3te/au3te	80	ei3teti/ei3ti
9	ni3en(e)/nine	90	ni3enti/nin(e)ti
10	ten(e)	100	hundred/hundreþ
11	eleven(e)/enleven	200	two hundred
12	twelf/twelve	1000	þousend
13	þrettene/þrittene	2000	two þousend

Sample Texts

The first sample text is one from the early Middle English period, *Piers Plowman*, the dream-vision, written in the mid-14th century CE, attributed to William Langland. As you can see, even in this early stage, a speaker of English can largely understand the original.

Piers Plowman	
Middle English	**Modern English**
In a somer seson, whan softe was the sonne,	In a summer season, when soft was the sun,
I shoop me into shroudes as I a sheep were,	I clothed myself in a cloak as if I were a shepherd,
In habite as an heremite unholy of werkes,	In a habit like a hermit unholy in works,
Wente wide in this world wondres to here.	Went far in this world to hear wonders.
Ac on a May morwenynge on Malverne hilles	But on a May morning on Malvern hills
Me bifel a ferly, of Fairye me thoghte.	A marvel of enchantment befell me, it seemed to me.
I was wery forwandred and wente me to reste	I was weary from wandering and went to rest myself
Under a brood bank by a bourne syde;	Under a broad bank by a brook's side;
And as I lay and lenede and loked on the watres,	And as I lay and leaned over and looked at the waters,
I slombred into a slepyng, it sweyed so murye.	I fell asleep, it sounded so merry.
Thanne gan I meten a merveillous swevene	Then I began to dream a marvelous dream,
That I was in a wildernesse, wiste I nevere where.	That I was in a wilderness, I knew not where.
Ac as I biheeld into the eest an heigh to the sonne,	As I looked to the east on high to the sun,
I seigh a tour on a toft trieliche ymaked,	I saw a tower on a knoll built skillfully;
A deep dale bynethe, a dongeon therinne,	A deep dale beneath, a dungeon therein,
With depe diches and derke and dredfulle of sighte.	With deep ditches and dark and dreadful of sight
A fair feeld ful of folk fond I ther bitwene	A fair field full of folk I found there between,
Of alle manere of men, the meene and the riche,	Of all manner of men the poor and the rich,

Piers Plowman (continued)	
Middle English	**Modern English**
Werchynge and wandrynge as the world asketh.	Working and wandering as the world asks.
Somme putten hem to the plough, pleiden ful selde,	Some worked the plow and played very seldom,
In settynge and sowynge swonken ful harde,	At setting and sowing they toiled very hard,
And wonnen that thise wastours with glotonye destruyeth.	And won what those who waste destroy with gluttony.

The next text is Chaucer's *Prologue to the Canterbury Tales*, the most famous work of the Middle English period, written from approximately 1380 to 1390 CE. Modern English glosses of underlined words are to the right of the text.

The Canterbury Tales, by Geoffrey Chaucer	
Middle English	**Modern English glosses**
Here bygynneth the Book of the Tales of Caunterbury	
Whan that Aprill, with his <u>shoures</u> <u>soote</u>	showers, sweet
The <u>droghte</u> of March hath <u>perced</u> to the roote	drought, pierced
And bathed every <u>veyne</u> in <u>swich</u> <u>licour</u>,	vein, such, liquid
Of which <u>vertu</u> engendred is the <u>flour</u>;	virtue, flower
Whan <u>Zephirus</u> <u>eek</u> with his sweete <u>breeth</u>	west wind, also, breath
Inspired hath in every <u>holt</u> and <u>heeth</u>	wood, heath
The tendre <u>croppes</u>, and the <u>yonge</u> <u>sonne</u>	new leaves, young, sun
Hath in the <u>Ram</u> his halfe cours <u>yronne</u>,	Aries, run
And <u>smale</u> <u>foweles</u> maken melodye,	small, birds (fowls)
That <u>slepen</u> al the <u>nyght</u> with open <u>ye</u>—	sleep, night, eye
(So <u>priketh</u> <u>hem</u> Nature in <u>hir</u> <u>corages</u>);	pierces, them, her, spirits
Thanne <u>longen</u> folk to <u>goon</u> on pilgrimages	long, go
And <u>palmeres</u> for to seken <u>straunge</u> <u>strondes</u>	pilgrims, foreign, shores
To <u>ferne</u> <u>halwes</u>, <u>kowthe</u> in <u>sondry</u> <u>londes</u>;	far, shrines, known, sundry, lands
And specially from every shires ende	

The Canterbury Tales, by Geoffrey Chaucer (continued)	
Middle English	**Modern English glosses**
Of Engelond, to Caunterbury they <u>wende</u>,	went
The <u>hooly</u> <u>blisful</u> martir for to <u>seke</u>	holy, blessed, visit
That <u>hem</u> hath <u>holpen</u>, whan that they were <u>seeke</u>.	them, helped, sick

The table below gives you an idea of what the *Prologue* sounded like in Chaucer's time. The words are written using Modern English spelling. Try reading this out loud to get a better flavor of what Middle English sounded like. While the pronunciation guide is not exact, it does give you an idea of what the actual *Prologue* my have sounded like at the time.

Pronunciation of the Prologue to The Canterbury Tales
here beginneth the boke of the tah-less of Cahnterboory
hwahn thaht Ah-pril, with his shoor-ess so-ta
the drukht off March hahth payr-sed toe the roh-ta
ahnd bahth-ed every vay-na in switch lick-oor,
off hwitch ver-too engend-red is the floor;
hwahn Zay-fear-uss ake with his sway-ta breath
inspeer-ed hahth in every holt ahnd heth
the tender crop-pess, ahnd the yoong-a soon-a
hahth in the rahm his hahlv-a course ee-roon-a,
ahnd small-a fool-ess mahk-en melody-a,
thaht slay-pen all the nikht with aw-pen ee-a
saw priketh hem nat-oor in hair coor-ahges;
thahn long-en folk to gone on pilgrim-ahges
ahnd palmer-ess for to say-ken straung-a strawn-dess
toe fairn hahl-wess, coath-a in soon-dree lawn-dess;
ahnd spess-ially from every sheer-ess end-a
off enga-lond, toe Cahnterboory they wend-a,
the hawly blissful martyr for toe say-ka
thaht hem hahth holp-en, hwahn thaht they where say-ka.

Following is the first stanza of *Sir Gawain and the Green Knight*, attributed to the Pearl Poet, written around 1400 CE in the Northwest Midlands dialect.

Sir Gawain and the Green Knight	
Middle English	**Modern English**
siþen þe sege and þe assaut watz sesed at troye	After the siege and the assault was ceased at Troy
þe bor3 brittened and brent to brondez and askez	the city destroyed and burned to cinders and ashes
þe tulk þat þe trammes of tresoun þer wro3t	the knight who the stratagems of treason there wrought
watz tried for his tricherie þe trewest on erþe	was tried for his treachery the truest on earth
hit watz ennias þe athel and his highe kynde	it was Aeneas the noble and his high kin
þat siþen depreced prouinces and patrounes bicome	who afterwards conquered provinces and became lords
welne3e of al þe wele in þe west iles	well nigh of all the wealth in the western isles
fro riche romulus to rome ricchis hym swyþe	when noble Romulus takes his way quickly to Rome
with gret bobbaunce þat bur3e he biges vpon fyrst	with great pomp that city he founds at first,
and neuenes hit his aune nome as hit now hat	and gives it his own name, as it now has
ticius to tuskan and teldes bigynnes	Ticius (goes) to Tuscany and begins (to set up) dwellings
langaberde in lumbardie lyftes vp homes	Langobard in Lombardy raises up homes
and fer ouer þe french flod felix brutus	and far over the French sea Felix Brutus
on mony bonkkes ful brode bretayn he settez	on many slopes very wide he founds Brittany
with wynne	with joy
where werre and wrake and wonder	where war and vengeance and marvel
bi syþez hatz wont þerinne	at times dwelt therein
and oft boþe blysse and blunder	and oft both bliss and blunder
ful skete hatz skyfted synne	have quickly shifted since

The final Middle English text is an anecdote printed by William Caxton in his preface to the *Eneydos* in 1490 CE. This very late example of Middle English can be understood almost in its entirety by a speaker of Modern English. In this anecdote he tells a story of merchants sailing down the Thames, stopping for food along the way. The story deals with a dialect difference and the misunderstanding it causes. The southern dialects of English used the native word "eyren" for our modern 'eggs'. The native term was displaced, however, in the northern dialects by the word "egges", via influence from Old Norse. The woman in the story has never heard this "new" word, and assumes it must be French. It is interesting to note that the term from the North eventually superseded the native word.

Caxton's Egg Anecdote	
Middle English	**Modern English glosses**
And ... a <u>mercer</u> cam into an <u>hows</u> and <u>axed</u>	textile merchant, house, asked
for <u>mete</u>, and specyally he <u>axyd after</u> eggys	food (meat), asked for
And the good <u>wyf</u> answerde that she <u>coude</u>	woman (wife), could
<u>speke</u> no <u>frenshe</u>. And the <u>marchaunt</u> was	speak, French, merchant
angry for he also coude speke no frenshe but	
<u>wold haue hadde</u> egges and she <u>vnderstode</u>	wanted to have, understood
hym not And thenne at laste a nother sayd	
that he <u>wolde haue eyren</u> then the good wyf	wanted to have, eggs
sayd that she vnderstod hym wel <u>Loo</u> what	lo
<u>sholde</u> a man in <u>thyse</u> dayes now <u>wryte</u> egges	should, these, write
or eyren certaynly it is harde to <u>playse</u> <u>euery</u>	please, every
man <u>by cause</u> of <u>dyuersite</u> & <u>chaunge</u> of	because, diversity, change
<u>langage</u>."	language

In the next chapter we will take a look at Early Modern English.

Early Modern English   5

My language! heavens!
I am the best of them that speak this speech,
Were I but where 'tis spoken.

—William Shakespeare, The Tempest, Act I, Scene II

History

early Modern English begins as the Middle English period ends, late in the 15th century CE and ends around the middle of the 17th century CE. This is the language of some of the best known literature in the English language, namely that of the King James Bible and the works of William Shakespeare. During this period the language changed considerably once again.

One hallmark of the beginning of this era was the end of the so-called "Wars of the Roses" and the ascension of Henry Tudor (Henry VII, father of the better known Henry VIII) to the English throne in 1485. Beginning in 1455, these civil wars, fought between the House of Lancaster and the House of York, lasted approximately 30 years. The wars became known as the "Wars of the Roses" because of the symbols for each house: a red rose for the House of Lancaster and a white rose for the House of York.

This period also marked a great change in the social order. After the Black Death ravaged England and other parts of Europe, feudalism gave way to a new system of workers who joined powerful guilds and unions, whose success resulted in part from the sudden dearth in supply of men to perform labor. Other socioeconomic changes of the time included a shift of wealth from inherited land to financial assets, which lead to greater social mobility, and an emerging middle class. Cities began to attract more and more laborers, helping to fuel the industrial revolution of the late 18th century. Living standards began to rise for the middle and upper classes, but fell for the lower classes living in the cities.

In the intellectual realm, scholarship became secularized with the advent of humanism. This shift from religious dogma to intellectual inquiry was the beginning of science as we know it today. Influenced by the Italian Renaissance, the English Renaissance saw a great blossoming of the arts, especially music and literature, including drama and epic poetry, in the beginning of the 16th century.

The Reformation, which began in continental Europe, also made its way to England at this time with Henry VIII's founding of the Church of England. The continental Reformation came about because of fundamental religious differences between the leaders of the various movements (such as Martin Luther, John Calvin, and Huldrych Zwingli) and the Roman Catholic Church. However, the split between the English and Roman Catholic churches largely came about because of Henry VIII's desire to divorce his wife because she had not given him a male heir.

With the advent of the printing press during Caxton's time, the language started to become standardized on a particular variety. Prior to its invention and wide use in England, each book had to be copied by hand. A normal person could not have afforded much of a personal library. But with the mass production of books, they became much more wide spread and much more accessible.

Along with the introduction of the printing press into England, another great influence on the standardization of English was the rise of a new economic and cultural center made up of Cambridge, Oxford, and London, forming a sort of triangle in the East Midlands region. The language of these new centers of education, commerce, and government became the language upon which English would eventually be standardized.

This was also the very beginning of what would become the British Empire. In 1497, just five years after Christopher Columbus's first voyage to the the Americas, John Cabot sailed to the northern shores of North America and claimed them for England, with the backing of Henry VII. It would be the beginning of a centuries-long quest to discover and conquer new lands for England. Spain and Portugal initially ruled the seas, bringing vast wealth back from their exploration and colonization of Africa and the Americas. Francis Drake (1540–1596) , a privateer, merchant, and sailor became known for pirating Spanish merchant ships coming from the Americas, and he came to be regarded as a national hero in England (and a villain in Spain). It was Drake who defeated the feared Spanish armada in 1588, earning him the favor of Queen Elizabeth I. The reign of Elizabeth (1558–1603) was the height of the English Renaissance. It was a time of relative peace, with the exception of several skirmishes with Spain.

The arts blossomed considerably under Elizabeth. With the establishment of public theaters such as the Rose, the Swan, and the Globe, theater became a more permanent fixture and allowed the likes of William Shakespeare, Christopher Marlowe, and Ben Jonson to flourish and become household names. Shakespeare is said to have been one of the greatest contributors to the vocabulary of English, either by coining new words, borrowing them from other languages, or giving cachet to "colloquialisms" (speech usage of the common people) of the time.

In 1589, in *The Arte of English Poesie*, George Puttenham suggests the establishment of a written standard for English, writing "...ye shall therefore take the usuall speach of the Court, and that of London and the shires lying about London within 1x. myles, and not much above..." With London as the city of origin for most printed documents, its dialect became the *de facto* written standard, though, even during this time, regional dialects still ruled the spoken language. It was also at this time that spelling became fixed, for the most part, though inconsistencies still occurred.

Literature

The works of the Early Modern English era are some of the best known in our language, and indeed, are known throughout the world. This was the beginning of a new era for the language and its literature.

Christopher ("Kit") Marlowe (1564–1593) was a playwright, poet, and translator. Marlowe was the foremost writer of tragedies before Shakespeare. In 1587, *Tamburlaine*, the story of Timur, the 14th century Turkic-Mongolian warrior who began life as a shepherd but was destined to conquer much of Western and Central Asia, was Marlowe's first play performed in London. It was one of the first English plays to use blank verse, a type of poetry which has a regular meter (usually iambic pentameter), but no rhyme. Other works included plays such as *Dido, Queen of Carthage, The Tragical History of Doctor Faustus*, poems such as *Hero and Leander, The Passionate Shepherd to His Love*, and translations of Ovid's *Amores* and the first book of Lucan's *Pharsalia*. Marlowe led an intriguing, if short, life. It is suspected that Marlowe was a spy for the English government. In 1593, Marlowe was arrested for heresy and shortly thereafter died under strange circumstances after a fight in which he was stabbed above his eye and died immediately.

As mentioned above, William Shakespeare (1564–1616) is probably the best known author and playwright of this period. Indeed, he is one of the best known authors of Western literature throughout the world to this day. Born in 1564 in Stratford-upon-Avon, Shakespeare was a prolific writer of plays and poetry. Shakespeare's plays, including tragedies, comedies, romances, and histories, were often adaptations of previous works. He is also well known for his sonnets, a special type of poem of 14 lines that followed a particular rhyming scheme and logical structure.

Although a prolific writer, very little information has survived about the man himself, leading some to believe that the William Shakespeare born in Stratford-upon-Avon was not the actual author of the many works attributed to him. Some have suggested that Edward de Vere, the 17th Earl of Oxford, was the actual author, while others believe it to have been Christopher Marlowe (although he died before some of Shakespeare's works were purportedly published).

A popular playwright in his own time, Shakespeare became even more popular after his death. His plays are performed all over the world and have been translated into many languages. He is perhaps the most quoted person in the English language today, and we use many of his own neologisms in our every day speech without even knowing their true origins. He introduced such words as "addiction", "apostrophe", "assassination", "domineering", "exhale", "frugal", "heart-sick", "hostile", "lack-luster", "obscene", "premeditated", "retirement", "survivor", and "unreal", and such phrases as "cheer up", "foregone conclusion", "good riddance", "household name", "salad days", "seamy side", and "tower of strength". His plays, especially, are still widely read and performed even today. They include such masterpieces as *Romeo and Juliet, Macbeth, Hamlet,* and *Othello.*

Ben Jonson (1572–1637) was another well-known playwright, poet, and actor of the time. He is best known for his plays *Volpone,* a black comedy, and another comedy, *The Alchemist,* as well as for his lyric poems, including *Epigrams* and *Underwoods.* Jonson was a friend and rival of Shakespeare. During his time, he was often regarded more highly than Shakespeare.

Although the King James Bible is perhaps the best known version of the Bible in the English language, it was actually not the first of this era. William Tyndale's translation in the early 16th century was the first English language Bible to make use of the printing press, which allowed it to be much more widely distributed than earlier translations. This pioneering vision was not without its downside, however, as Tyndale was tried for heresy and treason and burned at the stake in 1535. Tyndale is credited with coining such words as "Jehovah", "Passover", and "scapegoat", and such phrases as "let there be light", "the powers that be", "my brother's keeper" and "the salt of the earth".

The King James version (called the "Authorized Version" in the United Kingdom), first published in 1611, was created by a group of 47 independent scholars working in six committees. Translated from Hebrew and Greek texts rather than the Latin Vulgate, it was heavily based on the Tyndale translation, with, by some counts, up to 80% of it being unaltered from Tyndale's original. Each committee was tasked with translating a group of chapters, which were later revised for uniformity with the text as a whole. As a result of its being based so heavily on the Tyndale translation, the language of the King James version was itself somewhat archaic even for the time. No doubt the sound of this older language seemed more "elevated" to the creators of this new version, just as archaic usage often sounds more elevated to us today (think Shakespeare or even Modern English writers of the 19th century, such as Charles Dickens).

Language

During the Early Modern English period the language itself changed considerably, reflecting the vast changes going on in society, the arts, science, and religion during this time. Inflectional endings for case and verb conjugations, already drastically reduced in Middle English morphology had disappeared almost completely by the start of the Early Modern period. Many new words from Latin and Greek were added to the "lexicon" (the vocabulary of a language) during this time as well, a reflection of the renaissance occurring at the time, with its emphasis on Greek and Latin classics. While inflectional morphology was withering, new grammatical features were being added, such as the use of the auxiliary "do" for negative statements and questions. The second person singular pronouns (thou/thee/thy/thine) dropped out of usage during this time, and the possessive pronoun "its" was added, replacing the old genitive form "his", which no longer seemed appropriate once natural gender replaced grammatical gender in the language.

One of the greatest distinguishing features of this era was a phonological one. It is called "The Great Vowel Shift", a term coined by the great Danish linguist Otto Jespersen. It actually began late in the Middle English period but was not completed until Early Modern times. The shift, which only affected the long vowels, affected the quality of the vowel sound. In Old English and Middle English, vowels generally had the "continental" sounds of Latin (or most of today's modern European languages, such as Spanish, Italian, and German). After the Great Vowel Shift, the long vowel sounds acquired the sounds they have today—quite different from those of Latin.

The lexicon of Early Modern English grew significantly due to various influences. One influence was that of literary innovations by the great authors, playwrights, and poets of the day. Another influence was due to international trade and exploration, in which speakers of English had much greater contact with the outside world, and they encountered many things for which English had no native words, including plants, animals, and other concepts. In many cases English speakers simply borrowed the words or names directly from other languages, including Arabic, Dutch, Italian, and Spanish. Although it was no longer the language of the aristocracy in England, French was still a great influence on the Early Modern English lexicon, due to its status in law and government. During the Renaissance, French was the language of courtly culture. Latin also continued to wield great influence over English, as it remained the language of education and science. With the rebirth of classical thought during the Renaissance, both Latin and Greek continued to contribute words to the lexicon. English borrowed freely from these classical languages and used roots and affixes from both languages, often in combination with native words. Many borrowings from Latin had been previously borrowed via French, giving the language "doublets" such as "chamber" and "camera", "palsy" and "paralysis", and "frail" and "fragile" (in each case, the first word was borrowed from French and the second from Latin).

Early Modern English Orthography

The orthography of Early Modern English changed only slightly from the Middle English period. Yogh ("ȝ") was dropped in favor of the letters for the sounds that it eventually came to represent, "y", "w", "g", "f" (sometimes spelled "gh"), and the silent "gh": "yȝe" became "eye", "yhalȝed" became "hallowed", "ȝive" became "give", "roȝ" became "rough", and "niȝt" became "night".

Thorn ("þ") eventually became indistinguishable from "y" (it was often written without closing off the top loop) and was eventually dropped altogether. This is why we still see references to "*ye* old book shoppe" when referring to this period—the "y" is actually a thorn, and is thus our simple "the" (no one ever actually said "*yee* old book shop").

The letters "i" and "j" (originally just an elongated "i") were used somewhat interchangeably, as were "u" and "v", though "v" was generally used at the beginning of words and "u" elsewhere. The long "s" ("ſ") came into use at the beginning or middle of words, while the "small s" was only used at the very end of a word. As such, "sinfulness" was written "ſinfulneſs". The US Bill of Rights famously has the word "Congreſs" at the beginning. Due to its similarity to "f", this letter eventually fell out of favor (actually, it *fell* out of *favor*).

Spelling became fairly fixed during this period, with the increase in use of the printing press. Latin wielded its influence on the spelling of some words of French and Latin origin, further separating spelling from its phonetic origins. Words such as Middle English "i(s)le" (from Latin *insula*, via French), influenced the spelling of Middle English "iland", creating Early Modern "island". "Debt", originally Middle English "dette" (from Latin *debita* via French) added the current "b" despite the fact that it was never pronounced in English.

During this period, other orthographic changes also occurred that were not directly related to spelling. Nouns were often capitalized in all cases, regardless of whether they were common or proper nouns (this is still the case in Modern German today). In addition, punctuation was changed and new symbols were added. The comma replaced the virgule ("/") as the sign of a pause, and the apostrophe (" ' ") came into use as a symbol for replaced letters in contractions and the possessive.

Early Modern English Phonetics and Phonology

One of the defining linguistic events of the Early Modern English period is the completion of the Great Vowel Shift. The changes, which affected the long vowels, began in the Middle English period but were only fully realized in the standard language late in the Early Modern period. To this day, however, there are dialects in Great Britain that have not fully implemented this shift.

Why this shift happened is not entirely known, however, we can describe *what* happened. Essentially, all of the long vowels shifted "up" (referring to the tongue's position in the mouth when the sound is pronounced), or if there was no place higher up to go, the sounds shifted to a diphthong. There are two possible mechanisms for the shift, one called a "pull chain", the other a "push chain". Linguists argue to this day which mechanism was responsible for the shift. In actuality, the two "chains" are slightly different ways of looking at the same basic mechanism—a gap was created in the phonological system of the long vowels, and other sounds "moved" into those positions. The "pulling" and "pushing" refer to whether the long, high vowels (the "ee" sound in "see", and "oo" sound in "soon") first shifted to diphthongs, leaving a gap in their former positions, thus "pulling" the other vowels up with them in a sort of chain reaction in which lower vowels moved higher to fill in newly vacant spots; or whether the long, low back vowel sounds "ah" in Modern English "father" and "aw" in British "law", first raised and then "pushed" the other vowels out of their positions and upward.

Below is a diagram of the Middle English vowel system, called a "vowel quadrilateral". It basically mimics the placement of the tongue in the mouth. It shows the back of the mouth on the right and the front on the left. These locations are usually referred to as front (on the left), central (in the middle), and back (on the right), referring to which part of the tongue is involved in the articulation of the particular sound. In addition to horizontal placement, there are also vertical ones, corresponding the height of the tongue (high, mid, or low). The sounds below show Modern English spelling of the sounds.

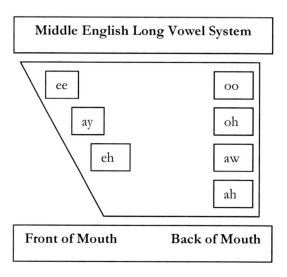

The table below shows the classification of the long vowels using this system.

Vowel Sound	Example	Classification
ee	bee	high, front
ay	bay	mid, front
eh	bed (elongated "e")	low/mid, front
oo	boot	high, back
oh	boat	mid, back
aw	law	low, back
ah	father	low, back

The vowel quadrilateral below shows the same quadrilateral as above, but with arrows to show the direction each sound shifted during the Great Vowel Shift. This time, instead of showing Modern English equivalents to the sounds, the diagram uses symbols from the International Phonetic Association (IPA). These symbols are used to show the phonetic pronunciation of all languages. The symbol in each box corresponds to the English sound you see in the prior diagram (note that the colon ":" simply means the sound is a long sound).

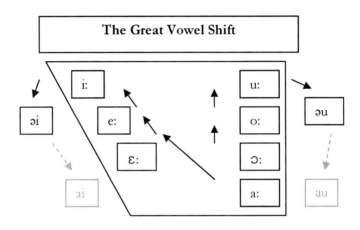

As you can see, each vowel sound essentially moved "up" in the diagram to a new position. In the case of the high vowels /iː/ and /uː/ (the slashes "/" are used to surround a phoneme when writing a phonological representation of a sound or sounds), since there is no place to move "up", these vowels changed into diphthongs. By the middle of the period these diphthongs both started with the schwa sound, /ə/. In gray, you can see the final diphthongs as they appeared towards the end of this period and the beginning of the Modern English period.

The table below shows the original pronunciation of example words from Middle English and how the pronunciation changed after the Great Vowel Shift. The center column shows the IPA transliteration of the Middle English pronunciation, with a transcription using modern spelling in parentheses. The Modern English column shows the current pronunciation of these words, with the full realization of the Great Vowel Shift and includes the IPA transcription as well.

Middle English	Middle English Pronunciation	Modern English
mys	/miːs/ ("mees")	mice /mais/
gees	/geːs/ ("gace")	geese /giːs/
break	/brɛːk/ ("breck")	break /breːk/
mous	/muːs/ ("moose")	mouse /maus/
goos	/goːs/ ("gose")	goose /guːs/
broke	/brɔːkə/ ("brawka")	broke /broːk/
name	/naːmə/ ("nah-ma")	name /neːm/

In effect, the entire inventory of long vowels shifted in sound quality. Since writing had already begun to be standardized late in the Middle English period when these changes were just starting, a disconnect arose between the original sounds that the letters represented and the current sounds those letters stand for. For example, in Middle English, "gees" was written much as it is today with "long e"; however during that time "long ee" was the sound "ay" in "day"; today "long e" is the vowel sound in "bee". It is because of the Great Vowel Shift that the letters used for our long vowel sounds differ so much from their continental European counterparts.

Vowels

Below is a table showing the vowel sounds of Early Modern English, with the Modern English pronunciations and IPA transcriptions. In final syllables with unstressed "e", the "e" (actually a schwa sound) was only pronounced in a few instances, such as certain plurals ("boxes", "judges"), possessives ("Ross's", "the fox's") (in these cases the apostrophe is simply taking the place of an "e"), and some weak verb past tense and past participle forms ("shouted", "granted", etc.). Final "e" at the end of a word was no longer pronounced at all by Early Modern times.

Early Modern English Vowels			
Spelling	**Example**	**Modern Pronunciation**	**IPA**
a a, ai	father place	"a" in "father" an elongated "a" in "hat" or the "a" in modern "place"	/a/ /æ:/, /e/
au, aw	law	"aw" in British English "law"	/ɔ:/
a	man	"a" in "man"	/æ/
e e, ee ea	bed be teach	"e" in bed "e" in "be" "ay" in "sway" (without the "y" sound at the end)	/ɛ/ /i/ /e/
ea (before "r")	hear	"e" in "bed" drawn out: "hehhhr"	/ɛ:/
i i	this I	"i" in "this" "ə-i", "eh-i", "I" (more on this diphthong below)	/ɪ/ /əi/, /ɛi/, /ai/
o	oft	"o" in British English "hot"	/ɔ/
o, oa o, ou	throne do	"o" in "throne" "o" in "do"	/o/ /u/
u u	but rule	"u" in "put" "u" in "rule"	/ʊ/ /u/

Diphthongs

The table below shows the diphthongs of Early Modern English.

Early Modern English Diphthongs			
Spelling	**Example**	**Modern Pronunciation**	**IPA**
i	I	"ə-i", "eh-i", "I"	/əi/, /ɛi/, /ai/
oi	toil	"oi" in "toil"	/ɔi/
ou	out	"ə-u", "ɔ-i", "ou"	/əu/, /ɔu/, /au/

The first example, "i" became a diphthong as a result of the Great Vowel Shift, but continued to be written as if it were still a simple vowel (i.e., with just one letter). The examples in the IPA column represent three various stages of the pronunciation of this new diphthong. The first, /əi/, is the schwa sound with a glide to the "ee" sound in "bee". This was probably the pronunciation late in the Middle English period. This pronunciation eventually gave way to the sound /ɛi/, which is similar to the prior pronunciation, but the schwa has turned into a short "e" sound as in "bed". By late in the period, this sound had its current sound, pronounced /ai/ as our current "I".

The last example also resulted from the Great Vowel Shift. The original "oo" sound became a schwa plus "u" sound early on, and eventually a sound very similar to that of today's "ou" sound in "house", though the initial sound was more like the British English "o" in "pot" initially. Eventually, it sounded like our current /au/ sound.

Consonants

Although the consonants did not change drastically from the Middle English period, there are some differences to note. Two new phonemes entered the language: the "ng" in "sing" and the "g" in "genre". The IPA symbols for these are /ŋ/ and /ʒ/, respectively. Prior to this period, the "ng" combination was pronounced as two separate sounds: "n" + "g" (although the "n" most likely had an /ŋ/ quality, /ŋ/ was not a phoneme itself, but an allophone of the /n/ phoneme—it only occurred in the position of /n/ + /g/). The sound in "genre" and "pleasure" came into the language due to French influence.

The /h/ sound was no longer pronounced except at the beginning of a word; its guttural alternative (the "ch" sound in German "Bach", symbolized by /χ/ in the IPA) disappeared altogether from the language. Other letters also became silent in certain positions: "l" after "a" in certain positions ("half", "talk"), "t" in combination with "s" ("castle", "hasten"), "g" and "k" before "n" ("gnat", "knight"), and "w" before "r" ("write", "wrong").

Early Modern English Grammar

Early Modern English grammar shows only minor changes from the Middle English period—nothing close to the drastic changes from Old English to Middle English.

Articles

There were no changes among the articles, except the change in spelling from the thorn in the definite article to a new spelling with "th".

Nouns and Adjectives

By this point, the morphology of nouns and adjectives became even more simplified in English. The plural marker became "–(e)s" in almost all instances except those that we still have today. The "-en" plural was lost in all words but "children", "oxen", and "brethren" (plus a few archaic and dialect examples). However, many "umlauted" plurals (that is, ones in which the internal vowel changed) remained, such as "foot"/"feet", "goose"/"geese", etc., as did those without different plural forms, such as "sheep". With the flowering of science during this period and the influx of more and more Latin terms from this field, the "-i" plural came into use for words ending in "-us" (a common noun class or "declension" in Latin, called the Masculine/Feminine Second Declension). So, the plural for the loanword "cactus" was "cacti" (this word originally designated a prickly plant from Sicily unrelated to modern cacti), "radius" had "radii", and "alumnus", "alumni". Some words that ended in "-s" in the singular dropped this "s" and added it back in the plural only. Examples of this phenomenon are the words "pea" and "cherry", originally "pease" (meaning a single "pea", from Latin *pisa*), and "cherise" (a single "cherry", from French), respectively. In both cases, the singular forms of the word ending in an "s" sound were re-analyzed by speakers as being plural. Thus, a new singular form was created without the "s" and the original singular form become the new plural.

The only other inflectional endings for the noun was the possession marker with " 's ". The apostrophe was introduced as a placeholder for the "e" that came from the Middle English period but was no longer pronounced in most instances (e.g., "John's book", "the dog's bone").

So essentially, nouns had only two cases in Early Modern English: possessive, which was the old genitive case, and common, for everything else.

The adjective, which had already lost most of its inflectional endings in Middle English times, lost them completely by the Early Modern period. The periphrastic use of "more" for the comparative and "most" for the superlative of adjectives with more than two syllables became fully entrenched in the language by this time, and the rules became more relaxed, as evidenced by the following examples that appeared in the literature of the time: "eminenter", "beautifullest", "more near", and "most foul". In addition, double and even triple comparatives and superlatives were still common: "the most unkindest cut" is from Shakespeare.

Pronouns

Pronouns in Early Modern English changed slightly from the Middle English period, and are fully recognizable by speakers of Modern English today. As in Middle English, pronouns continued to have three cases: nominative, possessive, and oblique (from the former two object cases).

Early Modern English Pronouns						
Number	**Case**	1st **Person**	2nd **Person**	3rd **Person**		
				masc.	**neut.**	**fem.**
Singular	**Nom.**	I	thou	he	it	she
	Pos.	my, mine	thy, thine	his	its	her
	Obl.	me	thee	him	it	her
Plural	**Nom.**	we	ye	they		
	Pos.	our	your	their		
	Obl.	us	you	them		

The only significant change to the first person pronouns was the complete disappearance of "ich" in favor of "I" (which had been capitalized in some texts as early as 1250 CE, but was only regularly capitalized during this period). The second person forms did not change at all, outside of spelling (and pronunciation), though significant changes were taking place with regards to their "pragmatic" use, that is, how they are used in a social context. We will discuss this in more detail below. The third person pronouns changed slightly during this period. The only major change in the singular was that of the loss of "hit" in favor of "it" in the neuter nominative and oblique cases, and the change from "his" to "its" in the neuter possessive case. This latter change was an analogical change. Since Middle English times, English no longer had grammatical gender distinctions, but rather natural gender—thus the use of "his" for non-animate objects lost favor, as this seemed to refer to something that was "male" rather than inanimate. In order to create this new possessive form, speakers of English created the new pronoun by analogy based on the fact that possessive case was generally created by adding "-s" to the end of a noun. So "it" plus possessive "-s" became "its". In the third person plural, the major change was the loss of the pronouns beginning with "h-" in favor of the newer borrowings from Scandinavian.

Perhaps the more significant changes were not those of the forms of the pronouns, but in their *use*, specifically in the second person pronouns. As early as the 13th century CE, the plural forms (Early Modern English "ye"/"your"/"you") had also been used to address individuals in addition to being used to address more than one person. This usage was likely influenced by courtly French. Many European languages do this to this day—the "polite" form of address is actually based on a plural form of the pronoun or some other third person plural. This usage was meant to show respect, and came to be used with strangers and people of higher social standing. The singular forms, "thou"/ "thy/thine"/"thee", came to be used for familiar or intimate situations, such as among family members and close friends. Eventually, the "thou" forms came to have a more negative, condescending connotation. By the late 1600's "thou" forms were used less and less commonly in favor of "you" forms in all situations.

Members of the Religious Society of Friends, also known as the "Quakers", continued to use a modified version of "thou" up until the 20th century. In later common use, they used "thee" for both nominative and oblique cases, and used the third person singular forms of the verb with it (e.g., "thee goes"). Initially, this so-called "plain speaking" was meant to show equality or solidarity among all people, directly opposing the newer use of "you" to symbolize higher social standing. Eventually, however, its use was no longer necessary when "you" became the norm for address regardless of class or other pragmatic factors, and its use was abandoned in the last century.

Today, "thou" forms are strictly used in certain religious contexts (e.g., certain prayers and ceremonies, such as marriage rites) and a few set phrases ("holier than thou"). Interestingly enough, as we will see in the chapter on Modern English, that is not the end of the story for the second person pronoun, as the current lack of plural distinction in these pronouns has led to the creation of newer forms.

Verbs

The changes in the Early Modern English verb from the Middle English period were almost as great as the changes from Old to Middle English. Below are the conjugations of our familiar strong and weak verb examples, "to sing" and "to love", respectively.

Early Modern English Strong Verb Conjugation: "to sing"							
Infinitive:	to sing			**Past Participle:**	sung		
Present Participle:	singing			**Imperative:**	sing		
Indicative				**Subjunctive**			
Present		**Preterite**		**Present**		**Preterite**	
I thou he	sing sing(e)st sings/ singeth	I thou he	sang sangest sang	*sg.*	sing	*sg.*	sang
pl.	sing	*pl.*	sang	*pl.*	sing	*pl.*	sang

As you can see, this conjugation of "to sing" looks very familiar—it is only slightly different from the conjugation of the verb as you know it in Modern English.

Early Modern English Weak Verb Conjugation: "to love"							
Infinitive:	to love			**Past Participle:**	loved		
Present Participle:	loving			**Imperative:**	love		
Indicative				**Subjunctive**			
Present		**Preterite**		**Present**		**Preterite**	
I thou he	love lov(e)st luves/ luveth	I thou he	loved lovedst loved	*sg.*	love	*sg.*	loved
pl.	love	*pl.*	loved	*pl.*	love	*pl.*	loved

A major change was from the single word infinitive (Old English "singan", Middle English "singen"; note Modern German and Modern Dutch: "singen" and "zingen", respectively), to a periphrastic infinitive with "to" + the verb root: "to sing". The "bare" infinitive (without the "to") is still used in some very common situations: with certain modal auxiliary verbs ("can", "should", "will", but *not* "want", "ought"), with some common verbs of perception ("see", "watch", "hear": "I saw him leave"), and some verbs of permission and causation ("make", "let", "have": "She made/let/had him do it").

The first person singular and all plural forms of the verb lost inflectional endings entirely. In addition, the "-(e)s" ending for the third person singular became more common. This originally Northern form competed with the Southern "-(e)th" (so prominent in the King James Bible and Shakespeare), for quite some time, until the Northern "-(e)s" eventually won out. There are several theories as to why this happened, from regular sound change to poetic ease in rhyming. However, the most plausible reason seems to be that the Northern form won out simply because it is slightly more "efficient". Adding "-eth" to many verbs adds an additional syllable, while adding "-s" does not: "fighteth" vs. "fights", "maketh" vs. "makes". While forms such as "doth" ('does') and "hath" ('has') held on longer than others, by the latter part of the 17th century, the "-(e)th" ending for the third person singular had entirely disappeared.

The ending for the present participle became "-ing", which won out over the former "-end(e)" forms.

The full conjugations for "to have" and "to be" are below.

Early Modern English Conjugation of "to have"				
Infinitive:	to have	**Past Participle:**	had	
Present Participle:	having	**Imperative:**	have	
Indicative			**Subjunctive**	
Present		**Preterite**	**Present**	**Preterite**
I thou he	have hast has/hath	I had thou hadst he had	*sg.* have	*sg.* had
pl.	have	*pl.* had	*pl.* have	*pl.* had

Early Modern English Conjugation of "to be"			
Infinitive:	to be	**Past Participle:**	been
Present Participle:	being	**Imperative:**	be
Indicative			
Present		**Preterite**	
I	am	I	was
thou	art	thou	wert/wast
he	is	he	was
pl.	are	*pl.*	were
Subjunctive			
Present		**Preterite**	
sg.	be	*sg.*	were
pl.	be	*pl.*	were

Note that the verb "to be" is still irregular, though quite similar to today's forms. In the second person singular preterite indicative, Shakespeare used "wert" in the indicative, while the King James Bible (with its archaic language) used "wast" in the indicative and "wert" in the subjunctive.

It was during the Early Modern period that the word "do" became fully "grammaticalized" for certain functions, that is, it was used in some instances strictly to perform a grammatical function, rather than as a "content" word (having a meaning in and of itself). It was used periphrastically as a helping verb in three situations: to ask a question, to form a negative, and in declarative sentences. In some instances, it still kept is own meaning, such as "I did my work", where it is the main verb and has meaning.

"Do" came to be used as an interrogative helping verb, but the alternative without the helping verb was also possible in Early Modern English: "Goest thou to church?" and "Dost thou go to church?" were equally acceptable and common usage. Likewise, "She goeth not to church" and "She doth not go to church" were common usage as well. During this period, it was also possible to use "do" for simple declarative statements: "He doth go to church" along side "He goeth to church"—the use of "do" in this context was not yet reserved strictly for emphatic meaning as it generally is today.

There is another instance where "do" could be used in Early Modern English where we would not use it today: in questions called "wh-questions". "Wh-questions" are questions that contain the usual "question words" of English, which mostly start with "wh": who, what, where, when, why, and how. When asking a question with one of these words as the subject, "do" cannot be inserted in Modern English, but it could in Early Modern English: "Who goeth there?" or "Who doth go there?". The latter would not be possible as a simple sentence in Modern English (but could if it were used as an emphatic rather than interrogative: "Who *does* go there? That's what I want to know!").

Numbers

Following is a table of the number system in Early Modern English.

Early Modern English Numbers			
1	one	20	twenty
2	two	21	one and twenty
3	three	30	thirty
4	four	40	forty
5	five	50	fifty
6	six	60	sixty
7	seven	70	seventy
8	eight	80	eighty
9	nine	90	ninety
10	ten	100	hundred
11	eleven	200	two hundred
12	twelve	1000	thousand
13	thirteen	2000	two thousand

As you can see, the numbers themselves are already identical to those in Modern English. The only difference at this time was the continued use of the format old Germanic format "one and twenty" and "two and thirty" for "21" and "32" respectively.

Sample Texts

Below are some sample texts from the period. The first is a very early piece, bordering on the Middle English period, the next three are renaissance examples, and the last one is from relatively late in the period. You should generally be able to understand the text, though the spelling in the first text is quite different from current usage. Where necessary, underlined words are glossed for you below the text.

This first text is from the play *Everyman*. The version below was edited by John Skot in the early 16th century. The author is unknown, though it was almost surely a translation from the original Dutch *Elckerlijc* (similarly meaning "everyone"), written around 1470 CE and first printed in 1495 by Pieter van Diest. A morality play, it makes use of allegory with "Everyman" (that is, any ordinary person) as the hero, and characters such as Fellowship, Knowledge, and Good Deeds. This text is from very early in the Early Modern era, and as such, the spelling is the least like our modern-day conventions compared to the other texts below. However, the language itself should be fairly easy to understand. If you substitute most of the "y's" with "i" and "u's" with "v" you will be able to figure it out fairly quickly.

Everyman, author unknown, edited by John Skot, ca. 1520

Here begynneth a treatyse how <u>yt hye</u>
fader of heuen sendeth <u>dethe</u> to <u>so-</u>
<u>mon</u> euery creature to come and
<u>gyue</u> counte of theyr liues in
this worlde and is in maner
of a morall playe.

I
Pray you all gyue your audyence
And here this mater with reuerence
By fygure a morall playe
The somonynge of euery man called it is
That of our lyues and endynge <u>shewes</u>

How transytory we be all daye
This mater is <u>wonders</u> precyous
But the <u>entent</u> of it is more gracyous
And swete to bere awaye
The story sayth man in the begynnynge
<u>Loke</u> well and take good heed to the endynge
Be you neuer so gay
Ye thynke synne in the begynnynge full swete
Whiche in the ende causeth the soule to <u>wepe</u>
<u>Whan</u> the body lyeth in claye
Here shall you se how <u>felawshyp</u> and <u>Iolyte</u>
Bothe strengthe pleasure and beaute
Wyll fade from <u>the</u> as <u>floure</u> in maye
For ye shall <u>here</u> how our heuen kynge
Calleth euery man to a generall <u>rekenynge</u>
Gyue audyence and here what he doth saye.

the (typesetter's abbreviation), high, death, summon, give, shows, wondrous, intent, look, weep, when, fellowship, jollity (a jolly mood), thee, flower, hear, reckoning

The next text is from one of the most famous plays in English, Shakespeare's *Romeo and Juliet* (1595). The scene below is one of the best known of this play, where a hidden Romeo sees Juliet lamenting their situation on her balcony. Appropriately enough for a book about our language, Juliet asks in the scene "What's in a name?" You should not even need any glosses for this text, written over 400 years ago. However, do keep in mind that Early Modern English is still a separate period from our current one, and even where things seem familiar, they may be falsely so. In many cases, there are "semantic" differences in words and phrases from those of today ("semantics" refers to meaning). As commonly known as this passage is, it is often misunderstood. In it, Juliet is asking why Romeo needs to be called a "Montague" (his last name), since the Montagues and Capulets (Juliet's family) are at odds. When she famously says "O Romeo, Romeo! *Wherefore* art thou Romeo?" she is not asking *where* he is, but rather *why* he is Romeo. In Early Modern English "wherefore" meant "why", not "where" (note Swedish "varför", Danish and Norwegian "hvorfor", all meaning "why"). (Another common example of our misunderstanding the meaning of Early Modern English is in the King James Bible, Psalms, 23:5, which states "my cup runneth over". Though many sermons over the past few hundreds years have dwelled on that "extra bit" running over, in Early Modern English, "my cup runneth over" simply meant "my cup is full"). Keep in mind that, when reading texts from this era, words and phrases do not always have the exact same meaning they have in our current stage of the language.

Romeo and Juliet by **William Shakespeare, Act II, Scene II, 1595**

Rom. She speaks.

    O, speak again, bright angel! for thou art

    As glorious to this night, being o'er my head,

    As is a winged messenger of heaven

    Unto the white-upturned wond'ring eyes

    Of mortals that fall back to gaze on him

    When he bestrides the lazy-pacing clouds

    And sails upon the bosom of the air.

Jul. O Romeo, Romeo! wherefore art thou Romeo?

    Deny thy father and refuse thy name!

    Or, if thou wilt not, be but sworn my love,

    And I will no longer be a Capulet.

Rom. [aside] Shall I hear more, or shall I speak at this?

Jul. 'Tis but thy name that is my enemy.

    Thou art thyself, though not a Montague.

    What's Montague? it is nor hand, nor foot,

    Nor arm, nor face, nor any other part

    Belonging to a man. O, be some other name!

    What's in a name? That which we call a rose

    By my other name would smell as sweet.

    So Romeo would, were he not Romeo call'd,

    Retain that dear perfection which he owes

    Without that title. Romeo, doff thy name;

    And for that name, which is no part of thee,

    Take all myself.

Rom. I take thee at thy word.

    Call me but love, and I will be new baptiz'd;

    Henceforth I never will be Romeo.

The next text, by the contemporary poet who rivaled Shakespeare, Kit Marlowe, is a poem about the Greek mythological characters Hero and Leander. Marlowe never finished the poem due to his untimely death in 1593. However, the poem was eventually completed five years after his death by George Chapman.

Hero and Leander by **Christopher Marlowe, 1593, 1598**

In Hellespont guiltie of True-loues blood,

In view and opposit two citties stood,

Seaborders, disioin'd by Neptunes might:

The one Abydos, the other Sestos hight.

At Sestos, Hero dwelt; Hero the faire,

Whom young Apollo courted for her haire,

And offred as a dovver his burning throne,

Where she should sit for men to gaze vpon.

The outside of her garments were of lawne,

The lining, purple silke, with guilt starres drawne,

Her wide sleeues greene, and bordered with a groue,

Where Venus in her naked glory stroue,

To please the carelesse and disdainfull eies,

Of proud Adonis that before her lies.

The next text is from the beginning of the King James Bible, probably the best known version in English. Despite the fact that it was printed *after* many of the greatest works of the era, it makes use of obviously archaic language, even for the time it was published. As noted above, this is due in part to its being based on the much earlier Tyndale version.

King James Bible, Book of Genesis, Chapter 1, verses 1-16, 1611

1 In the beginning God created the Heauen, and the Earth.

2 And the earth was without forme, and voyd, and darkenesse was vpon the face of the deepe: and the Spirit of God mooued vpon the face of the waters.

3 And God said, Let there be light: and there was light.

4 And God saw the light, that it was good: and God diuided the light from the darkenesse.

5 And God called the light, Day, and the darknesse he called Night: and the euening and the morning were the first day.

6 And God said, Let there be a firmament in the midst of the waters: and let it diuide the waters from the waters.

7 And God made the firmament; and diuided the waters, which were vnder the firmament, from the waters, which were aboue the firmament: and it was so.

8 And God called the firmament, Heauen: and the euening and the morning were the second day.

9 And God said, Let the waters vnder the heauen be gathered together vnto one place, and let the dry land appeare: and it was so.

10 And God called the drie land, Earth, and the gathering together of the waters called hee, Seas: and God saw that it was good.

11 And God said, Let the Earth bring foorth grasse, the herbe yeelding seed, and the fruit tree, yeelding fruit after his kinde, whose seed is in it selfe, vpon the earth: and it was so.

12 And the earth brought foorth grasse, and herbe yeelding seed after his kinde, and the tree yeelding fruit, whose seed was in it selfe, after his kinde: and God saw that it was good.

13 And the euening and the morning were the third day.

14 And God said, Let there bee lights in the firmament of the heauen, to diuide the day from the night: and let them be for signes and for seasons, and for dayes and yeeres.

15 And let them be for lights in the firmament of the heauen, to giue light vpon the earth: and it was so.

16 And God made two great lights: the greater light to rule the day, and the lesser light to rule the night: he made the starres also.

The final text for this period is by John Milton, *Paradise Lost*. This epic poem was written in "blank verse", a form of poetry that has a regular meter, but no end rhyme. It is a retelling of the Biblical "fall of man": the temptation of Eve by Satan in the Garden of Eden. In it, Milton intertwines the Judeo-Christian tradition with Paganism. It is from fairly late in the Early Modern English period.

Paradise Lost by John Milton, 1667

Of Mans First Disobedience, and the Fruit
Of that Forbidden Tree, whose mortal taste
Brought Death into the World, and all our woe,
With loss of Eden, till one greater Man
Restore us, and regain the blissful Seat,
Sing Heav'nly Muse, that on the secret top
Of Oreb, or of Sinai, didst inspire
That Shepherd, who first taught the chosen Seed,
In the Beginning how the Heav'ns and Earth

Rose out of Chaos. Or if Sion Hill
Delight thee more, and Siloa's Brook that flow'd
Fast by the Oracle of God; I thence
Invoke thy aid to my adventrous Song,
That with no middle flight intends to soar
Above th' Aonian Mount, while it pursues
Things unattempted yet in Prose or Rhime.
And chiefly Thou O Spirit, that dost prefer
Before all Temples th' upright heart and pure,
Instruct me, for Thou know'st; Thou from the first
Wast present, and with mighty wings outspread
Dove-like satst brooding on the vast Abyss
And mad'st it pregnant: What in me is dark
Illumine, what is low raise and support;
That to the highth of this great Argument
I may assert th' Eternal Providence,
And justifie the wayes of God to men.

In the next chapter, we will explore the current period of our language, Modern English.

Modern English 6

Language is wine upon the lips.

—*Virginia Woolf*

History

Another common term for what we call "Modern English" is "Present-Day English" or "PDE". The Modern English period began in the mid 17th century CE during a time of great political and social upheaval in England. The British Empire continued to grow and spread English to all corners of the globe. But it was likely the colonization of North America that contributed most to the spread of English as an international language with the eventual rise of the United States on the world scene, and the subsequent rise of English as the language of commerce, science, technology, and pop culture.

English has freely borrowed vocabulary from other languages since its very beginnings as a distinct language, however, this tendency continued to increase exponentially in the modern era. Facing new flora, fauna, and many other unfamiliar things in its new surroundings in America, Australia, Africa, and Asia, English borrowed words from the local languages. With the influx of immigrants to America in the 19th and 20th centuries, English speakers came in contact with more and more words from various languages. Greater mobility and the advent of mass media helped to spread English even further, and in many ways, helped standardize the language.

One question people often ask is why does English lend itself so well to borrowing from other languages? To be sure, other languages borrow vocabulary freely as well, but English seems to do this with special ease. One possibility might be the fact that, as a mostly isolating language with few morphological endings, foreign words simply "fit" into English more easily than in some others. In English, a word can become nearly any part of speech with very little change, if any, required. Another reason seems to be the lack of fear speakers of English have in allowing new words into their vocabulary. While many other languages have long standing academies that "oversee" the language and try to tell its speakers what proper usage is and what vocabulary can and cannot be used, English has never had such an organization. English also seems especially adept at coining new words as necessary, either creating new words from other languages (Latin and

Greek being the favorites) via compounding, or creating them from scratch (as is often the case with business products and technology).

After World War II, the United States began its rise in prominence, and it became much more influential in science and technology as well as in business and the arts. Movies and television spread American culture and its language all over the globe. Wall Street became a world financial center (along with London), and many of the greatest scientific breakthroughs of the 20th century happened in America. Perhaps the most important technological innovations, especially with regards to language and communication, involved the computer and Internet. The language of both of these technologies is English. All major computer languages are based on English vocabulary, from C++ and Java, to the web's HTML. And the growth of the Internet has spread English even further. English has truly become an international language.

English currently has over 350 million native speakers, and according to some estimates, a billion second language speakers (but compare this to Mandarin, which has about 885 million native speakers alone and is becoming a popular second language all over the world). You can travel almost anywhere in the world and get by in English. A speaker of Spanish from Uruguay at a conference in Paris is more likely to speak English to her colleague from Somalia than French. With the advent of the Internet, chat, and instant messaging, English has become a *lingua franca* (a language widely used as a means of communications among speakers of other languages), helping people all over the world to communicate more easily with each other. Suffice it to say that English is not going to die out any time soon.

Literature

English literature has blossomed since Shakespeare's time. From *The Compleat Angler* by Izaak Walton (1653) to today's blogs (yet another coined English word spread across the globe, originally "web log"), it seems as if speakers of English cannot stop writing. Alexander Pope was the master poet of the early 18th century, best known for his translation of Homer and satirical verse. Another great satirist of that era was Jonathan Swift, author of the classics *Gulliver's Travels* (1726) and *A Modest Proposal* (1729). William Wordsworth and Samuel Taylor Coleridge launched the Romantic Age at the turn of the 19th century with their *Lyrical Ballads* (1798). The so-called "Second Generation" of Romanticists are even better known: Lord Byron, John Keats, Percy Bysshe Shelley, and Mary Shelley. Popular novelists of the era were Sir Walter Scott (best known for *Rob Roy* (1817) and *Ivanhoe* (1819)) and

Jane Austen, one of the best known female novelists in English litera-ture (*Sense and Sensibility* (1811), *Pride and Prejudice* (1813), *Mansfield Park* (1814), and *Emma* (1816)). The Victorian Era (1837-1901) saw the en-trenchment of the novel as a staple of English literature. Great authors and poets of the era included: the Brontë sisters (*Jane Eyre*, by Charlotte Brontë, *Wuthering Heights* by Emily Brontë, and *Agnes Grey* by Anne Brontë, all self-published in 1847), William Makepeace Thackeray (*Van-ity Fair* (1847)), Henry David Thoreau (*Walden* (1854)), Nathaniel Haw-thorne (*The Scarlet Letter* (1850)), Herman Melville (Moby Dick (1851)), Walt Whitman (*Leaves of Grass* (1855-1892)), Emily Dickinson, Thomas Hardy (*The Return of the Native* (1878), *The Mayor of Casterbridge* (1886), and *Tess of the d'Urbervilles* (1891)), Mark Twain (*Adventures of Huckleberry Finn* (1885), *The Adventures of Tom Sawyer* (1876)), and perhaps the best known of the era, Charles Dickens (*The Pickwick Papers* (1836-1837), *The Adventures of Oliver Twist* (1837-1839), *A Christmas Carol* (1843), *David Copperfield* (1849 - 1850), *A Tale of Two Cities* (1859), and *Great Expecta-tions* (1860-1861), written in serial format, which was quite popular at the time). The Modernist Era included such authors as Joseph Conrad (*Heart of Darkness* (1902), James Joyce (*Ulysses* (1922)), Virginia Woolf (*Mrs Dalloway* (1925), *A Room of One's Own* (1929)), and Ernest He-mingway (*The Sun Also Rises* (1926), *A Farewell to Arms* (1929), *For Whom the Bell Tolls* (1940), *The Old Man and the Sea* (1952)). The era following World War II, the so-called "Postmodern Era", saw the rise of such authors as Kurt Vonnegut (*Slaughterhouse-Five* (1969)), Umberto Eco (*The Name of the Rose* (1980)), and Alice Walker (*The Color Purple* (1982)).

In the beginning of the 21st century, well-known authors include John Grisham, Stephen King, J.K. Rowling, Augusten Burroughs, Khaled Hosseini, Michael Crichton, Toni Morrison, James Patterson, Amy Tan, Tom Clancy, and Daniel Silva.

During the Modern English period, new media such as radio, televi-sion, and film have also helped to spread English across the globe. Movies and television especially have spread American culture and the American dialects of English across the globe. But perhaps the most influential new form of mass and personal communication is the Inter-net, where one can publish one's own writings, audio recordings, and video for millions to see, or communicate one-on-one via email, chat and telephone (via VOIP—voice over Internet protocol, in which the Internet essentially becomes a phone network as well).

In one sense, the development of the Internet has been akin to the invention of moveable type and the printing press with regards to the proliferation and availability of written works. The printing press al-lowed more books to be printed more quickly, and more people had access to literature. It also had the effect of helping to standardize language across broad geographic regions. With the advent of the Internet age, the ease of writing and having one's message seen or heard by millions all over the world has increased exponentially. As I write, the Internet is awash in blogs, essentially personal journals dealing with everything from politics, to celebrities, to technology, to pets. A blogger who ten years ago had almost no outlet at all to have her writing seen, can now be read daily by anyone in the world with an Internet connection and enough interest. An Internet user does not even need to seek out her writing, rather he can set up a "newsfeed" from her blog and it will appear in his newsreader any time the blogger writes a new article. A step beyond blogging is podcasting (the word "podcast" was derived from Apple's iPod MP3 player device, combined with the word "broadcast"). With podcasting, a blogger can skip the writing entirely and just speak his mind, a sort of everyman's radio show available on demand. And the very latest technology allows a person to create a "vlog" (based on the "blog" concept, this is a "video (web)log"). A vlogger can essentially create her own on-demand video show. Where there used to be a handful of radio stations in a given area, and a few dozen (or hundred) TV channels available throughout an entire country, there are now thousands, and potentially millions of such "stations" and "channels" available via the Internet, an unprecedented communications explosion. It will be interesting indeed to see what effect this has on the future of the language, something we will discuss more in the next chapter.

Language

This section will be much more brief than in prior chapters. We will focus mostly on the changes from Early Modern English, rather than get involved in a detailed discussion of Modern English grammar.

One important movement during this period was the rise of the so-called "prescriptive" grammarians. Towards the end of the 18th century, a tradition arose of "prescribing" what grammar should be. This tradition is still with us to this day—it is the bane of many school children taking English classes, and can be heard among friends, family, and co-workers. A presciptivist says such things as "you should not split an infinitive" (e.g., "...**to** boldly **go** where no one has gone before..."), "you should not end a sentence with a preposition," "you should not say "ain't", etc. However well-meaning these may seem, they are often arbitrary, and they have very little do with linguistics. One unfortunate side-effect of learning grammar from this perspective is that many people have been turned off by the study of grammar in school, and many people resent being "corrected" by others. It is the job of linguists to *describe*, rather than *prescribe* language, and as such, linguists are considered "descriptivists". The study of linguistics is actually quite different from what most of us experienced in junior high English class.

Modern English Phonetics and Phonology

Let's take a look at the phonetics and phonology of Modern English.

Vowels

Below is a table showing the vowel sounds of Modern English (General American). In addition to the spelling and examples, you can see the IPA symbol for each sound.

Note that what we consider a "long a" and "long o" are generally pronounced as diphthongs in English: "made" does not have a pure /e/ sound, but rather a slight glide into /i/ at the end: /eⁱ/; likewise, "road" does not have a pure /o/, but a glide into /u/ at the end: /oᵘ/. This is something to keep in mind when pronouncing these sounds in other languages—the glide on the end of /e/ and /o/ sounds will give you away as a native English speaker.

Modern English Vowels		
Spelling	**Example**	**IPA Symbol**
a	man	/æ/
a	father	/a/
a	place	/e(ⁱ)/ †
au, aw	law	/ɔː/
e	bed	/ɛ/
e, ee, ea	be	/i/
i	this	/ɪ/
i	I	/ai/
o	oft	/ɔ/
o, oa	throne	/o(ᵘ)/ †
o, ou	do	/u/
u	put	/ʊ/
u	rule	/u/
u	but	/ʌ/

† Note that these vowels are often realized as diphthongs

169

Diphthongs

The table below shows the diphthongs of Modern English.

Modern English Diphthongs		
Spelling	**Example**	**IPA Symbol**
i	I	/ai/
oi	toil	/ɔi/
ou	out	/au/

The diphthongs changed slightly since the Early Modern period to their present-day forms. The original "on-glide" (i.e., the first sound of the diphthong) after the Great Vowel Shift in the /ai/ and /au/ examples above was a schwa sound. With the completion of the shift, these sounds lowered to /a/, which is what we have in Modern English.

Consonants

The only significant change in consonantal pronunciation from the Early Modern to Modern periods is that of "r". In Shakespeare's time, the "r" was likely still pronounced in all positions much as it is in most American, Canadian, Scottish, and Irish varieties of English today, though Scottish varieties tend to use a tongue-trilled, or "apical r", whereas the other varieties use a "retroflex" or "alveolar approximant" "r" (properly transcribed as [ɹ]; the [r] symbol in the IPA is technically reserved for the apical "r", but many IPA transcriptions of English use [r] for simplicity. Note that brackets, "[ ]", surround phonetic transcriptions, much like forward slashes surround phonemes; for example, the phoneme /r/ can have two different pronunciations in English: [ɹ] and [r]).

The loss of "r" at the syllable's end (/far/ → /fa:/, /bɔrn/ → /bɔ:n/) in England likely began in certain dialects in the late Middle English period, but flourished late in the Early Modern and Modern periods. Shakespeare, for example, most likely spoke a "rhotic" dialect of English (again, from the Greek letter "rho", simply meaning he pronounced all of his "r's"). It is somewhat ironic that many a Canadian or American production of a Shakespeare play features actors speaking with a non-rhotic "British" accent, when Shakespeare's pronunciation was in many ways, and certainly in this respect, much closer to their native accent.

The non-rhotic varieties of English also spread to part of the United States (mainly New England and the South, and as a result of the latter, to African-American Vernacular English (AAVE)), as well as to English colonies in Australia and South Africa. Although the non-rhotic characteristic is fading among American speakers in New England and the South, the rise of Hip-Hop culture in the US has also fomented the increase in the use of non-rhotic pronunciation in places where the geography itself would not support it. In fact, the spread of AAVE via Hip-Hop culture seems to be one of the greatest influences on American English today, especially with regards to pronunciation and vocabulary (though it is influencing the grammar as well).

Modern English Grammar

Modern English grammar shows only minor changes from the Early Modern English period. We will focus on some of those changes in this chapter.

Nouns and Adjectives

Noun and adjective morphology had already been reduced drastically by the Early Modern period. One more recent change has affected the new plurals resulting from Latin loan words (such as "-i" for words ending in "-us", such as "radius"/"radii", and "-ces" for words ending in "-x", such as "index"/"indices"). As often happens, this new, irregular plural has dropped out of favor and is being replaced by the usual "-(e)s" plural: "radiuses" and "indexes".

For the adjective, double and triple comparatives and superlatives died out by the Modern English period. Shakespeare's "most unkindest cut of all" sounds somewhat odd to us today.

Pronouns

Pronouns in Modern English changed only slightly from the Early Modern English period, as you can see in the table below.

Modern English Pronouns						
Number	**Case**	**1st Person**	**2nd Person**	**3rd Person**		
				masc.	neut.	fem.
Singular	**Nom.**	I	you	he	it	she
	Pos.	my	your	his	its	her
	Obl.	me	you	him	it	her
Plural	**Nom.**	we	you	they		
	Pos.	our	your	their		
	Obl.	us	you	them		

The most significant change in the pronouns was the loss of the second person singular "thou" forms, which had been around in some form since Indo-European. This change had begun in the Early Modern period and, by the beginning of the Modern English period, it had disappeared almost entirely except for some religious purposes and in some dialects, as discussed in the prior chapter. Originally a plural form only, "you" became used more and more as a sign of respect when addressing an individual, and by the end of the Early Modern period, "you" became the sole second person pronoun for both singular and plural. In addition to this change, the pronoun forms themselves changed: the former nominative, "ye" disappeared in favor of the oblique form, "you", which came to be used for both nominative and oblique forms. (The same situation occurred in the group that used "thou" forms the longest, the Quakers, who used this form into the early 20th century. As we saw in the last chapter, the oblique form, "thee", was used for both nominative and oblique forms.)

Another change in the second person pronoun has been occurring in many American English dialects: the creation of new second person plural pronouns. As is often the case, when language change causes ambiguity, languages tend to make further changes to resolve the ambiguities. For example, since the decline of "thou", "you" has done double duty for both singular and plural, thus it is sometimes difficult to tell when the use of "you" refers to one person being addressed or more than one. As such, new plurals have gained popularity: "youse" in the Northeast (obviously an analogical change based on noun plurals: add "-s" to make something plural), "y'all", from "you all", in the South and AAVE, "y'uns", found in western Pennsylvania, and even the common "you guys" heard throughout the country. "Y'all" has especially gained ground over the past few decades as the preferred plural in the South and in AAVE. With the rise of Hip-Hop culture throughout the US and the world and its use of this term, "y'all" seems like a likely successor as the new second person plural pronoun.

Another interesting occurrence with personal pronouns in Modern English is the use of the third person plural pronouns used in the singular—the same thing that happened with "you". Ambiguity and the rise of so-called "political correctness" has spurred the use of "they", "their", and "them" in the singular. Traditionally, the singular, masculine third person pronouns "he", "his", "him" has been used when the party being referred to is unknown. Some speakers and writers have consciously altered their language to use "she" and "her" when referring to an unknown third person in an apparent attempt to make up for the historical lack of use of that pronoun. However, this has had the effect of sounding awkward for some, as if the speaker or writer is talking about a specific person, when the person is actually unknown. Over the past decade or so the use of the plural pronouns in ambiguous situations has grown: "I haven't met your new company vice president—how are *they* working out?" The speaker certainly knows that it is a single person, but does not want to use "he" and risk offending the person spoken to by using a sexist assumption (that a vice president would be a "he").

Verbs

The changes in the Modern English verb from the Early Modern English period are fairly minimal.

Modern English Strong Verb Conjugation: "to sing"			
Infinitive:	to sing	**Past Participle:**	sung
Present Participle:	singing	**Imperative:**	sing
Indicative			
Present		**Preterite**	
I	sing		
you	sing	*sg.*	sang
he	sings		
pl.	sing	*pl.*	sang

With the loss of the second person singular "thou", its ending, of course, died out as well. Early in this period the third person singular ending "-(e)s" finally won out over the former "-(e)th" ending. With these changes, the third person singular ending is the only verb inflection in the present tense, and there are no longer any inflectional endings in the preterite.

The weak conjugation below shows similar changes.

Modern English Weak Verb Conjugation: "to love"			
Infinitive:	to love	**Past Participle:**	loved
Present Participle:	loving	**Imperative:**	love
Indicative			
Present		**Preterite**	
I you he	love love loves	*sg.*	loved
pl.	love	*pl.*	loved

In addition to the changes noted above, verbs have lost a separate subjunctive form. Rather than using a separate form, Modern English now utilizes the bare infinitive form for formal requests ("He asked that she **leave** now.", "She requested that he **be** here on time."), and the preterite plural form of the verb for "present" unreal conditions ("If I **were** in school, I would be having more fun.", "If I **ate** that, I'd get sick."); and the past perfect for past unreal conditions ("If I **had gone** to college, I would have a better job.") The subjunctive in general is slowly dying out. The verb "to be" is still a major holdout, although one often hears "If I **was** there, I'd go along" alongside the more usual form "If I **were** there…". The subjunctive also still exists in the language in formulaic language such as "God **save** the queen", or "So **help** me God". While one rarely hears the older subjunctive form "be", as in "if she **be** a good woman" (we would use the present or preterite indicative here), the subjunctive can still be heard in formal requests, such as "he asked that she **be** here tomorrow".

The full conjugations for "to have" and "to be" are below. You will notice very few changes from Early Modern English, other than those already mentioned.

Modern English Conjugation of "to have"			
Infinitive:	to have	**Past Participle:**	had
Present Participle:	having	**Imperative:**	have
Indicative			
Present		**Preterite**	
I you he *pl.*	have have has have	*sg.* *pl.*	had had

Modern English Conjugation of "to be"			
Infinitive:	to be	**Past Participle:**	been
Present Participle:	being	**Imperative:**	be
Indicative			
Present		**Preterite**	
I you he *pl.*	am are is are	I you he *pl.*	was were was were

Numbers

Following is a table of the number system in Modern English.

Modern English Numbers			
1	one	20	twenty
2	two	21	twenty-one
3	three	30	thirty
4	four	40	forty
5	five	50	fifty
6	six	60	sixty
7	seven	70	seventy
8	eight	80	eighty
9	nine	90	ninety
10	ten	100	hundred
11	eleven	200	two hundred
12	twelve	1000	thousand
13	thirteen	2000	two thousand

The numbers themselves have not changed since Early Modern English times; the main innovation was the change from the Germanic system of "one and twenty" for "21" to the system we have today, where the numbers are reversed and there is no conjunction present: "twenty-one".

This change occurred surprisingly late in our history. As late as the 19th century, examples of the former inverted order were still quite common in both America (Thomas Jefferson, in a personal letter written in 1826, says in the same sentence "For *three-and-twenty* years of the last *twenty-five*") and Great Britain (the writings of both Jane Austen and Charles Dickens exhibit the use of both forms as well).

In the next chapter, we will assess some current linguistic trends in English, and try to predict the future of English.

The Future of English

7

> If we have learned one thing from the history of
> invention and discovery, it is that, in the long
> run—and often in the short one—the most dar-
> ing prophecies seem laughably conservative.
>
> —*Arthur C. Clarke*

Language change is constant. And although language change often adheres to various known processes and seems to work within a system of finite possibilities, it is impossible to accurately predict the future form of any given language. Nonetheless, in this chapter I will attempt to predict certain changes within the English language, in some instances based on current changes taking place within the language, and in others, based on changes that have occurred in other languages (especially Germanic languages) in the past.

It has really only been within the past century that English has become a dominant international language. With the rise of the Internet, innovations in science and technology, and the spread of American pop culture, English will likely have a place as a world language for quite some time. However, it is certainly also possible that English will succumb to the same fate as other "world languages" such as Latin and French, and eventually give way to another dominant language in the future. The most likely challenger at present is Chinese, but Spanish is also a possibility.

Both of these languages suffer from geographic isolation: Chinese is mainly spoken in China and neighboring Asian countries, and Spanish mainly in the Americas. China will undoubtedly become the next super power, and with such power comes cachet for a country's language as well. Spanish is also spoken by a large number of people, but mostly in poorer countries in North, Central, and South America. However, with more stable governments and economies now in place in most Latin American countries, and increasing populations, the future for Spanish looks good as well. Spanish is also becoming more and more prominent in the United States and it may eventually overtake English in number of speakers there. More and more products and services in the United States are already "bilingual" in both English and Spanish ("bilingual" means speaking or involving two languages, however, in the United States it is also used specifically to mean "English and Spanish").

The Chinese language is made up of several dialects that, when spoken, are not mutually intelligible. Standard Mandarin, based on the dialect of Beijing, is the official dialect of China. This dialect alone has over 850 million native speakers (compared to 380 million for English and around 400 million for Spanish). Chinese is written with "logograms" (also called ideograms, though technically, this designation is not entirely correct). A logogram is a single character that represents a word or "morpheme" (the smallest meaningful unit of language; this can be a word, an affix, a part of a compound word, etc.) This is much different from an alphabet, in which a letter represents a single sound, or a "syllabary" (in which a character represents a syllable, such as "la", "le", "li", "lo", "lu"), which Japanese uses for certain words (its syllabaries are called "hiragana" and "katakana"). Chinese has over 47,000 characters, though a university student can get by knowing 4,000 - 5,000 characters, and basic literacy is considered to be recognition of 1,500 - 2,000 characters. Each character must be memorized with the word it represents. The characters are essentially the same in all of the dialects, with each character having the same meaning across dialects, but a different pronunciation. This writing system is what unites the various dialects of Chinese and is the main reason the dialects are generally not considered separate languages (though they are about as different as English, German, and Dutch).

Spanish would likely need the backing of a future super power (possibly the United States itself) to achieve international *lingua franca* status. As previously mentioned, the language is quickly gaining ground within the United States, along with the increasing size of its Latino population. Over time, the number of speakers of Spanish in the US could overtake the number of speakers of English. Currently there are approximately 30 million speakers of Spanish in the US, and the Hispanic populations of several states are already rapidly approaching fifty percent (some examples are California, Texas, and New Mexico). But it seems more likely that, rather than being driven out by Spanish, English and Spanish would co-exist and possibly even merge in some fashion, as often happens today among bilingual speakers of the language in the US, giving rise to the term "Spanglish".

In any case, even if English does some day lose its status as an international language, it will likely live on regardless. Latin never actually died out, it simply turned into a dozen or so separate languages that were no longer mutually intelligible. Altogether, the Romance languages today claim over 700 million speakers. French, one of these daughter languages, is alive and well, and still holds the status of a second international language. So regardless of English's role in the future, it will likely continued to be spoken by hundreds of millions of people for centuries to come.

Literature

Just as the printing press was a revolutionary invention for literature and eventually enabled thousands of authors to have their works seen by millions, anyone with access to the Internet can publish their views and their art for anyone else in the world with Internet access to see. Our view of literature and writing in general as something committed to paper has already become outdated. Newspapers have migrated online as a way to continuously update the news, ebooks are becoming more and more popular, with even an author of Stephen King's stature testing the waters, and blogs, podcasts, and vlogs are commonly read, heard, and seen by millions of people daily. The invention of "electronic ink" is just around the corner. This invention will enable the use of flexible paper-like devices to display electronic texts, thereby resolving the issue of using cumbersome, bulky electronic devices such as laptops and PDAs. Some day not so far in the future you will be able to carry around a newspaper in your briefcase that constantly updates itself wirelessly via the Internet. You will be able to carry a small "book" in your book bag that can call up the text not only for all of your classes in school, but also every book ever published (or at least digitized). Imagine—the entire Library of Congress in your book bag. Google is already working on digitizing some of the largest university library collections in the US.

In the future, writing may be much more collaborative. Today, a book is usually written by just one author, unless it is a book dealing with business, the sciences, or technology. Literary works are rarely written by more than one person. However, the Internet allows people from all over the world to collaborate very easily on almost any type of project. In the future, your favorite novels may be written by a team of people who collaborated via the Internet to conceive, write, edit, and even publish their entire work online. Instead of publishing houses and agents, writers will be able to bypass the middle man and still reach millions via large online booksellers like Amazon.com and Barnes & Noble. With search engines such as Google Book Search indexing entire libraries, books will be instantly available on the Internet for searching via keywords and phrases, much like you search for web pages today. Indeed, books and web pages may not really be considered the separate entities they are today. In the future, anyone will be able to write whatever they want, and it will be made available to anyone who wants it (or is willing to pay for it), immediately.

There are some downsides to such things as well. A popular online encyclopedia, Wikipedia, allows virtually anyone to edit it online. While information is generally vetted through a number of different editors, that has not stopped false or even malicious information form being published. Likewise, without editors and publishers to edit and check facts, the validity of information you read will come into question more and more. Just as "you can't believe everything you see on the Internet" is true today, in the future, this may be true of e-publications in general. Perhaps at some point computers themselves will be intelligent enough to scour online writing, and do the editing and fact-checking for us.

Language

Just as English has changed greatly in the past, the language will continue to change in the future. There are many factors that will contribute to this change. Some of these will be language-internal, that is, normal change that happens over time, while others will be language-external, such as the mass media, and the spread of English as an international language, with the resulting influence from other languages.

In addition to the "original" English of Great Britain, distinct dialects grew in Britain's early colonial empire, giving us Canadian, American, Australian, New Zealand, Indian, and South African English. Later colonial pursuits involved African, Asian, Caribbean, and Pacific countries and territories, where further distinct dialects grew. For the most part, all of these dialects are mutually intelligible, and the greatest differences are in pronunciation and the lexicon (the English dialect situation is nothing like that of many other languages, such as German, French, Spanish, or Chinese, where one dialect is often not mutually intelligible with another). However, it might easily be the case that in the future, "American", "British", "Australian", "Hongkongese", "Indian English", etc. might become just as mutually unintelligible as Low German versus Bavarian, two dialects of Modern German.

The situation is changing now in another way, with a large number of people learning English as a second language, many of whom do not live in an English speaking area. English is used as a *lingua franca* throughout the world for communication, from tourists in English and non-English speaking countries, to bloggers and chatters on the Internet. Rather than everyone learning everyone else's language, it is considerably simpler to learn just one that everyone else is learning. Thus, there has been somewhat of a snowball effect in this respect over the past decade. It will be interesting to see how this influx of non-native speakers using the language with other non-native speakers will influence the evolution of English.

Spelling Reform

One of the most likely changes that will happen to English some day is spelling reform. At one time, spelling in English was fairly phonetic—one letter was approximately equal to one sound. The early use of the printing press was a boon for the language in most regards, but it turned out to be the bane of school children and people learning English as a second language today in at least one respect. Spelling began to be standardized before the Great Vowel Shift had completed, and, as such, our Modern English spelling basically still reflects Middle English pronunciation. In Chaucer's time "made" was pronounced much as a speaker of Modern German might guess using her own spelling rules: "mah-duh". But after the Great Vowel Shift, and with the loss of the pronunciation of final "e", this word has come to be pronounced as we do today. Few of the vowels have their original Latin-like pronunciation. In addition, there are silent letters galore, and spelling variations that make little sense anymore. As a result, learning to spell in English can be nearly as difficult as learning Chinese characters because, in many cases, one must memorize the spelling for any given word since there is not a true a one-to-one correspondence between a letter and its pronunciation. A common anecdote illustrating the absurdity of English spelling is that the word "ghoti" could be pronounced as "fish", taking the "gh" from "laugh", the "o" from "women", and the "ti" from "nation" (though often attributed to George Bernard Shaw, a champion of spelling reform, Shaw himself did not claim credit for it).

There have been many champions of spelling reform in the past, but most ideas set forth have met with little enthusiasm. Part of the problem is the vast amount of literature already available using the current spelling system, and the fact that hundreds of millions of current English speakers would need to relearn how to spell in their own language. (If you are old enough to remember the 1970's, consider that Americans tried and failed to adopt the metric system, a system much simpler than our current one, and one which is used by every other country in the world but the US, and you will see what a formidable task changing something as basic as spelling will be.) These issues will likely be resolved in the not-so-distant future when literally everything that has ever been published will be scanned electronically and thus could likewise be programmatically converted to use the new spelling system. Likewise, in the future, people will not sit down at a computer and type in words letter by letter as I am doing now. They will simply speak to their computer and the computer will create the words for them. This solves the problem of current speakers' issues with writing text, however they will still need to learn how to read the text. Unless of course we simply allow our computers to read for us, which they can already do reasonably well today. In fact, for the slow learner (or merely a stubborn one), a computer could simply re-spell a text on-the-fly using the old spelling system. In any case, technology will eventually be able to resolve most of the issues hindering spelling reform.

While there have been numerous suggestions for spelling reform, I will posit my own here. As a linguist, I will admit to having some bias towards the International Phonetic Association alphabet, introduced in an earlier chapter. While it has its limitations, linguists have been successfully using it to transcribe the languages of the world for over one hundred years. It was in 1886 that a group of British and French language teachers formed what would eventually become the International Phonetic Association. Originally based on an alphabet called the "Romic" alphabet (appropriately enough devised for English spelling reform), the IPA alphabet has been changed and enhanced to make it suitable for all languages. The IPA makes periodic changes to the alphabet to keep up with the latest phonetic research. As of the writing of this book in 2007, there are 107 letters and 56 diacritics and suprasegmentals (symbols that further describe the pronunciation, such as aspiration, rounding, nasalization, etc.) in the IPA alphabet.

The IPA symbols are mostly based on Latin and Greek letters, but new symbols have also been devised as needed. Ideally, a new spelling system for English would involve mainly letters that speakers are already familiar with. But, given that there are more phonemes in English than letters in the current alphabet, I will need to use some IPA symbols that are not based on the current alphabet. Again, keep in mind that in the future, keyboards, if used at all, will be "virtual" (you can change them with the click of a mouse button, or the command of your voice), and technology will be able to overcome most hurdles (in fact, you can easily change the virtual keyboard on your computer today, though changing the physical display is more difficult). I also want to stick with the original idea of an alphabet, that is, one symbol equals one and only one sound, as much as possible. Given the variety of pronunciations in the different English dialects, we do not want the alphabet to represent every single actual sound, as the IPA would, but each symbol should represent the sound in such a way that it will be properly interpreted by any given native speaker. For example, even though a Scottish speaker of English pronounces the letter "r" as /r/, and an

American speaker, as /ɹ/, we will use the common symbol "r" and an American and Scottish person will pronounce them according to their own dialect. This could be somewhat problematic where pronunciation differs vastly from dialect to dialect, but we will not tackle that question here.

The following tables show the spelling system of English after spelling reform.

English Spelling Reform: Vowels			
Current Spelling	Modern English	New Spelling	Example
a	father	a	faðər
a	mad	æ	mæd
e	bed	ɛ	bɛd
a, ai, ay	made	e	med
i	bit	ɪ	bɪt
e, ee, ea	mean	i	min
o, ou	often	ɔ	ɔfən
o, oa	boat	o	bot
u	put	ʊ	pʊt
oo, ou, u	boot	u	but
a, e, i, o, u	sofa	ə	sofə

In our reformed spelling for English, each vowel sound has its own symbol. Whereas in Modern English, one letter could represent a short and a long vowel, our future spelling system will separate these out in order to conform with our "one sound, one symbol" rule. This will necessitate the introduction of a few new symbols, all based on the original letters with slight modifications. I have also included the schwa symbol to stand for all of the indistinct vowels such as "a" in sofa, "e" in "butter", "io" in "nation", as well as the "u" in "butter" (in the actual IPA, there is a separate symbol, /ʌ/, used, for example, in the transcription for "but" /bʌt/, used in my dialect as a sort of schwa in a stressed position, but for simplicity's sake, we will use schwa for both).

The diphthongs of English after spelling reform are below. In our future spelling, the "long i" sound is now spelled out appropriately as a diphthong. Note that in our spelling system we will not yet spell out the "o" and "a" sounds of English as dipthongs.

English Spelling Reform: Diphthongs			
Current Spelling	Modern English	New Spelling	Example
i	bike	ai	baik
ou, ow	house	au	haus
oi, oy	boy	ɔi	bɔi

Below are the consonants of English after spelling reform.

English Spelling Reform: Consonants			
Current Spelling	Modern English	New Spelling	Example
b	bin	b	bɪn
c, k	cat	k	kæt
ch	chin	tʃ	tʃɪn
d	dog	d	dɔg
th	thin	θ*	θɪn
th	the	ð*	ðə
f	fat	f	fæt
g	go	g	go
h	hat	h	hæt
g, j	jump	dʒ	dʒəmp
l	let	l	lɛt
m	man	m	mæn
n	nip	n	nɪp
ng	king	ŋ	kɪŋ
p	pin	p	pɪn
qu	queen	kw*	kwin
r	run	ɾ	ɾən
c, s	sit	s	sɪt
sh	show	ʃ	ʃo
t	ten	t	tɛn

Future English Spelling: Consonants (cont.)			
Current Spelling	Modern English	New Spelling	Example
v	van	v	væn
w	win	w*	wɪn
x	six	ks	sɪks
y	year	j	jɪr
x, z	zoo	z	zu
g, s, z	genre	ʒ	ʒanrə

*Note: these letters will eventually be obsolete after the phonetic changes described below.

In general, these consonants are not terribly different from those with which an English speaker is already familiar. The new consonants are: θ (this is the Greek letter "theta", used for the voiceless dental fricative in "thin", rather than the Germanic thorn, "þ" that Germanic linguists commonly use), ð, ŋ (called "eng"), ʃ (this symbol, an elongated "s" is called "esh") and ʒ (called "ezh", the "zh" representing the "g" in "genre"). In addition to these new letters, there is one, "j", which is used in a different way than we use it in English (the symbol "y" is used for a high, front, rounded vowel, as in German "ü" or French "u"; "j" represents the English "y" sound). Also, a few digraphs are new, reflecting the actual sounds of theses combinations: "tʃ" for "ch" , "dʒ" for "j" and some instances of "g", "kw" for "qu", and "ks" for "x". There will no longer be capital or lower case letters. A capital could be made by simply increasing the size of the letter, but there will be no separate symbols (I could have used capital letters for our new alphabet instead of adding new symbols, but part of the reason for not doing that is so that speakers of English will get used to the IPA symbols, enabling them to quickly pick up the pronunciation of any other language that adopts this sort of alphabet for their language in the future).

For the most part, learning the new alphabet will not be overly difficult. Whereas the old alphabet has 26 letters, our new alphabet will have 33 symbols (11 vowels and 22 consonants). The difficult part will be in quickly interpreting these new symbols grouped together as words.

To see just how difficult this might be, here is the previous paragraph spelled with the new spelling rules:

fɔr ðə most part, lərnɪŋ ðə nu ælfəbɛt wɪl nat bi ovərli dɪfəkəlt. weræz ðə old ælfəbɛt hæz 26 lɛtərz, aur nu ælfəbɛt wɪl hæv 33 sɪmbəlz (11 vaulz ænd 22 kansənənts). ðə dɪfəkəlt part wɪl bi ɪn kwɪkli ɪntərprətɪŋ ðiz nu sɪmbəlz grupt tugɛðər æz wərdz.

You can probably immediately see some difficulties here. The pronunciation is based on American English (and my own dialect, in particular). A speaker of British English would probably expect "for" to be spelled "fɔ", "new" as "nju", and "not" as "nɔt". In the future, these differences will need to be ironed out and a compromise selected. This will not be limited to speakers of dialects outside the US. If I had used the word "on" above, I would have spelled it "ɔn", whereas many speakers in the US who are not from the Northeast might have written this as "an" (pronounced "ahhn"). Another difficulty pops up with differences in pronunciation that we do not currently note in our orthography. For example, the word "ðə" near the beginning of the second line would be pronounced "ði" by most speakers of English (though not all). Rather than introducing a second article in our spelling (even though it is there in our speech), it might be prudent to simply choose one (this issue may eventually resolve itself, as you will see below). Similarly, even though we write the plural of most nouns with "-s", in actuality, it is /z/ as often as it is /s/ (if it comes after a vowel or voiced consonant it is /z/). Thus, we have "kansənənts" but also "lɛttərz" and "wərdz". So this may take some getting used to. If you simply say the words to yourself, the correct letter is obvious, but it would require people to pay more attention to their actual pronunciation. The same issue would occur with the past tense and past participle forms for weak verbs, which can be /-t/ or /-d/ depending on the environment before it (i.e., whether it is voiced or not, e.g., "sewed" would be "so**d**", but "walked" would be "wɔk**t)**". Alternatively, we could go the route of the definite article here and just decide upon using "-s" for plural and "-d" for weak verbs. There are arguments for and against both possibilities.

Conceiving of and implementing spelling reform in English will be a long, hard task, but it will eventually be necessary. Without it, the language will eventually have changed so much that the words themselves will simply be graphemes that have no connection to the words they symbolize, defeating the purpose of using an alphabet at all.

Future English Phonetics and Phonology

In this section, we will take a look at the phonetics and phonology of a possible Future English.

Vowels and Diphthongs

Vowel sounds change much more easily than do consonants in a language over time. As you saw in the snippets of Indo-European and Germanic reconstructions, and throughout the history of English itself, the vowel sounds have changed considerably, whereas consonant sounds have remained more steadfast. Some consonants like /l/, /r/, /m/, /n/, and /s/ (in certain positions) have come down to Modern English from Indo-European relatively unchanged. Those consonants that underwent Grimm's Law changes in Germanic have also remained fairly close to their original Germanic sounds in all of the modern Germanic languages except German (because of the High German Consonant Shift), that is., for several thousand years. But in general, the vowel sounds have always been in flux. Even today, with the many varieties of Modern English, including American, Canadian, British, Irish, Scottish, Australian, New Zealand, and South African English, it is generally the vowel sounds that differentiate the accents from one another the most. American [hoᵘm], British "Received Pronunciation" [həʊm], and Australian [həʉm] ([ʉ] is a high, central vowel) all feature the same consonants, but quite different vowel sounds. As such, it is safe to say that the vowel sounds of Future English will probably change the most.

A trend in English vowel sounds over time has been the diphthongization of what were once "monophthongs" (simply meaning a single, pure vowel sound). As you can see in the example above with "home", American English has a simple /u/ glide at the end of the sound, while British and Australian English have changed this sound to a diphthong beginning with schwa. I predict this trend will continue, changing some current vowels to full-fledged diphthongs, such us /e/ and /o/ (which would become /ei/ and /ou/).

Consonants

Although consonants are somewhat hardier than vowels over time, linguistically speaking, they can and do change as well, as you saw with the various consonant shifts in the second chapter. The most likely candidates for changes in English would seem to be /θ/, /ð/, /r/, and /w/.

The two sounds represented by English "th", /θ/ and its voiced counterpart, /ð/, are relatively uncommon sounds in the world's languages and cause learners of English as a second language a great deal of difficulty. Most learners will substitute a /d/ or /z/ for this sound. These sounds come down to English all the way from Germanic, but of all the modern Germanic languages, only English and Icelandic (the most conservative of all the Germanic languages) have preserved them (though Faroese has the grapheme "ð", it represents a glide rather than the phoneme /ð/; Danish has a similar sound, but it is a secondary development, rather than a sound preserved from Germanic). In the other Germanic languages, these sounds have generally become /d/ or /t/. The well-known Cockney dialect of London uses substitutions for these sounds in certain instances: /θ/ becomes /f/, and /ð/ becomes/v/ medially and word finally, thus [dɛf] for 'death' and /bʊvə/ for 'bother'. Except for word initial /θ/, these sounds have also disappeared in African-American Vernacular English: initial /ð/ is pronounced /d/ ("this" is /dis/), medial and final /θ/ is pronounced /f/ or /t/ ("birth" is /bəf/ or /bət/), and medial and final /ð/ is pronounced /v/ or /d/ ("smooth" is /smuv/, "father" is /fadə/). Jamaican English regularly substitutes /t/ for /θ/ and /d/ for /ð/: "with that thing" would be /wɪt dæt tɪŋ/. So, even within dialects of English itself, these sounds are disappearing in favor of more common sounds. If any consonants were to disappear in English in the future, these are likely candidates. Likely changes are: initial /θ/ → /t/, medial and final /θ/ → /f/, initial /ð/ → /d/, and medial and final /ð/ → /v/.

The /r/ of English also seems to be susceptible to loss. A major distinction among dialects of English today is rhotic status, that is, there are rhotic dialects like American (except Southern, New England, and AAVE), Irish, and Scottish dialects, and non-rhotic one like most British, Australian, New Zealand, and South African dialects. Given the number of North American speakers of English, the /r/ is not in any danger of dying out soon. Nor is it really in danger of dying out entirely: even in the so-called non-rhotic dialects, /r/'s are still pronounced in certain positions. It is only at the end of a syllable that they are not pronounced: "car" becomes /ca:/, "dark" becomes /da:k/, but "red" is still /rɛd/. African-American Vernacular English is also a non-rhotic dialect, and it seems to be a dialect on the rise as the language of Hip-Hop culture. So it is possible that at some point, other North American dialects of English could become non-rhotic as well.

This would not be an isolated occurrence. In Modern German the standard "uvular r" (articulated with the uvula at the back of the throat, just like the French "r") is mainly heard at the beginning of a word or between vowels. In similar situations to non-rhotic English (syllable final), it has generally become a glide and has become somewhat like a schwa in many dialects.

The English /w/ is unique among the modern Germanic languages. Among all of the modern Germanic languages, this sound has invariably become /v/. This is also the most common substitution used by speakers of English who have acquired it as a second language. There is certainly a possibility that English will also succumb to this change some day and that /w/ will become /v/.

Future English Grammar

Grammatical change, like phonological change, is as constant as it is hard to predict. I will make some educated guesses here, keeping in mind our spelling and phonological changes as well as current trends.

Articles

Although articles occur quite frequently in English usage, we have seen that they have changed greatly since Old English times, from sixteen or more possibilities for the definite article to our current one, "the". And the indefinite article has changed from a fully declinable number to an actual article that has two possible forms today.

As discussed earlier, the definite article, "the", has two separate pronunciations in standard English today: /ði/ when it comes before a word beginning with a vowel sound or when emphasized: /ði æpl/ for "the apple", and /ðə/ in all other circumstances. In some dialects, it is /ðə/ in all circumstances. It is possible that this will eventually become the sole form of the definite article. With our phonological changes, I predict that the future of the definite article will be /də/, written "də" in our new orthography.

Likewise, "an" (/æn/ or /ən/) is used before a noun beginning with a vowel sound, and "a" elsewhere (/ʌ/; again, we will use the schwa for this sound). And in many dialects, we already see that "an" is slowly disappearing with examples such as /ə æpl/ ('a apple') in some dialects. It is plausible to assume that the future of the indefinite article will be a non-changing form, written "ə" with our new spelling system.

Nouns and Adjectives

The noun in English has gone from one that could be declined for various cases and numbers to one that has just two possible inflectional endings, plural (usually "-(e)s") and possessive ("-'s"). It is certainly possible with continued regularization of the language that the "-(e)s" plural ending will simply become "-(ə)s" for all nouns, including those that currently have a unique plural, such as a zero plural (sheep/sheep → ʃip/ʃips), plural in "-en" (child/children → tʃaild/tʃailds), and plural in "-i" (alumnus/alumni → əlɔmnəs/əlɔmnəsəs). (Note that I am keeping the "-s" as an "s" in our new orthography, however in reality, we would continue to pronounce it as /z/ in the same circumstances we do today, when it comes after a vowel or voiced consonant; "ʃips" would be pronounced /ʃips/ but "tʃailds" would actually be pronounced /tʃaildz/ as we would pronounce it today.)

Another possibility is that plural markings could die out altogether. There are many languages in the world where you simply say "I read two book yesterday" where the adjective shows the plurality. Some languages simply repeat the singular word when referring to the plural: "book book".

As we have seen, when former morphological markers of the past have died, new periphrastic constructions arose in their place. This has already happened for the possessive case. You can say "Jane's car" or "the car of Jane". The latter may sound a little strange (but in many languages, including French and Dutch, this is how possessives are constructed). It is considerably more common to use such a construction in English when referring to inanimate objects: "the book's cover" or "the cover of the book". My guess is that this phrase will eventually win out over this last vestige of a morphological genitive marker in English. So our possessive phrases in the examples above will become "də ka əv dʒein" and "də kəvə əv də bʊk".

Our adjectives are already as simple as we can make them morphologically, with no inflectional endings. However, when comparing, we still have "-er" and "-est" in competition with "more" and "most". Again, the periphrastic constructions seem to be the trend in English, so the morphological endings will possibly die out altogether some day. Instead of "good/better/best" we will have "gʊd/mɔ gʊd/moust gʊd".

Pronouns

Pronouns have remained closer to their original forms since Old English times than perhaps any other part of speech. For instance, it is the only place where we mark three cases instead of two (with the addition of the oblique cases, marking indirect and direct object use). However, in the future, even these may become more simplified. There is already a tendency to use the oblique forms where one would expect nominative forms: "Who's coming along?" "*Me!*". "*Him and me* are going too" is not terribly uncommon in colloquial speech either. This is often the case used in English pidgins in place of the nominative (a pidgin is a language that comes into existence through the attempts by the speakers of two different languages to communicate; it is primarily a simplified form of one of the languages, with a reduced vocabulary and grammatical structure): in Tok Pisin, an English pidgin spoken in Papua New Guinea, "I'm sick" is "*Mi* pilim sik". My prediction is that case distinctions will some day be lost in the pronouns, largely in favor of their current oblique forms, as seen in the table below.

Future English Personal Pronouns					
Number	**1st Person**	**2nd Person**	**3rd Person**		
			masc.	**neut.**	**fem.**
Singular	mi	ju	hɪm	dɛm	hə
Plural	əs	jɔl	mɔl		

In addition, the plural "dɛm" (from Modern English "them") will be used as a neuter third person singular pronoun (our current "it"), and for situations where the referent (called the "antecedent") is unknown. English will also resolve the ambiguity it currently has in the second person—with two separate pronouns for singular and plural, it will be clear whether one or more than one person is being addressed.

Since this new use of "dɛm" (doing double duty as a singular and plural pronoun) will eventually cause ambiguity, just like singular and plural "you" do in Modern English, a new third person plural pronoun will evolve. Based on the new second person plural, construction (i.e., via analogy), this new third person plural pronoun will be constructed from "dɛm" + "ɔl" ('all'), written "mɔl".

Verbs

The verb in English has changed greatly over time. The trends have included increasing use of auxiliary verbs for periphrastic constructions and simplification of the morphological system (that is, fewer inflectional endings). Over time, the number of tenses has actually increased, but in our Future English, this trend will be reversed.

Modern English still has the strong/weak characteristic of the Germanic languages. In the future, this distinction will disappear as well. To begin with, the preterite form of the verb will disappear completely. In order to form the past tense, Future English will use the auxiliary verb "hæv" plus the bare infinitive (which is essentially the verb stem), much like our current construction of the present perfect tense, which uses a form of "to have" plus the past participle. "I saw" or "I have seen" will become: "mi hæv si". "hɪm hæv rait" is "he has written" or "he wrote". If it seems unreasonable that these two different tenses would collapse into one, it is not—this has actually already occurred, at least in colloquial speech, in German and Dutch, and for all intents and purposes, in French as well. And in Afrikaans, a language that grew out of Dutch in South Africa, this very thing has happened in the standard language. Perfect or imperfect meaning (i.e., whether or not an action is complete) can simply be gleaned from the context.

You may have also noticed that the conjugation for "he has" is "hɪm hæv". The last vestige of person marking on the verb, the third person singular "-(e)s", will also disappear, making the verb entirely uniform for all persons and numbers.

With no more preterite forms or past participles (since the bare infinitive is now used in its place), the strong/weak distinction will also disappear from the language. The infinitive will lose its "to" particle, and will become just a bare infinitive, formed by the verb stem alone.

Tenses will change too. The new past tense construction will be used for the current preterite, present perfect and past perfect, with context being the key to understanding the exact meaning. The present participle will be replaced by the simple verb stem as well and the latter will be used in progressive tenses. Future tense will use the auxiliary "vɪl" + the verb stem, and this will take the place of both the current future and future perfect tenses.

Below is a sample conjugation of a verb in Future English.

Future English Verb Conjugation of "sɪŋ" ('to sing')			
Infinitive:	sɪŋ	Infnitive:	sɪŋ
Present Participle:	sɪŋ	Past Participle:	sɪŋ
Present Tense:	sɪŋ	Past Tense:	hæv sɪŋ
Present Progressive:	bi sɪŋ	Past Progressive:	hæv bi sɪŋ
Future:	vɪl sɪŋ	Imperative:	sɪŋ

"To be" and "to have" will still be important verbs in the language, but they will eventually also become fully regular.

Future English Conjugation of "bi" ('to be')			
Infinitive:	bi	Infnitive:	bi
Present Participle:	bi	Past Participle:	bi
Present Tense:	bi	Past Tense:	hæv bi
Present Progressive:	bi bi	Past Progressive:	hæv bi bi
Future:	vɪl bi	Imperative:	bi

Future English Conjugation of "hæv" ('to have')			
Infinitive:	hæv	Infnitive:	hæv
Present Participle:	hæv	Past Participle:	hæv
Present Tense:	hæv	Past Tense:	hæv hæv
Present Progressive:	bi hæv	Past Progressive:	hæv bi hæv
Future:	vɪl hæv	Imperative:	hæv

As you can see, the verb here is considerably simpler than even in Modern English. Although it may seem "too simple" to create all of the various meanings we have in our verb system today, it really is not. Afrikaans has also lost its strong/weak distinction in a similar manner, and other languages have conjugations not terribly dissimilar to the one proposed for Future English.

Numbers

The numbers in Future English will change as well. In the list below, I have transcribed them with the new spelling system, and I have taken several phonological changes into account. In addition to the changes outlined above, I've simplified many of the consonant clusters in the current language. This is not an uncommon occurrence—certain consonant clusters in the history of English have undergone simplification (the flipside of this is that, when vowels disappear, new consonant clusters can develop). As an example, the number 50 below in Future English is "fɪdi". In fact, this is not far off from the pronunciation of a popular rap artist's name at this time, "50 Cent", commonly pronounced "fitty cent". So in this instance, the second /f/ disappears entirely. Another way a consonant cluster can be broken up is by the insertion of a vowel, called "epenthesis" (this can include the insertion of vowels or consonants). In the number 12, "tvɛləv", the schwa is inserted between the "l" and the "v" at the end. This type of epenthesis is also fairly common in dialects of English and other Germanic languages. Another common type of sound change which we have already discussed, metathesis, where sounds within a word are reordered, might also occur. In the case of 100 below, metathesis will occur at the end of the word at one stage, our current /hʌndrəd/ → /hʌndərd/ (the schwa and the "r" switch places), and eventually this will result in our Future English "həndə".

The following table shows the proposed numbers for Future English.

Future English Numbers			
1	vən	20	tvɛni
2	tu	21	tvɛnivən
3	tri	30	tədi
4	fɔ	40	fɔdi
5	faiv	50	fɪdi
6	sɪs	60	sɪdi
7	sɛvə	70	sɛvədi
8	eit	80	eidi
9	nain	90	naidi
10	tən	100	həndə
11	lɛvə	200	tu həndə
12	tvɛləv	1000	tauzən
13	tritin	2000	tu tauzən

Sample Texts

Following are some sample texts in Future English.

---

də preə əv də lɔd

favə əv əs ɪn hɛvə, neim əv ju bi houli. mei kɪŋdəm əv ju kəm, mei vɪl
əv ju bi du, ɔn əf æz ɪn hɛvə. gɪv əs deili fud əv əs tudei ɛn fɔgɪv sɪns
əv əs, æz əs fɔgɪv sɪns əgɛnst əs. ɛn dount lid əs tu tɛmt, bət dilɪvə əs
frəm ivəl. eimɛn.

---

roumio ɛn dʒuliɛt bai vɪljəm ʃeikspiə, ækt 2, sin 2

roumio hə spik.

ou, spik əgɛn, brait eindʒəl! fɔ ju bi

æz glɔriəs tu dɪs nait, bi ouvə hɛd əv mi,

æz bi ə vɪŋ mɛsəndʒə əv hɛvə

tu də vait-əptən vəndə ais

əv mɔtəls dæt fɔl bæk geiz ɔn hɪm

vɛn hɪm bistraid də leizi-peis klauds

ɛn seil ɔn də bʊzəm əv də eiə.

dʒuliɛt ou roumio, roumio! vai du ju bi roumio?

dinai favə əv ju ɛn rifjuz neim əv ju!

ɔ, ɪf ju vount, bi sveiə ləv əv mi,

ɛn mi vɪl nou lɔŋgə bi ə kæpjulət.

---

nout frəm də ɔfə

mi houp ju hæv ɛndʒɔi bʊk əv mi. dɛm hæv bi ə laiflɔŋ drim əv mi
rait dɛm. ɛvə sɪns mi hæv rid də siris əv bʊks bai də lɪŋgvɪst mariou
pei æz ə tʃaild, mi hæv bi ɪntrɪst ɪn də hɪstri əv də ɪŋglɪʃ læŋvɪdʒ. dɛm
bi houp əv mi dæt dɪs bʊk vɪl spak də seim ɪntrɪst ɪn əvəz stədi
læŋgvɪdʒ ɛn lɪŋgvɪstɪks.

Final Words

In this book, you have learned not only about the history of English, but you have also been introduced to various concepts in historical and theoretical linguistics. What you have learned here is just the beginning—we have only scratched the surface of the study of Indo-European, Germanic, and English linguistics. The bibliography of this book contains many reference works for readers of all levels of knowledge in the field of linguistics—I encourage you to check them out and to read more about the topics that interest you the most.

It is my hope that this book has sparked even more of an interest in you to further your studies of the history of English, as well as in historical and theoretical linguistics.

I will leave you with an Old English greeting that could be used for both hello and goodbye. It means something like "be healthy" or "be safe", though a more literal translation would be the antiquated "be hale" or the modern "be whole":

Wes hāl!

Bibliography

Baker, Peter S. *Introduction to Old English*. Malden, MA: Blackwell Publishing, 2003.

Barber, Charles. *The English Language: A Historical Introduction*. Cambridge: Cambridge University Press, 1993

Beekes, Robert S. P. *Comparative Indo-European Linguistics*. Philadelphia: John Benjamin Publishing Co., 1995.

Bennet, William H. *An Introduction to the Gothic Language*. New York: The Modern Language Association of America, 1980.

Bentley, G. E. *Shakespeare and Jonson: Their Reputations in the Seventeenth Century Compared*. Chicago: University of Chicago Press, 1945.

Braune, Wilhelm and Hans Eggers. *Althochdeutsche Grammatik*. Tübingen: Max Niemeyer Verlag, 1987.

____. *Althochdeutsches Lesebuch*. Tübingen: Max Niemeyer Verlag, 1994.

Burgess, Anthony. *Shakespeare*. New York: Carroll & Graf, 2007.

Bush, Douglas. *English Literature in the Earlier Seventeenth Century, 1600-1660. Oxford History of English Literature*. Oxford: Clarendon Press, 1945.

Campbell, Lyle. *Historical Linguistics: An Introduction*. Cambridge, MA: The MIT Press, 1998.

Campbell, Lyle and Mauricio J. Mixco, *A Glossary of Historical Linguistics*. Salt Lake City: The University of Utah Press, 2007.

Cathey, James E. (Ed.). *Héliand: Text and Commentary*. Morgantown, WV: West Virginia University Press, 2002.

Crystal, David. *The Cambridge Encyclopedia of the English Language*. Cambridge: Cambridge University Press, 1987.

Dobson, E. J. *English Pronunciation, 1500-1700*. Oxford: Clarendon Press, 1968.

Fennell, Barbara A. *A History of English. A Sociolinguistic Approach.* Oxford: Blackwell, 2001.

Fischer, Olga, Ans van Kemenade, Willem Koopman, and Wim van der Wurff. *The Syntax of Early English.* Cambridge: Cambridge University Press, 2000.

Gallée, Johan Hendrik. *Altsächsiche Grammatik.* Halle: Max Niemeyer, 1910.

Godden, Malcolm. *The Making of Piers Plowman.* London: Longman, 1990.

Handbook of the International Phonetic Association: A guide to the use of the International Phonetic Alphabet. Cambridge: Cambridge University Press, 2002.

Heuser, Wilhelm. *Altfriesisches Lesebuch mit Grammatik und Glossar.* Heidelberg : Carl Winter's Universitätsbuchhandlung, 1903.

Jucker, Andreas H. *History of English and English Historical Linguistics.* Stuttgart : Ernst Klett Verlag, 2000.

Kolve, V. A. and Glending Olson (Eds.). *The Canterbury Tales: Fifteen Tales and The General Prologue; Authoritative Text, Sources and Backgrounds, Criticism* (2nd ed.). New York: W.W. Norton and Co., 2005.

König, Ekkehard and Johan van der Auerwa (Eds.). *The Germanic Languages.* New York: Routledge, 2005.

Kyes, Robert L. *The Old Low Franconian Psalms and Glosses.* Ann Arbor: The University of Michigan Press, 1969.

Marsden, Richard. *The Cambridge Old English Reader.* Cambridge: Cambridge University Press, 2004.

Mayhew, A. L., and Walter W. Skeat. *A Concise Dictionary of Middle English From A.D. 1150 to 1580.* Clarendon Press: Oxford, 1888.

Mitchell, Bruce, and Fred Robinson. *A Guide to Old English.* Sixth Edition. Malden, MA: Blackwell Publishers, Inc., 2002.

Nevalainen, Terttu. *An Introduction to Early Modern English.* Oxford: Oxford University Press, 2006.

O'Grady, William, John Archibald, Mark Aronoff, and Janie Rees-Miller. *Contemporary Linguistics: an Introduction*. Fourth Edition. New York: Bedford/St. Martin's, 2001.

Pei, Mario. *The Story of English*. New York: J. B. Lippencott, 1952.

Penzl, Herbert. *Englisch: Eine Sprachgeschichte nach Texten von 350 bis 1992*. Berlin: Peter Lang AG, 1994.

Prokosch, Eduard. *A Comparative Germanic Grammar*. Philadelphia: Linguistic Society of America, 1939.

Rauch, Irmengard. *The Gothic Language: Grammar, Genetic Provenance and Typology, Readings*. New York: Peter Lang Publishing, 2003.

____. *The Old Saxon Language: Grammar, Epic Narrative, Linguistic Interference*. New York: Peter Lang Publishing, 1992.

Robinson, Orrin W. *Old English and its Closest Relatives: A Survey of the Earliest Germanic Languages*. Stanford: Stanford University Press, 1992.

Schoenbaum, S.. *William Shakespeare, A Compact Documentary Life*. London: Oxford University Press, 1977.

Sievers, Eduard. *Heliand*. Halle: Verlag der Buchhandlung des Waisenhauses, 1878.

Szemerényi, Oswald J. L. *Introduction to Indo-European Linguistics*. Oxford: Oxford University Press, 1990.

Quak, A. and van der Horst, J. M. *Inleiding Oudnederlands*. Leuven: Universitaire Pers, 2002.

Thomason, Sarah G. *Language Contact: An Introduction*. Washington: Georgetown University Press, 2001.

Ule, Louis. *Christopher Marlowe (1564-1607): A Biography*. New York: Carlton Press Corp., 1995.

Vinaver, Eugène. Sir Thomas Malory. In Roger S. Loomis (ed.) *Arthurian Literature in the Middle Ages*. Clarendon Press: Oxford University, 1959.

Voyles, Joseph B. *Early Germanic Grammar: Pre-, Proto-, and Post-Germanic Languages*. New York: Academic Press, Inc., 1992.

Watkins, Calvert (Ed.). *The American Heritage Dictionary of Indo-European Roots* (2nd Ed.). New York: Houghton Mifflin Co., 2000.

Williams, Joseph M. *Origins of the English Language: A Social & Linguistic History*. New York: The Free Press, 1975.

Wright, Joseph. *An Elementary Middle English Grammar*. Oxford: Oxford University Press, 1962.

___. *An Old High German Primer*. Oxford: Clarendon Press, 1906.

___. *Grammar of the Gothic Language*. Oxford: Clarendon Press, 1997.

Glossary

A

ablative A grammatical case that generally marks motion away from something.

ablaut Also known as vowel gradation or apophony, a vowel alternation denoting grammatical contrast.

accusative A grammatical case that marks the direct object.

adjective A word that modifies a noun.

affix A bound inflectional or derivational morpheme (a prefix, infix, or suffix) added to a base or stem that changes the meaning or syntactic use of a word.

affricate A phonetic sequence formed by a stop plus a fricative, e.g., /dʒ/ (the "g" sound in "gym"), /tʃ/ (the "ch" sound in "child").

African-American Vernacular English (AAVE) A dialect of English spoken by some African-Americans and popularized via Hip Hop culture.

Afrikaans A West Germanic language descended from Dutch spoken in South Africa and some surrounding countries.

agglutinating language A language in which affixes that encode a single grammatical contrast are added onto a base or stem.

Alemannic An Upper German dialect.

alliteration The repetition of the same sounds or the same kinds of sounds at the beginning of words or in stressed syllables in a line of poetry, common in ancient Germanic poetry.

allophone A variation of a phoneme, usually in complementary distribution with other allophones; in English, the "p's" in "pit", "spit", and "stop" (all pronounced with a slight difference) are allophones of the phoneme /p/.

analogy A source of language change in which speakers generalize a certain grammatical feature based on similar characteristics from one word to another.

aorist A verb tense that expresses action without indicating its completion or continuation.

aspiration A slight release of air after the articulation of a stop.

Angles One of the three Germanic peoples who conquered England in the 5th century CE.

assimilation The influence of one sound on another in a word, causing one sound to become more like the other.

attested A description denoting that a language has been written down.

auxiliary verb Also called a helping verb; a verb that occurs with a main verb in a sentence to show a change in meaning or tense.

B

Beowulf An Old English epic poem likely composed in the early 8th century CE, concerning the exploits of the warrior Beowulf and containing tales of the Geats, Danes, and other ancient Germanic peoples.

bilabial A consonant articulated using both lips, e.g., /b/, /m/.

borrowing A source of language change involving the adoption of words or grammatical structures from one language to another.

C

Canterbury Tales, The An incomplete series of tales written from approximately 1387-1397 CE by Geoffrey Chaucer; the best known work in Middle English.

case A morphological category that encodes information about a word's grammatical role within a sentence.

Chaucer, Geoffrey The 14th CE author of the Canterbury Tales.

cognates Words from different languages that have descended from a common source.

colloquial Characteristic of informal speech or writing, rather than formal speech or writing.

Comparative Method, the A set of methods used by historical linguists to reconstruct a dead language based on systematic comparison of its descendant languages.

conjugation A verbal paradigm; a set of verbal inflections for a given verb.

consonant   A type of sound exhibiting obstruction within the vocal and/or nasal tracts.

D

Danelaw   A part of England under Danish rule in the 9th century CE.

Danish   A North Germanic language spoken in Denmark.

dative   A grammatical case marking the indirect.

declension   A paradigm of forms associated with a noun or adjective.

definite article   A determiner that indicates a specific reference, such as English "the".

demonstrative   A word that indicates something being referred to, such as "this" or "that".

dental   A consonant articulated with the tongue against or near the teeth, e.g., /t/, /d/.

descriptive grammar   A grammar that seeks to describe a language as it actually exists (the opposite of "prescriptive grammar").

determiner   A limiting adjective that usually precedes a descriptive adjective, including articles, possessive pronouns, and other words such as "some" and "each".

dialect   A regional or social variety of a language with unique phonological, lexical, and syntactic properties.

diphthong   Two vowel sounds comprising a single syllable, with one sound gliding into the other.

diphthongization   The creation of a diphthong from a monophthong.

direct object   The object in a sentence that receives the verb's action.

Dutch   A West Germanic language spoken in the Netherlands.

E

epenthesis   The insertion of a sound into the middle of a word.

Early Modern English   The stage of English from approximately the 15th to the 17th centuries CE; preceded by Middle English and followed by Modern English.

edda   Poetic and prose stories written in Iceland in Old Norse during the 13th century CE.

F

final devoicing   A phenomenon in which the final consonant sound of a word becomes voiceless.

First Sound Shift   Also known as Grimm's Law, this shift involved changes of the plain and aspirated stops from Indo-European to Germanic.

fricative   A consonant sound characterized by audible friction within the vocal tract, e.g., /f/, /z/.

Frisian   A West Germanic language spoken in the Netherlands, Germany, and Denmark; it is the closest living relative to English.

fusional   A type of language in which a bound morpheme (affix) that can mark several different grammatical categories at the same time is added to a word.

futhark   The name of the runic alphabet, named after its first six letters.

G

gender   A grammatical marking of category that does not always coincide with natural gender.

genitive   A grammatical case marking possession.

German   A West Germanic language spoken in Germany, Switzerland, Austria, and many surrounding countries.

Germanic   Also called Proto-Germanic, the parent language of all modern-day Germanic languages; a daughter language of Indo-European; the name of a family within Indo-European.

gerund   A noun derived from a verb, formed by adding "-ing" to a verb.

glide   A sound that has both consonant- and vowel-like qualities, e.g., /j/, /w/.

glottal   A consonant articulated using the vocal folds, e.g., /h/.

Gothic   An East Germanic language that has become extinct; best known for a Biblical translation by Wulfila, documented from the 4th century CE to the 8th century.

grammar   A mental system of rules and categories that allows a speaker of a language to create and understand words and sentences within a language.

Great Vowel Shift, the   A shift in the long vowel sounds of English that began late in the Middle English period and was completed by the Modern English period; in this shift, all long vowels moved higher up in the vowel quadrilateral, while those already at the highest level became diphthongs.

Grimm, Jacob   A 19th century Germanic linguist, best known for his elucidation of the First Sound Shift and as an editor of fairy tales.

Grimm's Law   See "First Sound Shift".

H

helping verb   See "Auxiliary Verb".

High German Consonant Shift   Also known as the Second Sound Shift, a shift in the stops from Germanic to Old High German.

historical linguist   A linguist who studies the history of a language, primarily focused on language change, language reconstruction, and comparison of languages.

I

Icelandic   A North Germanic language spoken in Iceland; it is the most conservative of the modern Germanic languages.

imperative   A grammatical verb mood used primarily for commands.

indefinite article   A word used before singular nouns to denote any member of a group, such as "a"/"an".

indicative   A grammatical verb mood indicating real action.

indirect object   An object in a sentence that indicates who or what is receiving the direct object.

Indo-European   Also known as Proto-Indo-European, a prehistoric language that is the parent of most modern European languages, as well as some languages of West Asia, India and the Middle East.

infinitive   A verb form that is not conjugated and often appears in a sentence with auxiliary or other finite verbs.

inflection   The modification of a word's form, generally by adding an affix, to mark its grammatical use in a sentence.

instrumental   A grammatical case marking the means by which something occurs.

International Phonetic Association   Also known as the IPA, a group that created and maintains a special phonetic alphabet used to transcribe the world's languages.

isolating   A type of language that uses syntax rather than inflections to show grammatical relationships within a sentence.

J

Jutes   One of the three Germanic peoples who conquered England in the 5ᵗʰ century CE.

K

King Alfred   The Anglo-Saxon king responsible for many works written in Old English.

King James Bible   The best-known English translation of the Bible, published in 1611; written in Early Modern English; also known as the "Authorized Version" in the United Kingdom.

L

language family   A group of languages related by descent from a common ancestor; the evidence of relationship is observable shared characteristics.

laryngeal theory   A generally accepted theory that certain vowel differences among cognates in Indo-European daughter languages resulted from a set of sounds, called laryngeals, that influenced the vowel sounds, but disappeared in all daughter languages but Hittite.

lexicon   The vocabulary of a language.

lingua franca   A common language used by diverse populations, often for purposes of commerce.

linguist   A person who studies language.

linguistics   The study of language.

liquid   A frictionless consonant sound that can be prolonged like a vowel, e.g., /l/ and /r/.

locative   A grammatical case marking location.

long vowel   In most languages, a vowel sound that is pronounced longer in duration than a short vowel; English has lost this distinction of duration in its long vowels.

M

Mandarin   The dialect of Chinese with the greatest number of speakers; the official Chinese dialect.

medio-passive   A grammatical voice which includes both the middle voice and the passive voice.

metathesis   A type of sound change in which two sounds switch places.

Middle English   The stage of English from approximately the 12th to the 15th centuries CE; preceded by Old English and followed by Early Modern English.

Modern English   The stage of English from approximately the 17th century to the present; also know as Present-Day English (especially when referring to the current time period); preceded by Early Modern English.

mood   A grammatical concept describing a verb's relationship to reality and intent.

morpheme   The smallest linguistic unit that has meaning; it can be a word, a part of a compound word, or an affix.

morphology   The study of the internal structure of words.

N

nasal   A consonant that is articulated with a lowered velum (soft palate), allowing air to escape through the nasal passage, e.g., /n/, /m/, and /ŋ/.

neologism   A newly coined word.

nominative   A grammatical case marking the subject of a clause.

Normans   A people from Normandy in northern France, originally of Scandinavian heritage, who conquered England in the 11th century.

Norwegian   A North Germanic language spoken in Norway.

noun   A part of speech denoting a person, place, or thing.

number A grammatical concept of nouns, pronouns, adjectives, and verb agreement expressing a distinction of countable quantities.

O

oblique A grammatical case marking an object.

Old English The earliest stage of the English language (approximately the 5th to the 12th centuries CE); also known as Anglo-Saxon; preceded by Germanic and followed by Middle English.

Old Frisian The earliest stage of the Frisian language (approximately the 11th to the 16th centuries CE).

Old High German The earliest stage of the German language (approximately the 6th to the 11th centuries CE).

Old Icelandic An Old Norse dialect; the earliest stage of the Icelandic language (approximately the 8th to the 14th centuries CE).

Old Low Franconian The earliest stage of dialects related to modern Dutch (approximately the 6th to the 12th centuries CE).

Old Norse The earliest stage of the modern Scandinavian languages (approximately the 8th to the 14th centuries CE).

Old Saxon The earliest stage of some modern Low German dialects (documented from the 9th to the 11th centuries CE).

optative A grammatical mood indicating a wish or hope (related to the subjunctive mood).

orthography A set of conventions used to represent language in written form.

P

palatalization Changing a sound by raising the tongue towards the hard palate (near the front of the mouth) while articulating the sound.

passive A grammatical voice in which the noun phrase that receives a verb's action in a clause becomes the subject of the sentence.

past participle A non-finite verb form used with an auxiliary verb to create periphrastic past tenses; an adjectival verb.

past perfect A verb tense that denotes action begun and completed in the past before another action; also known as the pluperfect.

Pennsylvania Dutch   A language spoken throughout the US and Canada, made up of various German (mostly from the Palatinate) and Swiss dialects; also known as Pennsylvania German.

periphrastic   Denoting a grammatical concept expressed by more than one word, i.e., as phrase.

person   A grammatical concept of pronouns and verbs denoting roles such as the speaker(s), the person(s) spoken to, or the person(s) spoken about.

philologer, philologist   A somewhat antiquated term for a linguist (especially an historical linguist).

phoneme   A contrastive phonological segment with predictable phonetic variants; made up of a set of allophones; the phoneme /p/ in English is made up of the different "p" sounds (allophones) in "pit", "spit", and "stop" (among others).

phonetics   The study of the sounds of a language.

phonology   The study of the sound system of a language.

pidgin   A language with a simplified grammar that develops as a means of communication between two or more groups who do not share a common language; it is not a native language of any speakers.

pluperfect   See "past perfect".

possessive   A grammatical case marking ownership.

pragmatics   The study of the ability of a speaker to communicate more than what is explicitly stated.

prefix   An affix that is prepended to the root or base of a word.

preposition   A word typically designating relationships in space or time.

present   A grammatical tense denoting action that is happening at the current time.

present participle   A non-finite verb form used with an auxiliary verb to create periphrastic tenses; an adjectival verb.

present perfect   A verb tense that denotes action begun in the past and continuing to the present; also known as the perfect.

Present-Day English   Also known as PDE; another term for Modern English, especially as it is used today.

prescriptive grammar A grammar in which rules are given for how a language *should* be spoken, rather than how it actually is (the opposite of "descriptive grammar").

preterite A verb tense denoting a single occurrence in the past; also known as the simple past.

pronoun A word that takes the place of a noun phrase, e.g., "I", "she", "you".

R

rhotacism In Germanic linguistics, the change of /z/ in certain positions to /r/, which occurred in all Germanic languages except Gothic.

root The morpheme that exists after all affixes are taken away.

rune A letter in the runic alphabet.

runic alphabet An alphabet, called the futhark, invented by Germanic peoples, characterized by straight lines and sharp angles, usually carved in wood or stone.

S

saga An epic tale, written in Old Norse prose, detailing the adventures of the ancient Germanic peoples.

Sanskrit An ancient Indo-European language spoken in India; a classical and liturgical language of India; the parent of many languages in present-day India.

Saussure, Ferdinand de A famous Swiss linguist of the 19th and early 20th centuries, often considered the "father of modern linguistics".

Saxons One of the three Germanic peoples who conquered England in the 5th century CE.

schwa An unstressed mid-central vowel, represented as "ə"; the "a" sound in "sofa".

Scots A variety of English spoken in Scotland.

Second Sound Shift See "High German Consonant Shift".

semantics The study of meaning in language.

Shakespeare, William   Regarded as the greatest playwright of the English language; lived in England during the Elizabethan period; wrote in Early Modern English.

short vowel   In most languages, a vowel sound that is pronounced shorter in duration than a long vowel; English has lost this distinction of duration in its short vowels.

simple tense   A tense constructed without the use of auxiliary verbs, such as the present and preterite in English.

sound law   A regular sound change, ideally with no exceptions; the basis for the comparative methods used by historical linguists.

stop   A type of consonant in which the air flow is completely stopped within the vocal tract, e.g., /p/, /b/; also known as a plosive.

subjunctive   A grammatical mood marking unreal situations, wishes, commands, and necessity, among others.

suffix   An affix appended to the end of a word.

suppletion   The use of one word as the inflected form of another word when the two words are not genetically related, e.g., "go" in the present tense and "went" in the past tense.

Swedish   A North Germanic language spoken in Sweden.

syllable   A unit of spoken language that consists of a single uninterrupted sound formed by a vowel, diphthong, or syllabic consonant alone, or by any of these sounds preceded, followed, or surrounded by one or more consonants.

syntax   The study of the rules of clause and sentence structure.

T

tense   A grammatical concept of verbs that marks the time an action occurred, relative to the time of the utterance.

typology   The study and classification of languages according to their structural features.

U

umlaut   Denotes the movement of articulation of a vowel due to the influence of another vowel sound within a word (most often /i/ or /j/; in this context it is also known as i-mutation).

V

variety a form of language that differs from other forms of the language systematically and coherently, such as a standard language versus a dialect of the language.

velar A consonant articulated with the tongue touching or near the soft palate, or velum, e.g., /k/, /g/.

verb A part of speech denoting the action occuring within a clause.

Verner, Karl A 19th century Danish linguist best known for the discovery of Verner's Law.

Verner's Law An historical sound change in Germanic in which the voiceless fricatives became voiced when immediately following an unstressed syllable in the same word.

vocal tract The oral cavity, nasal cavity, and pharynx.

vocative A grammatical case marking a person or thing being addressed.

voice (verbs) A grammatical marker of verbs describing the relationship between the action (or state) a verb expresses and the participants in the action (subject, object, etc.).

voice (phonology) A feature of consonants marking the use of the vocal folds (voiced) or absence of their use (voiceless).

vowel A sound produced with little constriction in the vocal tract.

vowel quadrilateral A diagram showing the location within the vocal tract that a vowel is articulated; shows a side view of the human head (front, central, back) with tongue position (high, mid, low).

W

Wulfila Also known as Ulfilas, a 4th CE century bishop best known for his creation of the Gothic alphabet and the translation of the Bible into Gothic.

Y

Yiddish A West Germanic language descended from Middle High German, influenced by Hebrew and various Slavic languages, written in the Hebrew alphabet.

Index

Printed in the United States
148265LV00002B/92/P